The Films of Martin Ritt

The Films of

MARTIN

Fanfare for the Common Man

RITT

by Gabriel Miller

University Press of Mississippi / Jackson

www.upress.state.ms.us

Copyright © 2000 by University Press of Mississippi
Manufactured in the United States of America

08   07   06   05   04   03   02   01   00   4   3   2   1

⊗

Library of Congress Cataloging-in-Publication Data

Miller, Gabriel, 1948–
    The films of Martin Ritt: fanfare for the common man / Gabriel Miller.
      p.   cm.
    Includes bibliographical references and index.
    ISBN 1-57806-276-4 (cloth : alk. paper) — ISBN 1-57806-277-2 (pbk. : alk. paper)
    1. Ritt, Martin, 1920–

    PN1998.3.R578 M55   2000
    791.43'0233'092—dc21   00-027342

British Library Cataloging-in-Publication Data available

For Kathy, Lizzie, and Jessica

Contents

Foreword

I cannot talk to you about Marty Ritt's body of work. I can't analyze how his early work changed to the films toward the end of his career. I can only tell you about my experience with him as an actress and as a woman who was lucky enough to call him my friend. He had a profound and lasting effect on me in both categories. "If you're lucky, every piece of work you do will in some way represent who you are or at least who you were at that moment," Marty told me. He felt it was important to stand for something, to have a moral point of view—especially if you work in the arts. He changed my work and how I thought about my work. His voice remains in my head.

I first met Marty Ritt in 1979. I received a message that he wanted to meet with me while I was working on a film in Tuscaloosa, Alabama (acting in a small role). I had been in very few films, mostly playing "the girl" (faceless, character-less roles you try to bring to life with the force of your personality). I had never carried a film. It had been a tremendous struggle for me to shed my TV situation-comedy persona, having starred in three television series; but I had been lucky enough to be cast in the lead in an exquisitely written mini-series, "Sybil." That's what Marty had seen.

I, of course, knew of Martin Ritt. I had been studying at the Actors Studio for years and he was highly touted as an "actor's director." Not only had he been an actor himself at one time, but he was an early member of the Studio and he knew the work.

I jumped on the next flight to Los Angeles and didn't have time to read the script before meeting with Marty. But my mother had. As I was running out the door, I asked her, "What's the character?" "Well, she's a southern girl who works in a cotton mill." The film was *Norma Rae*. Marty and I didn't talk very long. He asked me how serious I was about my work. I was so grateful to have the opportunity to tell someone how deeply I felt about acting and how desperately I wanted to be good. He told me it had been offered to several other actresses, all of whom had turned it down. The studio didn't want me, he added; but if I wanted it, he would fight for me and he would win.

Marty said directing was 80 percent casting. The goal was to find that actor whose essential ingredients fit that of the character, an actor whose "vein of gold" illuminated the character. The "vein of gold" is that quality a person exhibits the moment he walks in the room. It's what an actor radiates. He can try to play against it but the colors are most always present. Some actors' gold veins are deeper and richer than others. And some, through hard work, skill, and tenacity, tap and stretch their gold more than others.

Marty liked to rehearse, and I've never worked with a director who used the time more productively. He preferred a two-week rehearsal schedule that started with table readings and would eventually put three or four scenes on their feet—which means the actors get on their feet and start to block out the scene. These were usually the scenes Marty found most essential for the characters' development. Marty felt if an actor could conquer these few scenes, he'd have the character. In *Norma*, for instance, they were most of the scenes in the motel with Reuben. The first scene when Norma and Reuben meet after Norma has been hit in the face by a disgruntled lover, and the scene in which Norma finally comes to Reuben's room to join in his cause.

Marty taught me when to work and when to stay away. It's common for an actor, especially an untrained or inexperienced one, to over-think a role. When you're working in film, what's important is the "now." Marty would rehearse a scene until it was almost *there*, but save the arrival for that one or two or three takes where it comes alive and the camera is rolling. Unlike the theatre, an actor does not have to recreate the moment night after night. Each scene just has to be magic once, preferably outside of rehearsal. During the McCarthy era, when Marty had been blacklisted, he supported his family and many of his friends by playing the horses, and he was quite a good handicapper. Marty used to compare an actor's preparation to horse racing: get the horse warmed up and heading into the gate, but as a director he was careful not to ring that bell until the cameras were rolling.

I wasn't anyone's vision of Norma Rae, an uneducated, promiscuous, southern mill worker who stumbles into becoming a hero. I wasn't even Marty's. But he felt I could act and my vein of gold fit Norma's fierce strength. I also had a built-in vulnerability which I need never play. Whatever aspects of Norma I didn't start with, Marty helped me find. I slowed my natural tempo by focusing on heat—physical heat. This kind of work I had learned at the Actors Studio. Recreating for yourself the physical aspects of being in a heated atmosphere. When I did this correctly, it slowed my speech and walk in an organic way. Marty constantly reminded me to lower the pitch of my voice. My "little girl" quality was something we were constantly trying to play against by focusing on something that would either dilute it or complicate it. At one point, when we needed Norma to respond in a very earthy way, he gave me what he admitted was an odd suggestion. He asked me to think of Pat Neal in *Hud*. We were halfway through the film by that time and he knew I would love that kind of direction. (I work very internally and love having something outside of myself to visualize). Marty had great skill in both complicating the actor's work and simplifying it at the same time. To complicate it he might suggest an actor say one thing and do another. If an actor, for example, had a scene in which he was playing a character who was angry and performing an activity, the actor would have a tendency to deliver the dialogue and do the activity rapidly. Marty might ask the actor to continue doing the activity with speed but slow the dialogue down so that the activity and the dialogue were at different rhythms. To simplify a performance, Marty would never allow an actor's body to underline or say the same thing as the dialogue. For instance, saying "No" and shaking his head "no." "Do not capitulate to the moment," he would say. He understood the use of activity and the use of stillness. Delivering an emotional performance that is also extremely economical was what Marty Ritt taught.

He loved acting and was filled with wonderful stories of his early days with the Group Theatre, studying acting with Michael Chekhov (Anton's nephew). He told endless and wonderful stories about the early days at the Actors Studio. But when he told a story, I realized, it would usually pertain to something he wanted in the scene we were about to film. Many times I would take the story and try to "use it" in my work. Marty watched his actors so intently it was not unusual for him to get caught in a shot. He'd forget to move as the camera and actors headed his way. Frequently, I would be in a scene and out of the corner of my eye catch sight of Marty diving under a bush or ducking behind a chair. My focus would immediately shift from whatever intense thing I was working on to trying not to laugh.

He never took "film by" credit. He said he never would, unless he had written the film, and photographed it, and edited it, and acted in it, playing all the roles. He valued everyone's specific participation in the making of a film and liked to have the writer or writers on the set every day, which is extremely rare. If some-one did something stupid or they weren't up to his standards, he would certainly let them know. And anyone else who might be standing within a three-block radius.

Marty's heart was always with the working class, and he had nothing good to say about management. He had faith in "the people." He always said to me, "If given the chance and the proper information, the people will always do the right thing." But during the eighties, when the country was so conservative, Marty had a hard time believing the people could elect a government that seemed so like the one he had struggled to live through during the fifties. I remember having lunch with him one day on the old MGM lot, before it was purchased by the Sony Corporation. Ronald Reagan had just been elected and Marty was very upset. He put his arm around me and said, "The country is in for trouble. Especially the arts. I don't believe they will recover in my lifetime." He was right.

He didn't like organized religion or the Republican party (called many of them "aggressively illiterate") and didn't adhere to anyone's book of etiquette. If you were invited to dinner, you'd better be on time. If you were twenty minutes late, you might very well find that Marty had already eaten.

A no-nonsense man, who wore a one piece jumpsuit, often food-stained, he bluntly said what was on his mind. He didn't chit-chat and never coddled or patronized. Many times, after I had come to him with a complaint, he'd say to me, "I'll run a benefit, Sal." Which basically meant, get on with it. Toward the end of filming *Norma* he came to my dressing room, sat down, and said, "I just wanted you to know, Sally, you're first-rate." Never have three words meant so much to me. It changed how I saw myself.

He was extremely generous with his intelligence and passion, his delicious sense of humor and his wisdom. Martin Ritt was magical. I loved him and I will always miss him.

Sally Field

Preface

Martin Ritt was an important filmmaker whose career in Hollywood spanned three decades. Before directing his first film in 1957, he had a successful career in television, acting in, producing, or directing more than one hundred television shows and helping to develop the medium during its formative decade. He had also put together an impressive theater resumé, working with the Federal Theater Project, the Theater of Action, and, most important, the Group Theatre. It was the Group Theatre that shaped his working and social philosophy; the people he met there—notably, Elia Kazan, Harold Clurman, Clifford Odets, Luther Adler, Robert Lewis, and Sanford Meisner—taught him much about acting, directing, the humanistic theater, and the importance of the ensemble.

Many of Ritt's twenty-six films were well received. Some, like *Hud, The Spy Who Came in from the Cold*, and *Norma Rae*, garnered high critical praise and large audiences. Ritt's actors invariably did well—three won Oscars and many more were nominated. Major stars like Paul Newman, Richard Burton, Jane Fonda, Kirk Douglas, Sally Field, Jon Voigt, and Sean Connery did some of their best work under his direction. He ranks among the most important directors of social films this country has ever produced, and he was surely one of the most sensitive chroniclers of the South.

Throughout his life Ritt was labeled a political filmmaker, but he tended to dismiss the label. He thought of himself as a liberal and his films as liberal in spirit, but while he conceded the liberal concerns of a few of his films, his primary concern was to capture how people lived as truly, realistically, and humanistically as possible. He had great empathy for minorities and the disenfranchised; few American filmmakers have so vividly celebrated the variety and multiplicity of America. Ritt's was truly a democratic cinema. With the possible exception of his mentor Elia Kazan, no American filmmaker has incorporated the democratic aesthetic of the common man so effectively into his art.

Ritt's films, however, have received no serious critical consideration; there has been virtually no scholarly attention to his work. The only book yet published on Ritt, Carlton Jackson's *Picking Up the Tab: The Life and Movies of Martin Ritt* (Bowling Green University Press, 1994), offers a reliable recounting of events in Ritt's career, but it does not examine any of the films to gauge their aesthetic dimensions or thematic development. While calling Ritt "the greatest maker of social movies up to this point in American history," (1) Jackson does not attempt to define Ritt's accomplishment as a filmmaker. This is the gap this study is intended to fill, providing the first in-depth analysis of all of Ritt's films—indeed, the first critical explication that even some of his best-known films have ever received. Although the study of the films is the main concern here, I have set these discussions within a narrative of the important events in Ritt's life and some stories from the production histories of the films; I hope that a sense of the man and the artist emerges from these pages.

Acknowledgments

In writing a book like this, one accumulates many debts of gratitude. First, to Val Almanderez, of the Margaret Herrick Library of the Academy of Motion Picture Arts and Sciences, who was always generous with his time and help, before and during my visits to the library. Thanks as well to Barbara Hall, who arranged to send me copies of items from the collection, and to the various members of a very helpful staff at the library.

This book also owes a great debt to Adele Ritt, who was consistently kind and helpful in numerous ways, including setting aside an afternoon for an interview. Meeting her was one of the chief joys I experienced while writing this book. Sadly, Adele Ritt died before this book went to press. I hope it proves to be worthy of the interest and time she devoted to it. Another thank-you goes to Tina Ritt, Martin Ritt's daughter, who, like her mother, was always gracious and generous with her time.

Some of Ritt's collaborators were also helpful, particularly Robert Radnitz, who granted a number of lengthy telephone interviews as well as meeting with me in Los Angeles and buying me lunch. Walter Bernstein met with me twice in New York and kindly answered follow-up questions on the phone. Irving Ravetch, Joseph Stefano, Julius Epstein, and Lawrence Turman also gave of their time. Many thanks to Paul Newman and Kirk Douglas, who also granted me interviews.

I am grateful to Hal Kantor, who sent me copies of two of Ritt's films, Rod Merl of the American Film Institute for a copy of the seminar Ritt gave there, and Alan Adler of Twentieth Century Fox for being supportive and helpful.

A very special thank you goes to Sally Field, who agreed to write the foreword for this book even while preoccupied with the editing of her first film. I know that for her this was a labor of love, and I appreciate both her generosity and her loyalty to Ritt's memory.

Other thank-yous go to the Office of Research and Sponsored Programs at Rutgers University for various grants that helped in the research for this book and to Steven Diner, Dean of the College of Arts and Sciences at Rutgers, Newark, for additional financial support. I also want to thank my colleague H. Bruce Franklin for his constant encouragement and belief in this project and my friend Jim Verniere, who read parts of the manuscript, very patiently listened to me kvetch on the phone, and yet remained helpful and encouraging.

My greatest debt is to my family. My children, Lizzie and Jessica, endured hearing me talk about Martin Ritt in between their requests for rides and money. And, as always, to Kathy, stronger and more wondrous than all of Ritt's heroines, my love and gratitude always.

The Films of Martin Ritt

Discovering a Vocation: Childhood, College Years, Work in the Theater and Television

Despite a long and successful career in Hollywood, Martin Ritt remains a director whose work has gone largely unnoticed by film scholars and critics. This is all the more remarkable in that Ritt came into his own as an artist just when the auteur theory and the cult of the director were taking hold as central tenets of cinema's critical vocabulary. Ritt was an established figure who maintained his artistic independence into the eighties, when young directors could become powers in the industry on the basis of two or three films, yet somehow his films have always been more celebrated than their creator. Ritt made twenty-six films between 1957 and 1990, in addition to the countless television dramas and Broadway and non-Broadway plays he had directed before coming to Hollywood. A dedicated professional whose credits include some of Hollywood's most distinguished work, he fashioned for himself an extraordinary life in film.

When Ritt came to Hollywood, the studio system was breaking down. In 1958 domestic box-office receipts dipped below $1 billion, down from a $1.7 billion peak in 1946. Four years later they fell below $900 million, about half the studios' income in 1946. Two major contributors to the slump, from which Hollywood would not emerge until the mid-sixties, were television and the blacklist, both intimately tied to Ritt's own career. Television robbed the movies of much of their audience, despite such innovations as 3-D, Cinemascope, and Cinerama, all essentially attempts to do what television could not, in the hope of luring viewers back into the theaters. At the same time, the blacklist robbed the studios of

3

significant talent, but more important it fueled and then fed on suspicions that Hollywood was turning out pro-Communist, subversive products.

Having learned how to be a director by working on numerous television shows as an actor, producer, and director during the fifties, Ritt found his career cut short when he was blacklisted in 1952. Yet he managed to survive both of these cultural onslaughts and carve out a successful movie career on his own terms. Coming to Hollywood at a time when big, expensive films were considered essential to Hollywood's survival, Ritt succeeded with mostly smaller films that focused on families and individuals. When 1950s' Hollywood, again in reaction to television, converted almost exclusively to color, Ritt continued to make films in black and white, including two of his greatest artistic and commercial achievements, *Hud* and *The Spy Who Came in from the Cold*. The tenacity (or perversity) of this aesthetic vision is especially apparent in that he made six films with Paul Newman between 1958 and 1967, and half of them are in black and white!

Ritt managed to thrive within the system despite never having an enormous popular success. Instead, he persisted in making the kinds of films that interested him, projects dealing with social issues and focused on individuals and loners who operate outside the system. Most of his films retain a small, intimate look, without big Hollywood effects or self-conscious camera angles. Ritt rarely calls attention to his camera, instead focusing on character and story; it was both an ethic and a style that he maintained throughout a career that spanned three decades and multiple changes in fashion. He always stayed true to himself and to a company of collaborators, including screenwriters Walter Bernstein, Irving Ravetch, and Harriet Frank; cinematographers Sidney Levin, John Alonzo, and James Wong Howe; art director Tambi Larson; and others who worked with him on numerous projects.

Steadfastly maintaining that film was a collaborative process, Ritt refused to put his name above the title like so many of his colleagues, even though he could have commanded such billing. He was equally independent and iconoclastic in his choice of projects—he was a Jew who never made a film about Jews or the Jewish experience, a city boy who rarely used the city as a primary setting. Born and raised in New York City, he found his subject matter and filmic locale in the rural South. He lived his entire life in New York or Los Angeles and yet he was preoccupied with the romance of an American past rooted in rural communal values. He earned considerable respect in the Hollywood system while making films about people who thrived outside systems or who rejected them entirely.

Ritt's roots and early work experiences shaped the attitudes that remained with him throughout his life. He was born on March 2, 1914, in New York City, the first child of Morris and Rose Lass Ritt. Their second child was a daughter, Dorothy.[1] Morris Ritt, himself a recent immigrant from Russia, opened an employment agency for newly arrived immigrants on Avenue B and Tenth Street. And after the birth of their daughter, Rose (who had emigrated from Poland) embarked on her own career, becoming an agent for chorus girls, with an office on Forty-sixth Street.

Martin Ritt had a fairly typical upbringing for a child of immigrants, combining exposure to an Old World lifestyle at home and an Americanized life on the street. He went to Public School 64 and in the afternoons was sent to Cheder, or Hebrew school. Ritt and his classmates were attacked almost daily on their way home from Hebrew school by members of other ethnic groups, particularly the Italians. Remembering being in a fight practically every day, Ritt considered himself a "tough kid."

The family prospered and moved to the Bronx, while Ritt attended the Rhodes Preparatory School and then DeWitt Clinton High School. His two interests were literature and sports: he excelled in English, impressing his teachers with his reading ability, and he played halfback on the varsity football team and participated in boxing, baseball, and basketball (he had ambitions of becoming a coach), while holding down a job at a butcher shop after school.

Ritt's toughness would be needed in facing a very unpleasant family episode when he was in high school. Growing weary of his wife's extramarital affairs, Morris Ritt asked for a divorce and insisted that his son testify against his mother in court. Ritt had never been close to his father, and this incident estranged them further. This trauma was followed a few years later by Morris's sudden death, probably of a heart attack, shortly before his son's graduation from high school. Morris left the family nothing, and Rose found herself with two children and no money just as the depression reached full swing in 1932.

Ritt feared that his dream of going to college and preparing for a career as a coach might have to be postponed. But looking for a small school and in desperate need of an athletic scholarship, he received the offer he wanted from an unlikely source, Elon College near Burlington, North Carolina. Although Ritt's recollections of this arrangement varied over the years, in all probability, he attended Elon in his first year as a tuition-paying student (though the fees were minimal as Elon was then operating under bankruptcy laws) and then won a football scholarship in his second year, playing for a team called "the Fighting Christians of Elon College." Despite attending Cheder and being bar-mitzvahed, Ritt had not been raised in a religious home, and he never displayed any interest in his Jewish heritage, so being a Jew in this environment never caused him any real problems. Ritt found playing football for Elon disappointing—he was not a starting player and the team lost most of its games—but as he had done in high school, Ritt excelled in literature and in German. He was an accomplished debater, and he dabbled in the theater, acting in a few productions as well as attending plays at the University of North Carolina at Chapel Hill. Elon apparently affected Ritt more than his own urban upbringing, for it provided him with the dual inspiration that would later infuse his film work: the dream of a rural, peaceful, bucolic America and a sensitivity to the degradations of racism and rural poverty.

His concept of the land and the rural community as repositories of value forms the bedrock of his pastoral ideal. His films generally idealize the life of the country, and his later films display a strong tendency to move his characters away from urban settings toward the rural, from sophistication and complexity toward natural simplicity. Many of Ritt's characters find in the land the potential for change, even regeneration.

Leaving Elon, Ritt enrolled for a brief time at St. John's Law School in Jamaica, New York, but, he said, "I didn't have to spend too much time there to know that law wasn't for me" (Jackson 13). His disaffection for the law was in no small part fueled by his growing attraction to the life of the theater. In 1935 he traveled around the "Borscht Belt" in New York's Catskill Mountains, drawn by the memory of his experiences in college theater and by the chance to make some money developing fitness programs for the players. At the Hotel Waldemere, he was offered the part of Crown in *Porgy and Bess*, which he played in blackface. Now Ritt was hooked on acting, and he decided to make it his career.

In 1935, after his stint in the Catskills, Ritt found work at the Federal Theater Project, an outgrowth of FDR's Works Progress Administration. Although the Federal Theater Project had its origin in economic necessity, its head, Hallie Flanagan, felt that art was an integral part of the social fabric of the community, and her vision of theater as a social force profoundly influenced both the Theatre Union and the Group Theatre. Art was defined as a fulfillment of the social need that gave it life; it was therefore impelled to recognize and reflect the implications of social change. Ritt's experiences with the Federal Theater Project and the Group Theatre, which he joined in 1937, were seminal and lasting, shaping his theory of film until the end of his career. All of his mature work is informed by a consciousness of the interdependence of art and the social forces that shape human society, and this socio-aesthetic sensibility remained the prime factor in his choice of projects.

The political consequences of his association with the Federal Theatre, a major outlet for radical expression—its foes characterized it as under Communist-dominated leadership—would also affect Ritt's career in later years. At this time, he also worked for the Theatre of Action, one of the many left-wing theater groups that proliferated during the thirties—one of the first productions he appeared in took place during the May Day parade of 1935. Although Ritt commuted in from the Bronx, many of the actors lived together in Greenwich Village; among them were Nicholas Ray and Elia Kazan, who would become a great influence on Ritt's career.

Ritt's affiliation with the Theatre of Action opened doors to other theater groups, among them the Glasgow Theatre, where he won a part in William Saroyan's *The Time of Your Life*. The part required him to dance—Ritt had become and was considered for the rest of his life an accomplished dancer—but after a few rehearsals, he found himself replaced by a spectacular new kid, Gene Kelly, who remained a lifelong friend.

The strongest formative influence on Ritt, however, was his association with the Group Theatre. The communal spirit of the Group is reflected in Ritt's attitude toward filmmaking, which he always considered a collective enterprise, categorically rejecting the cult of the director. The Group's philosophy is echoed most forcefully in his choice of projects and in his convictions about the relationship of art to the commercial enterprise. Ritt clearly acknowledged the depth of this influence, "[Y]ou've got to be lucky that something exists which, in some way, mirrors what you want to be about. If the Group Theatre hadn't been there, I might have evolved into what I have but it probably would have taken longer and I would not have had as firm a base" (SMU 2).

Although the Group Theatre shared with the Federal Theatre and the Theatre Union its origins in the social ferment of the thirties, the Group Theatre parted company with the more political aims of the Theatre Union. Its cofounder, Harold Clurman regarded theater not as a weapon for social change but rather as an art that reflected life. The Group's real ancestors were the great art theaters of Europe and Russia, from which Clurman adapted his theater as a vehicle for both art and communion, a collective expression of life experience.

The Group Theatre was committed to American plays that articulated contemporary social problems, but it did not advocate particular solutions. Its aims were more moral than political, as it strove to reflect issues and questions rather than to provide answers. Unlike other theater groups that emerged from the thirties, the Group, while rejecting Broadway values, chose to present its productions on Broadway, and thus throughout its short history had a complicated relationship with the commercial framework of that enterprise.

Ritt's recollections of the Group reflected Clurman's aims: "They were definitely not a political group. I mean, I could tell that because I was fairly political. . . . But they were totally committed to doing American work, American plays.

. . . it was in the true tradition of what they conceived to be a democratic America, and what they conceived to be serious work, creative work" (SMU 3–4).

Ritt's cinema, with few exceptions, was likewise rooted in American themes—history, and most specifically, the American landscape. His articulated aim was to explore and reflect the American experience. Ritt himself was politically involved, but his films are never dogmatic. Ritt's aim was to open the eyes of his audience, to make them learn and think about the world around them. And while his best work presents well-constructed, interesting stories and characters, the plots serve the interest of themes and ideas. Like the work of his spiritual godfather, Clurman, Ritt's cinema is more moral than political: his characters are tested by events, and they are measured by how they acquit themselves.

Ritt was brought into the Group Theatre in 1937 by Elia Kazan, who recommended him as a boxing coach for Luther Adler, who was to play Joe Bonaparte in Clifford Odets's *Golden Boy*. During the performance it was Ritt's job to beat tattoos on the punching bag and provide sound effects during the ring scenes; he was eventually promoted to assistant stage manager and later got a small role in the play.

Elia Kazan, who also had a part in *Golden Boy* (and who went on to become America's most important director of the fifties) became another important influence. Ritt and Kazan remained close until Kazan, whose nickname was Gadge, named names before HUAC (House Committee on Un-American Activities): "All of us who have been around this business as long as I have realize that judgment is just as important as talent. If you look at the history of Tennessee Williams, you'll see that Gadge only did his good plays, the other ones he didn't do. So you have to give him credit for extraordinary judgment, which did desert him at a certain point in his life" (SMU 5).

If there is any filmmaker whose work and style parallels Ritt's, it is Kazan. There are personal parallels as well. Both were children of immigrants, raised in New York City, and both came of age artistically in the left-wing theater. Kazan cofounded the Actor's Studio, where Ritt taught in the fifties, and both were considered superior teachers of acting, actors' directors with the ability to draw exceptional performances from their casts. (Ritt directed numerous actors in Academy Award–nominated and –winning performances, although he was nominated only once for his direction.)

Both were masters at location shooting, which in Kazan's case began with *Boomerang* in 1946 and in Ritt's in his very first film, *Edge of the City*, in 1957. Because of their ability with actors, both were able to integrate local inhabitants effectively into their films, thus achieving a degree of authenticity that is rare in the American cinema. Kazan's work in films such as *Boomerang, Panic in the Streets,* and *On the Waterfront* clearly influenced Ritt, whose artful use of local characters is especially noteworthy in *The Molly Maguires, Sounder, Conrack, Casey's Shadow,* and *Norma Rae;* and his talent for evoking local color increases his stories' verisimilitude and power.

Closely related to this shared sense of local color was Kazan's use of the Deep South as the locale for four of his films—*Panic in the Streets, Baby Doll, A Face in the Crowd,* and *Wild River*—which remained unequaled in their regional accuracy until Ritt adopted the South as his own artistic milieu, making eight films there, including *Hud, Sounder, Conrack, Casey's Shadow,* and *Norma Rae.*

The two directors also shared an interest in films that reflect the social and political vagaries of the American experience, shot in a straightforward, unadorned style. (Kazan's style shifted dramatically in the sixties, when his films took a more personal turn, while Ritt's remained fairly constant throughout his career.) Both also meditated on the blacklist, a defining event in both men's lives—Kazan most dramatically in *On the Waterfront* and *The Visitors,* and Ritt in *The Front* and *The Molly Maguires.*

Finally, both of these directors liked to filter their stories through father-son relationships. Ritt announced this theme in his first film and then returned to it in at least six others. Kazan explored the father-son theme most effectively in *East of Eden,* but it contributed a central element to his other work, particularly the autobiographical *The Arrangement.* These relationships lay at the heart of both directors' ruminations about the American past and present, particularly the relationships between social progress and the intransigent individual and between a bucolic past and an industrial present. Ritt's first great film, *Hud,* incorporated all of these issues, as did Kazan's *East of Eden* and the haunting, elegiac *Wild River.*

Another important association that Ritt formed at the Group Theatre was with its premiere playwright, Clifford Odets, author of *Golden Boy* as well as other Group successes such as *Waiting for Lefty* and *Awake and Sing!* Like Ritt, Odets had started out as an actor but went on to achieve fame by pursuing another talent; he would go on to direct his own plays (*The Country Girl* and *The Flowering Peach*) as well as two films (*None but the Lonely Heart* and *The Story on Page One*). When Ritt met him in 1937, Odets was New York's preeminent playwright and the toast of Broadway, a position he was soon to secure with the success of *Golden Boy.*

Odets liked Ritt enough to offer him a part in *Night Music,* which starred Elia Kazan, but Ritt turned it down; years later he claimed the part was only one line. Odets was to be the only one of his friends whom Ritt would forgive for cooperating with the House Committee on Un-American Activities. According to his wife, Ritt had always considered Odets a little crazy, and so he found it difficult to hold a grudge. When Ritt was blacklisted from television in the early fifties, Odets offered him a part in what was to be his last play, *The Flowering Peach*. Ritt played Shem, Noah's oldest son, in Odets's retelling of the story of Noah and the flood, and he also helped Odets direct the play during its pre-Broadway run in Boston. Prior to the opening there, Odets sent him a letter thanking him for his "shrewd and tough assistance" and offered him 1 percent of the show "as a little gift to you" (RC 12-6-54). Ritt continued to befriend Odets and dined with him regularly until Odets's death from stomach cancer in 1963.

Ritt worked in various capacities for the Group Theatre. In 1939 he appeared in Irwin Shaw's *The Gentle People*, which starred Franchot Tone, Sylvia Sidney, and Sam Jaffe. In 1940, he played Samuel Brodsky in Elmer Rice's *Two on an Island* for the Playwrights Company. That year was especially notable for Ritt, for on September 25, he married Adele Wolfe, a dancer who was known professionally as Adele Jerome. Adele, whom he met at one of the many radical clubs that they both attended, was a member of the Young Communist League, a John Reed unit, and an organizer for the National Committee for the Arts, Sciences, and Professionals, which made the U.S. Attorney General's list of Communist front organizations in the fifties.

In 1942 Ritt appeared in Maxwell Anderson's *The Eve of St. Mark*, one of the first American plays to raise serious questions about American involvement in World War II. Detailing the story of a young man who leaves his family and fiancée to join the army and is eventually reported missing in action in the Philippines, the play starred William Prince, Aline Macmahon, and Mary Rolfe.

Ritt was himself drafted and then inducted into the Air Force on April 13, 1943, and he served until he was honorably discharged as a corporal on January 3, 1946. (He had tried to enlist to go to Spain in 1938, but the American volunteer forces had a full complement of troops at the time.) At first assigned to study weather patterns in Champaign, Illinois, he was preparing to be sent to China to report on weather for American troops in Asia when he was suddenly tapped by a talent scout to appear in a play sponsored by the Air Force. Transferred to Special Services, he lived in a special barracks with other theatrical GIs. Ritt played Gleason in Moss Hart's *Winged Victory*, a play tracing the careers of three young men aspiring to be pilots. The cast was made up of servicemen on special leave and included fellow Group Theatre alumni Karl Malden and Lee J. Cobb as well as Barry Nelson, Red Buttons, Edmond O'Brien, and Gary Merrill. Ritt remembered the play as basically a "soap opera" and attributed its success—it opened in New York in November 1943—to "the American commitment to soap opera" (SMU 16). He also appeared in the film version, which was produced by Darryl F. Zanuck and directed by George Cukor and was released by Twentieth Century Fox in 1944, but he thought little of that effort as well, deciding that George Cukor "was a little out of his element" (SMU 16).

More important to Ritt at this time was his opportunity to direct Sidney Howard's *Yellow Jacket*, about Walter Reed's efforts to develop a vaccine for yellow fever. The Group Theatre had been interested in producing the play when it was written in 1934, but Howard, scared off by the Group's string of failures in 1931 and 1932, gave it instead to Katharine Cornell and Guthrie McClintic. Ritt was chosen to direct a special performance at the Forty-fourth Street Theatre (where *Winged Victory* had opened a year earlier) on April 6, 1944, with John Forsyth, Gary Merrill, and Alfred Ryder. He would direct the play again in 1947 for the American Repertory Company, and he took the play to hospitals, where it was performed for the patients.

After his discharge from the Air Force, Ritt directed *Mr. Peebles and Mr. Hooker*, a theological morality play about the confrontation between good and evil in a small Tennessee town. Ritt found it an "interesting play" that "didn't quite work," but it opened at the Music Box Theater on Broadway on October 10, 1946. That year he also directed *The Big People* by Stanley Young and Nancy Wilson Ross at the Lyric Theatre in Bridgeport, Connecticut, and at the Falmouth Theatre in Conamessett, Massachusetts. In 1947 he directed *Eastward in Eden*, by Dorothy Gardner, a play about Emily Dickinson and her search for love.

Ritt's major undertaking as a stage director was Dorothy Heyward's historical drama *Set My People Free*, which chronicled the true story of Denmark Vesey, a powerful and dynamic ex-slave who planned an uprising that almost succeeded in liberating slaves in Charleston, South Carolina, in the early nineteenth century. Starring Juano Hernandez (who would act again for Ritt in Hemingway's *Adventures of a Young Man*) and Canada Lee, the play opened in New York at the Hudson Theatre on November 22, 1948. In 1949 Ritt also directed Terrence Rattigan's *The Winslow Boy*, starring Cedric Hardwick and Dennis King.

His last play before devoting himself almost exclusively to television was a melodrama, *The Man*, by Mel Dinelli, which opened on January 20, 1950, at the Fulton Theatre. The play chronicles the relationship between a psychotic handyman and the kindly old lady who hires him to work at her rooming house. The landlady, played by Dorothy Gish, takes a motherly interest in him, but he proceeds to dominate and kill her. Ritt remarked that he thought that play "worked very well" (SMU 18).

By this time, Ritt had already picked up a few jobs in the emerging new television industry. In a 1985 interview, he agreed that the early days of the medium had been a "golden age": ". . . because a lot of very gifted people came out of that period. A lot of extremely good work was done. It was done because the full economic ramifications of television had not yet taken over. And it was a place to function on a very creative level" (Berkowitz 40).

Ritt's first job in television was directing "The Fight Game," a twelve-and-a-half-minute documentary for Intercity Television, followed by a sequel entitled "They Came out Fighting." Soon he was under contract to CBS, where he worked on the drama anthology series *Danger*, a weekly live broadcast that specialized in psychological drama and murder stories. Ritt served primarily as a producer of shows directed by his friend Yul Brynner, but his greatest acclaim on that show came as an actor in an episode called "The Paper Box Kid." Written by his close friend Walter Bernstein, who created the role for Ritt, the story focuses on a petty hoodlum who wants to prove his toughness but who also has a dreamy side. As the play opens, he is dancing alone to music from a juke box, but the kid is a bit crazy and he gets mixed up in a barroom holdup. In an attempt to prove how tough he is, he convinces his companion to shoot the bartender; soon he is in jail, on death row.

The teleplay, based on a story by Mark Hellinger, was directed by Sidney Lumet. Bernstein described the story as "sentimental," but he remembered that Ritt's acting "just exploded." In a column devoted to the show in the *New York Herald Tribune*, John Crosby wrote that Ritt, "may be the best actor on television" (June 9, 1952). Fred Rayfield of *The Compass* wrote, "The performance of Martin Ritt as a sort of Hairy Ape primitive young thug in 'The Paper Box Kid' on *Danger* last Tuesday night was one of the finest pieces of acting I've seen on TV." The episode was so popular that Bernstein wrote another episode for Ritt, but it was only "half as good." Bernstein recalled that Ritt tended to "over-intellectualize" his acting roles but that he was an "arresting physical presence" (Interview).

Ritt also directed and produced episodes for the *Somerset Maugham Theatre*, originally called *Teller of Tales* when it premiered in 1950. Another live series presenting a new drama every week, this show had the distinction of having Maugham himself introduce each play and return at the end to thank the audience for watching and then announce the next week's title. Maugham's appearances, however, were filmed from his home on the French Riviera.

Ritt enjoyed the freedom, the sense of discovery and experimentation, and the improvisational air of live television. In a busy year, he remembered directing from twenty-five to fifty live half-hour shows: "There was only one studio, above Grand Central Station in New York City. We had one camera to do every show and we didn't even have a standby camera in case something went wrong. The shows never went further than the Ohio River at that point [1947]" (Berkowitz 40).

In directing with one camera, Ritt remembered, when you finished a scene, you "went black and just stayed there until the camera got over to the other set." There was no postproduction. "Everything had to happen right there." The average time for rehearsing a half hour show was one week. "The audience forgave an occasional boom dropping into the shot, or something sloppy in the physical production, because the excitement of doing it the way we were doing it and the quality of the material overcame the mechanical lapses" (Berkowitz 41).

During this time Ritt also directed "No Time for Comedy" on *The Celanese Theatre*, a series dedicated to presenting quality plays by leading playwrights; and he worked, with Yul Brynner, as a producer-director for CBS's *Starlight Theatre*, another anthology series that specialized in stories of romance. Ritt was also contracted to "act as consultant to the producer-director on all phases of production" for a series entitled *The Aldrich Family*, the television version of the long-running radio comedy about the adventures of teenager Henry Aldrich and his "typical American family," but this arrangement would not come to pass, because Ritt himself was soon to be branded "un-American."

After producing, directing, or acting in some one hundred television shows, Ritt showed up at CBS one day in 1952 to work on *Danger* and found himself abruptly fired. Recalling those days, Ritt put it succinctly: "One day I was working and the next day I was out on my ass" (Jackson 27). He had suspected that something was up that morning because on his way to see Donald Davis, the head of television, he saw a producer with whom he had worked for two weeks at the behest of management, helping him to smooth out the problems in an upcoming show. When the producer recognized Ritt walking down the long hallway, however, he just disappeared. Ritt would utilize that incident twenty-five years later in *The Front*.

When Ritt got to Davis's office, he was told, "Marty, you haven't been renewed." When Ritt asked why, he was told, "I have no idea." Ritt, of course, knew what was going on and told him so. Davis's reaction was one Ritt always remembered: "Marty, this is the United States of America. Those things don't happen here." A year later Davis called Ritt and said, "I'm terribly sorry, I now know that everything you said to me that day was true." Ritt replied, "There's nothing you can do about it. Nobody can do anything about it. It's going to run its course" (SMU 20). HUAC's business did eventually run its course, but not before it ruined countless lives and destroyed many others. Ritt was unable to work in television or film for six years, but unlike the character Hecky Brown in *The Front*, he was a survivor.

HUAC, though the most visible, was not the only agency of the anti-Communist crusade. Its activities were restricted by legislation that permitted pursuit of only Communists and fellow travelers, not liberals, but its work was facilitated by a variety of extremist groups that, emboldened by HUAC and not restricted by cumbersome rules, widened the scope of the investigation. One of the most powerful of these organizations was American Business Consultants, formed by three ex-FBI agents in 1947. This group put out *Counterattack*, a newsletter, on a regular basis, and in June 1950 published what would become the bible of the "greylist," *Red Channels*, the names of 151 people in show business and Communist front organizations.

In 1947 *Counterattack* alleged that Ritt had helped Communist Party locals of the Retail, Wholesale, and Department Store union stage their annual show. Ritt claimed that a man in Syracuse who owned a number of grocery stores had accused him of donating large sums of money to the Communists, but he always denied the charge. He had directed a show for Russian War Relief at Madison Square Garden and this effort was also listed. But as Ritt put it—a sentiment echoed by Hecky Brown in *The Front*—"[T]hey were on our side at the time" (Berkowitz 42). His associations with the Group Theatre and the Federal Theatre didn't help either. *Counterattack* also mentioned Ritt in 1951, describing him as "a lecturer at the Communist Party's . . . school run by People's Drama."

Unlike many of his friends, however, Ritt was never named or subpoenaed; it was all guilt by association. One of his friends even appealed to the right wing of the director's union, defending him on the grounds that he had never been named. Ritt recalled that the union replied, "Well, we know he's not on our side. And we don't want him to get a big influential job. So we're not going to do anything unless he lets us know he's on our side" (Berkowitz 42). Ritt resolutely refused to do that.

In 1955, when he was preparing to direct Arthur Miller's *A View From the Bridge*, an FBI agent asked him, "Why are you being so difficult? Everybody wants to hire you." Ritt replied, "I'm not being difficult. I haven't done anything. What do you want me to do?" Ritt gave two different versions of the agent's reply. In one he said, "Name names" (Berkowitz 42). In another, "I can't really tell you at this point. I want to organize it" (SMU 21). In both versions, however, Ritt walked away.

The act of informing on others was distasteful to Ritt, and he returned to it again and again in his films. *Edge of the City, Five Branded Women, The Spy Who Came in from the Cold, The Brotherhood, The Molly Maguires,* and, of course, *The Front* all deal either tangentially or directly with the issue of informing. The informer who had the profoundest effect on Ritt was his friend and colleague

Elia Kazan, who has emerged in the folklore of the left as, in Victor Navasky's words, "the quintessential informer" (199). Kazan first testified before HUAC in January 1952, answering all questions except one about the people he knew when he was a member of the Communist Party. In April, he recanted and named names, including Clifford Odets. Kazan, however, was not content just to capitulate to the committee; in addition he provided an annotated bibliography of the twenty-five productions that he had directed, with explanations of their histories. He then published an ad in the *New York Times* (April 12, 1952) entitled "A Statement," in which he justified his actions and denounced the Communist Party. Ritt, like many others, never forgave his mentor.

Ritt stated years later that he had never been a member of the Communist Party. "I was always a very left-wing liberal, and I agreed with the Communists a lot of the time, but I *didn't* agree with them some of the time, and that was bitter and angry" (SMU 24). Prior to Kazan's informing, Ritt had helped him form the Actor's Studio and had taught acting there—the "naturalistic" style that he had learned from Kazan and fellow Group Theatre alumnus and acting teacher Robert Lewis. Among Ritt's students were Eli Wallach, Anne Jackson, E. G. Marshall, Lee Remick, Paul Newman, and Joanne Woodward, some of whom would later appear in Ritt's films.

In addition to teaching at the Actor's Studio, Ritt directed several out-of-town plays while he was blacklisted from television. He was particularly busy at the Playhouse in the Park in Philadelphia. In 1953 he directed Sidney Kingsley's *Detective Story*, and in 1954 *Boy Meets Girl*, a play by Bella and Sam Spewack about a baby film star whose services are contracted before his birth, starring Robert Preston. Next came a revival of *The Front Page*, also with Preston, with whom Ritt had co-starred a year earlier in Richard Condon's *Men of Distinction*, directed by Martin Gabel. He also co-starred with Sallie Gracie in Garson Kanin's *Born Yesterday*. That same year (1954) he directed *Put Them All Together* by Theodore Hirsch and Jeannette Patton at the Tower Playhouse in Spring Lake, New Jersey.

During these years the family income was supplemented by Adele's selling advertisements for the phone company and Ritt's frequent attendance at the racetrack, where he became a talented handicapper. When he became a successful director, he bought a number of racehorses and spent his summers at Delmar, where he could race his own horses and handicap other races. Ritt liked to go to the races with his friend Walter Matthau; they became known as the "Odds Couple," he being the best and Matthau the worst (Rickey 40). The two also made a racing film together in 1978, *Casey's Shadow*, which provided a relief for Ritt after his work directing *The Front*.

Ritt's biggest break as a theater director came in 1955. In 1954, while appearing in *The Flowering Peach*, he telephoned Arthur Miller to say that producer Robert Whitehead would let him have his theater every Sunday for a one-act play using the cast of Odets's play. Miller was intrigued by the idea, and within two weeks he wrote *A Memory of Two Mondays*, "a kind of elegy for my years in the auto parts warehouse" (353). In his autobiography *Timebends*, Miller remembered that time: "Stout and cheerful, a gifted poker and horse player, Ritt was high on the new one-act but thought I needed a curtain raiser for it, something to round out a full evening. I loved this promising atmosphere of sheer play and enjoyed my own power to give actors roles without commercial worries to dampen the happiness of work. Besides one-act plays were never done in the Broadway theatre, and rarely in the rest of the country, and this added to the attraction of the project" (353). The "curtain raiser" that Miller came up with was *A View from the Bridge*. The play, clearly influenced by the times, concerns a Sicilian waterfront worker who, in a jealous rage, informs on his nephew, an illegal immigrant. As in *The Crucible*, the act of informing was still a major issue for the playwright as well as the director.

Because *The Flowering Peach* closed sooner than expected, these two Miller plays were put into rehearsal for Broadway, but casting proved to be a problem. For the title role of Eddie Carbone, Miller suggested Lee J. Cobb, who had starred to great acclaim in *Death of a Salesman* seven years earlier. Although Cobb had been his colleague at the Group Theatre, Ritt balked at casting an informer; Miller believed that attitude only perpetuated the blacklist mentality. Cobb's agent solved the problem, however, declaring that Cobb could not appear in a Miller play lest he incur the wrath of the American Legion. Miller was then dissatisfied with the casting of Van Heflin as well as J. Carrole Naish (as the narrator), who, according to Miller, "scrambled his lines like a juggler who keeps dropping his Indian clubs" (354).

The double bill opened in New York at the Coronet Theatre on September 29, 1955. Brooks Atkinson of the *New York Times* found *A Memory of Two Mondays* "pedestrian" but *View* "grim and rasping." Miller himself was not fond of this original production of what was to become one of his most often revived and most successful plays. He felt the play's presentation made it seem like "an academic and irrelevant story of revenge" (354), and he thought Ritt had gone along with the producer Kermit Bloomgarden's desire for a Broadway hit rather than remaining faithful to the play's spirit. "Marty Ritt . . . went along, as he thought he must, rather than aggressively pursuing his own vision of what the production ought to be. In a word, the play on the stage had no tang" (354–55).

A View from the Bridge had a respectable run, but it was not a hit. It did, however, catch the eye of producer David Susskind, who asked Ritt to direct Robert Alan Aurthur's *A Very Special Baby*, a play about a dictatorial father who tries to dominate his family, his thirty-four-year-old youngest son in particular. (Its theme of father-son confrontation would recur often in Ritt's later work.) This contact led directly to the beginning of Ritt's film career. When Susskind decided to film Aurthur's teleplay, *A Boy Is Ten Feet Tall*, he defied the blacklist by offering the job of director to Martin Ritt.

CHAPTER 2

The Making of a Film Director:
Edge of the City and
No Down Payment

Familial conflict, especially between father and son, is one of the subplots of *Edge of the City*, Ritt's first film. Written by Aurthur, whose source was his television play *A Man Is Ten Feet Tall* (Philco Television Playhouse, October 2, 1955, NBC), and produced by Susskind, the film featured Jack Warden, this time in the role of the villain.

Blacklisted from working in television, Ritt was teaching at the Actors Studio. Aurthur wanted Ritt to direct the film, but Susskind at first balked because of Ritt's outlaw status. Metro-Goldwyn-Mayer was involved in a proxy fight, however, and so Ritt was hired because he was willing to work for ten thousand dollars. Fearful of his taint, no one from the studio talked to him. Ritt made the film in about a month, filming in a railroad yard in New York City and at the Fox-Movietone Studio; its cost was less than a half a million dollars. In the film Sidney Poitier retained the role of Tommy Tyler, which he had played in the television production, while John Cassavetes replaced Don Murray in the central role of Axel Nordmann, and Jack Warden replaced Martin Balsam as Charlie Malick.

Unsure of how to make a movie—"I didn't even know where to look in a camera"—Ritt nonetheless found himself able to tell his crew, "This is what I want. He's going to be walking down here, this is what I want to see, this is the size I'd like to see, and I got what I wanted." Ritt recalled that when the film was finished, he had shot so little film that the cutter told him, "You are crazy. If you had made a single mistake we wouldn't have been able to put this one together"

(SMU 27). Ritt's novice status was shared by the production company, for this was the first effort of the group that composed Jonathan Productions (named for Robert Alan Aurthur's son): Aurthur, Susskind, and Alfred Levy, who was later to become Frank Sinatra's manager but who at the time was a contract-budget specialist for Susskind's Talent Associates.

The working title for *Edge of the City* was *A Man Is Ten Feet Tall*, and the film retained that title for its British release. It was an auspicious directorial debut. Energetically paced by the jazz-like contrapuntal rhythms of Leonard Rosenman's score, the film displays Ritt's fondness for the closed, tight construction that he would utilize more subtly in his later urban films. The overuse of symbolic shots, such as those of Axel Nordmann (Cassavetes) framed by gates and gate-like doors that emphasize his psychological entrapment, reflects the first-time director's struggle to find his own style. Ritt does, however, let his camera dwell on the New York setting, making it more of a presence than he would later in *The Brotherhood* or *The Front*, where exterior shots are minimized.

This film introduces a number of important themes that would recur in Ritt's work. Both Nordmann and Tommy Tyler (Poitier) are outsiders. A deserter from the army, Nordmann is estranged from his family and devoid of any other personal relationships, while Tyler is a black man who tries to embrace life, but finds himself harassed on the job by Charlie Malick (Warden). In addition to the outsider theme, race is explored, though minimally, while Ritt concentrates instead in his presentation of the city, on an early delineation of pastoral and anti-pastoral motifs that would dominate his later films. There are also references to the blacklist and informing, subjects that were to shadow much of his work until he managed to exorcise them in *The Front*.

The subject of informing, the character of a corrupt boss extorting money from workers, and the loading dock setting evoke *On the Waterfront*, which had been released three years earlier, directed by Ritt's former Group Theatre colleague and friend Elia Kazan. Each film's protagonist struggles under the thumb of a corrupt boss, and each finds his life and his sense of self expanded through a significant relationship. Terry Molloy (Marlon Brando) is forced to confront both his lost innocence and his unsavory relationship with the union when he falls in love with Edie Doyle (Eva Marie Saint), the sister of a man he was indirectly responsible for killing. Axel Nordmann is brought out of his shell by the friendly overtures of Tyler and by his attraction to Ellen Wilson (Kathleen Maguire), a friend of Tyler and his wife (Ruby Dee).

Aurthur's teleplay *A Man Is Ten Feet Tall* reveals closer ties to *On the Waterfront* than does Ritt's film. The original story takes place on the piers and docks of New York's waterfront, while the film's locale is the railroad yard, and there are references to the workers organizing a union to combat oppressive, boss-controlled working conditions. Tommy Tyler suggests that Malick's hatred of him is due in part to his support of a union. After Tommy's death, the investigating detective tells the workers, "Let the hoods run the racket and you pay the penalty. . . . Only you can stop it." In the teleplay, Axel Nordmann challenges Malick and tells the boss that he is going to call the police, thus defying the code of silence, but this scene was cut from the film version. There are also references to seventy-three unsolved deaths on the waterfront; Axel is determined that Tommy's will not be the seventy-fourth.

While the political issues remain in the foreground of the teleplay, Aurthur's focus, like Ritt's in the film, is on Axel's evolution into a man who can rise to the moral stature of "ten feet tall." His mentor is Tyler, who talks more in the television drama about the need for man to evolve. Tyler urges Axel to stop looking down, to look up toward the heavens, and Axel responds by confiding his dreams of sailing to far-off places and his recognition of the life-transforming power of love. Having left a girlfriend back home in Minneapolis (Gary, Indiana, in the film), Axel openly envies Tyler's home life.

The conclusion of *Edge of the City* is less problematic than that of Kazan's film because its main focus has been on the evolution of the protagonist, leaving the union theme secondary. Axel's consciousness is nurtured and expanded through his relationship with Tyler, and Ritt's presentation of the interracial friendship, although muted and unremarked, was courageous for its time. During a fight Tyler is killed, but his death is reported as an accident because the men, including Axel, refuse to cooperate with the police by informing on Malick, the racist boss who is responsible for his death.

Soon afterward, Axel reconciles with his family and plans to return home, but first, to placate his guilt for not reporting his friend's killer to the police, he visits Tommy's widow to give her some money. After a heated argument, she throws him out of her apartment, whereupon Axel decides to return to the yard to confront Malick. Again there is a fight; Axel manages to strangle Malick into unconsciousness, and then picking the villain up by his collar, he drags him away toward the police station as the camera focuses on Axel, his act of courage complete.

Ritt's film, unlike Kazan's, is essentially a personal story, as Ritt's emphasis remains focused on the individual's need to come to grips with his conscience and assert his own convictions in the face of repressive group pressure. In this act of moral courage, Axel is the prototype for the heroes of Ritt's mature films. In the films of the sixties, however, the heroic action will destroy the individual;

here the implication is that Axel will be redeemed. His parents are prepared to welcome him back, and Tyler's family, one assumes, will applaud his bravery.

If Axel is sullen and repressed, Tyler is his opposite—open and ebullient. Character oppositions such as this are another device that Ritt would use often, most successfully in *Hud*, *The Brotherhood*, and *The Molly Maguires*. Tommy is an outsider by virtue of his color, but he has managed to overcome it by embracing life and family. Sidney Poitier described him as "symbolic of what people would like to be. . . . He was a strong man. He was a just man. He was a well-loved man. . . . And these ingredients in his character made his colour invisible" (Gow 97). The sacrifice of this noble individual offers Axel the chance to redeem himself. Early in the film Tyler tells him, "A man's gotta make a choice. There are the men and there are the lower forms. . . . You go with the men and you're ten feet tall. You go with the lower forms and you are down in the slime."

Ritt's archetypal protagonist must make a choice that involves a moral alternative. Axel must reintegrate himself with family and society, for, as Tyler tells him, being "alone is the worst." In subsequent films, Ritt would come to see "alone" with more complexity, sometimes recognizing it as the only viable alternative. Here, however, remaining outside all groups is tantamount to spiritual suicide. The decision to confront Malick enables Axel to reunite with his family, to confront his past, and, perhaps, to build a healthy relationship with his girlfriend.

The scene establishing the relationship between Tyler and Axel takes place on a pier overlooking the water. Away from the railroad, the men relax, enjoying food and a few laughs. This is the first of many such water settings wherein Ritt's characters are able to share an ideal moment divorced from the harsh social or political reality of the rest of the film. Tyler refers to the spot as "freedomsville."

The concept of freedom experienced as a respite from modern life is at the core of this film and of *On the Waterfront* as well. Both films employ the image of workers hemmed in and regimented as they load cargo under the control of bosses as metaphors for repression in the city and in society as a whole. The chain-gang symbolism is further colored by reference to the House Un-American Activities Committee, whose specter haunts both *On the Waterfront*, with its subtext of informing, and *Edge of the City*. In a scene following the idyll at the pier, Axel tells Tyler that his real name is Nordmann, not the North that he uses on the job. Tyler replies that he likes North better because it is more American, and "these days it pays to be 110 percent American."

One other parallel to a later work is notable. Axel's estrangement from his rigid, moralistic father (a policeman) prefigures Hud's troubled relationship with his father, Homer Bannon. In both cases the estrangement is due in part to the father's holding his son responsible for the death of an older brother in a car accident. In *Edge* Ritt ultimately brings father and son back together, as Axel is able to atone for his past by performing an act of bravery. In the later work, however, Hud never reconciles with his father, remaining unrepentant to the end. The distance Ritt had moved in his assessment of human nature can be measured by the differing fates of these two protagonists.

Edge of the City was an impressive film debut, although when the executives at Metro saw the film, they hated it, and for a time would not even place it on the release list. When eventually released, however, it received excellent reviews and was even nominated for awards by the London Academy. Soon after its opening, Buddy Adler of Twentieth-Century Fox invited Ritt to come to Hollywood to direct *No Down Payment*, based on a novel by John McPartland. Having worked only sporadically from 1951 to 1957, broke and in debt, Ritt was happy to get a job in Hollywood.

Jerry Wald had purchased rights to the novel in manuscript, and production started on the film before the book was published. Ritt's film, with a screenplay by Philip Yordan, moves the story from San Francisco to Los Angeles, which has no real effect on the novel's themes or characters. Set in a middle-class subdivision called Sunrise Hills, the story focuses on four young couples who are shown to be victims of the rat race that was consuming the upwardly mobile after World War II. The narrative touches on the related issues of automation, buying on credit, and racial integration. If the film bites off more than it can chew, these themes are for the most part effectively presented, and *No Down Payment* thus serves as a primer on many motifs Ritt would return to later in his career.

Among the families the film focuses on are Herman and Betty Kreitzer (Pat Hingle and Barbara Rush). Herman, the owner of a hardware store, argues with his wife over his not going to church. Their neighbors are Jerry Flagg (Tony Randall), a used car salesman with a big-shot complex, and his patient, long-suffering wife, Isabel (Sheree North), and Troy and Leola Boone (Cameron Mitchell and Joanne Woodward), a couple from Tennessee. Troy is a war hero who misses the violence and the camaraderie of the military and desperately wants to become the town's police chief; Leola just wants a child. As the film opens, these three couples are settled and sociable, indulging in a round of cookouts and get-togethers. Into this placid group come David and Jean Martin (Jeffrey Hunter and Patricia Owens), who are immediately integrated into the social world of their neighbors.

Ritt is most interested in exploring the lives of these affluent suburbanites in order to show how the pursuit of money and status erodes character and destroys relationships. The film's varying focus on the lives of the four couples, however, works against the dramatic power the creators were after, dissipating any emotional involvement in their stories.

The Flaggs are the primary exemplars of the single-minded pursuit of wealth that destroys lives. The last of the four families to be introduced, they eventually disappear from the story with no apparent resolution to their plot segment. Jerry Flagg first appears at noon on Sunday, already preparing his first cocktail. Berated by his wife for this indulgence, he excuses it with the claim that he is preparing for a busy day. He next appears at the Kreitzers' barbecue, where he arrives quite drunk. As Isabel greets him, she notices lipstick on his shirt. He then asks Jean Martin to dance and becomes so aggressive in his attentions that Troy has to break them up. Isabel confronts her husband, insisting that he is drinking too much despite a doctor's recommendation that he quit. Jerry responds that he is sick of himself. They fight; Isabel slaps him and leaves the party.

The next day Jerry stumbles back into his house after sleeping in the car. He promises to buy his son a bike, although he obviously can't afford it, and he apologizes to Isabel, who suggests that he get a job selling new cars so that he can bring home a steady pay check. But Jerry longs for the "big killing" that he can only get on commission. Dreaming of a bigger house in a better neighborhood, he relives the week when he once made eight hundred dollars in commissions.

Desperate to raise thirty dollars to buy the bicycle, Jerry turns to his boss for a loan, who turns him down saying, "You're already into me for two hundred dollars." (At the barbecue it had been revealed that Jerry was five hundred dollars in debt.) He then pressures a financially strapped couple into buying a car on credit, involving an unscrupulous finance company, and he gets them to give him enough money for the bicycle. To celebrate, Jerry persuades his wife to give a barbecue. As they toast living on credit and having everything they want, Jerry's boss interrupts the party, demanding that he return the money he took on the car.

The climactic bedroom scene between Jerry and Isabel is a variation on a scene in Arthur Miller's *Death of a Salesman*. When Jerry comes home from another night of bar hopping and begins to boast about a big business scheme that will make them millionaires, Isabel tells him again to get a regular-paying job and to accept the fact that he is only an average man. Angrily, Jerry rejects his own mediocrity: like Willy Loman, Jerry denies that he is "a dime a dozen"—he is Jerry Flagg, a man who has bought into the success ethic without giving it much thought, believing that he can succeed on the strength of a "smile and a shoeshine." Despite its derivative structure, the scene is effectively handled by Tony Randall, and Ritt's staging, employing the couple's bed as the central prop, lends poignance and power to a moment in which family and home disintegrate before an inadequate and self-defeating philosophy.

The film's designated protagonists are the Martins. Ritt opens the film with his characteristic establishing shot—this time of the Los Angeles freeway, which is crowded with cars. As he cuts to the Martins in their car, they pass billboards advertising various communities, including Sunrise Hill Estates, which they soon pull into. Their first impression, of a church from which the congregants are departing, resembles a Norman Rockwell painting; it is not dissimilar to Hitchcock's setting for Santa Rosa in *Shadow of a Doubt*. Next the Martins are seen moving into their new home; they arrive along with the moving van, to be immediately greeted by the Kreitzers and invited to a barbecue. Entering the house, David looks out a window and sees the Boones kissing in their bed in the house next door.

Later at the barbecue, David mentions that he worked at Los Alamos during the war, although he claims that he never knew what was being done there and that he never left the country. In the resentment expressed by Troy, a decorated veteran, Ritt introduces a hint of secrecy underlying the placid surface, involving the bomb and American paranoia, but then he does little to develop this theme, which nevertheless remains as a sinister undercurrent throughout much of the film.

The Martins' story revolves around sex and money. David is an engineer and a scientist dedicated to research, but his wife, like Jerry Flagg, is enamored of money and status. Jean wants her husband to earn more and thinks he should go into sales. She misses her carefree days and still enjoys flirting and showing off her looks. When the drunken Jerry makes advances toward her at the party, David is visibly agitated, but he does nothing. It is Troy who steps between Jean and Jerry, and there is a suggestion that he, too, is attracted to her.

These strands come together in the film's climax. David, having agreed to try sales in order to please her, is sent to San Francisco to see a client. Troy, who is discouraged and angry because the town council has turned him down for police chief, gets drunk and walks into the Martin house, where he rapes Jean. Staging the scene much like Kazan does a similar one in *Streetcar*, Ritt shoots the frightened face of Jean and then cuts to a close-up of Troy as he moves closer toward the camera, and this is followed by a fade. Setting up the scene in this way seems to have been Wald's idea. In a memo to Ritt, he wrote: "The scene could be shot with the camera behind Troy's back and following him closer and closer to Jean, who is up against wall and who, because of the fear of what she knows is going to happen, cannot scream, even though she tries to. It could be deeply emotional if we ended the scene on the camera coming closer to Jean's face" (RC 5-31-57).

When Jean tells David about the rape, the scene is staged in the bathroom as David is shaving, and Ritt frames his face in the mirror. Realizing that he must confront Troy, David finds him in his garage and starts to choke him, but he is soon overwhelmed by the stronger man and knocked unconscious. Recovering, David walks back home, and Jean watches him through a window—Ritt's dual frame technique both emphasizes their marriage trap and makes their reconciliation more dramatic. When Jean cries, "I'm no good for you," David insists that they will face their problems and overcome them, and he proclaims his love for her without reservation. Jean, moved, does the same.

Wald felt that the Martins' story was the backbone of the film. In a lengthy memo to Ritt, he stressed the importance of an emotionally satisfying resolution of David and Jean's story and articulated his theory of film: "To me, all great films have to provide entertainment, enlightenment and exaltation. If it were not for the former, movies would not exist; without the latter, I don't think they could survive. The greatest films have a generous measure of all three—but, if a film contains a great measure of any of the three, it might have a possible chance of being remembered for a long, long time. We are on the verge of hitting the jackpot. What we need is a feeling of exaltation in the film in the final scene between David and Jean" (RC 6-14-57).

Wald's enthusiasm was contagious, though Ritt took it with a grain of salt, perhaps realizing that Wald's grand designs for his films were invariably undercut by his even stronger desire to please his audience. This film never achieves the kind of catharsis that Wald envisioned, and it certainly never comes close to tragedy. Wald's lofty aspirations for the Martins' story is undone by the multilayered structure of the plot.

No Down Payment is an effective melodrama that weaves together a series of stories in a suburban soap opera, and the emotional impact of the Martins' experience is absorbed into the rest of the film's action. Their reconciliation is immediately linked with the destruction of the Boones' relationship. When Leola finds out about the rape, she also confronts him in the garage. During their fight, Leola pushes him toward the car (a symbol of what all suburbanites are striving for) and it falls on him and kills him. Troy has not been a sympathetic character, and so neither his contrived death nor the Martins' juxtaposed declaration of love carries much emotional weight, although in combination they do achieve some melodramatic closure.

The film's conclusion reflects Wald's insistence on a happy ending, but it ends with Leola, rather than with the Martins, which confuses the dramatic structure.

In the final scene Leola gets into a cab to leave the development, and Ritt follows her with shots of Sunrise Hills, particularly the church. Herman Kreitzer, who had refused to go to church with his family, has become a church-goer, presumably because the minister helped to get Herman's Japanese employee Iko and his family into Sunrise Hills, a move opposed by some members of the community. With the apparent triumph of marital and racial harmony and the elimination of the violent (and racist) Troy, Sunrise Hills seems ready to become all that it appears to be on the surface.

Ritt hated the ending of the film. "I didn't want to shoot the end of the film, and for two days they fired me. They brought in another director and said, 'He's going to shoot the end we want.' So I went back and shot the ending they wanted. So I think the first half of that film works pretty well, and the second half is a lot of shit" (SMU 29).

Despite its structural flaws, *No Down Payment* offers an insightful portrait of the American middle class, exploring the problems of adjustment to the lifestyle of leisure created by automation and technology. Ritt even introduces that most pervasive aspect of American culture, television, even allowing sets showing programs to dominate some scenes. He also manages, through references to Los Alamos, Troy's chauvinism, and the conformist state of mind at Sunrise Hills, to reflect upon the national paranoia over Communism and its continuing effects on the national agenda. This, of course, was an issue Ritt would return to again and again.

CHAPTER 3

William Faulkner and Jerry Wald:
The Long Hot Summer and
The Sound and the Fury

Ritt was to make three more films for Jerry Wald between 1958 and 1962. Having announced that he planned to make film versions of literary classics, Wald asked Ritt to direct adaptations of William Faulkner's *The Hamlet* and *The Sound and the Fury.* Faulkner had worked for Wald while both were at Warner's, and the producer was a great admirer of the novelist's work. Now at Fox, Wald persuaded the studio to pay fifty thousand dollars for the two novels, which he planned to shoot in color and cinemascope.

The first film, based on *The Hamlet,* was renamed *The Long Hot Summer* to avoid confusion with Shakespeare's play. This was an auspicious project for Ritt, teaming him for the first time with writing partners Irving Ravetch and Harriet Frank Jr., who would go on to collaborate with Ritt on seven more films, including some of his best work. It also marked Ritt's first film association with Paul Newman, who had studied with him at the Actor's Studio and who would star in five more of the director's films. The cast included other Actor's Studio alumni: Joanne Woodward, Lee Remick, and Anthony Franciosa. Filmed in Clinton and Baton Rouge, Louisiana, this was also the first of eight films in which Ritt made use of the southern setting that would strongly flavor his career.

Much of the publicity surrounding the making of this film revolved around the casting of Orson Welles as Will Varner. Fox executives did not want Welles because he was considered difficult and temperamental, but Ritt insisted that he would be "terrific in this part," and the studio relented. Welles remembered, "There was a note of suspicion. I did not know what kind of monkeyshines I would have to put up with and the cast did not know what kind of caprices they would have to put up with me" (Brady 494). There were occasional battles over Welles's reading of the lines, camera placement, and scene blocking—Ritt observed, "Two weeks after we started you could bet we wouldn't finish the film"—but the two men developed respect for each other and managed to get the film made.

In 1965 Ritt related an incident to a reporter from the *Toronto Star:* "So when it's finally time [to shoot the scene] I find him just sitting and reading a Spanish language newspaper. He's not prepared for the scene. I'm pretty mad so I tell everyone, that's it. Let's strike the setup. We'll shoot something else. That night Welles calls me and says, 'Marty, why'd you do that? You humiliated me in front of everyone.' 'I humiliated you? What the hell do you think you did to me?' Then I told him the facts of life. We got along fine afterward" (Jackson 51).

Reflecting on the inevitable tension involved in working with an actor who brought a considerable reputation (and ego) as a director himself, Ritt went on to say: "He kept saying to me, 'You don't know a hell of a lot about making movies.' I said, 'I know a hell of a lot about people and what their behavior has to be in order to make my film work.' He said, 'Yes, you know that.' We had that kind of relationship all through the film" (Jackson 51).

The Long Hot Summer might be more accurately termed a transformation of Faulkner's work than an adaptation. While both versions focus generally on themes of sex and money, their approaches are quite different. The movie builds to a conclusion along the lines of a social comedy, as the hero wins the heart of the girl and all misunderstandings and complications are cleared up, whereas the novel is dominated by an antihero who, as the story ends, has successfully conned one of the town's more intelligent citizens out of a large sum of money. The novel's protagonist, Flem Snopes, is described as having "a pair of eyes of a cold opaque gray between shaggy graying irascible brows and a short scrabble of iron-gray beard as tight and knotted as a sheep's coat" (Faulkner, *Hamlet* 8). This character metamorphoses into the film's hero, renamed Ben Quick (after a minor character in the novel); he is played by Paul Newman, whose blue eyes and good looks were not the stuff Snopeses were made of, although better suited to wooing and winning Joanne Woodward. (It would be a few years yet before Ravetch, Frank, and Ritt could turn Newman into a more Snopes-like character and call him Hud.)

An aggressive white-trash family who dominate three Faulkner novels, *The Hamlet, The Town,* and *The Mansion,* as well as a number of short stories, the Snopses function as symbols of the degeneration of the capitalist ethic and as the forefathers of a modern South. Ravetch and Frank worked with *The Hamlet* and the short story "Barn Burning" in fashioning their script—*The Town* was not published until they were well into their work, and *The Mansion* was published in 1959, a year after the film's release. *The Long Hot Summer* was not conceived as an exposé of a corrupt social system, as are Faulkner's novels and Ravetch and Frank's later films, but as a rather conservative Horatio Alger–like comedy that resolves its conflicts in love and marriage. Ravetch and Frank commented, "*The Long Hot Summer* was a comedy about appetites, about love and sex, courtship and mating, ebullient young men and brainy young ladies, the yearning of parents for their children. It departs in fact, but not in faith, from William Faulkner's attitudes" (Wald, "Faulkner in Hollywood" 131). On its own terms it is a lively and entertaining film, one that Faulkner himself liked.

"Barn Burning" is the story of the vulgar tenant farmer Ab Snopes, who sets fire to the barns of landlords who cross him. His two sons are Flem, who helps him with the burning, and ten-year-old Sarty, who warns their newest landlord, DeSpain, that his barn is in danger. Going to DeSpain's house to introduce himself, Ab Snopes tracks manure onto an expensive and valuable rug, and when DeSpain gives him the rug to clean, he ruins it. DeSpain then takes Snopes's crop as payment, and Ab sues. When he loses the case, he goes to burn DeSpain's barn. After warning the landlord, Sarty runs away.

The Hamlet opens a few years after that story, when Ab rents a farm in Frenchman's Bend. The town is dominated by Will Varner, a veterinarian who owns a lot of property, including the general store run by his overweight son, Jody, who spends most of his time guarding his sexy sister, Eula. When the Varners learn who has rented the farm, they decide not to anger Snopes by evicting him. Flem is eventually hired as a clerk in the store, and there he soon starts loaning money and conning people out of theirs. Flem also agrees to marry Eula, who is pregnant by another man, if Will will give him the Old Frenchman Place, a decaying Civil War mansion on whose grounds there is rumored to be buried treasure. Flem then plants bags of "treasure" in the earth and cons some men into buying the place. The novel ends with the buyers frantically digging for treasure as Flem and Eula leave town and head for Jefferson.

The Long Hot Summer was Ravetch and Frank's first important screenplay, initiating what was to become their signature method of adapting literary sources to the screen—picking up some characters and scenes from the original and then inventing a new plotline, which in some cases bore no resemblance to the source material. This modus operandi is demonstrated again and again in the screenplays they prepared for Ritt (except *Conrack*, a streamlining rather than a transformation of Pat Conroy's *The Water Is Wide*). Ravetch and Frank explained their methodology: "We have found that as screenwriters, we've often needed an outside story to get us started. It sparks us; it sets us in motion. In the end, we may salvage only one or two elements—a character perhaps, or a situation, or a few strong scenes—and on this we build a whole new drama" (*Three Screenplays* xii).

For this film Ravetch and Frank did utilize some of Faulkner's scenes and some character names, although recasting them to suit the purposes of their own story. Flem Snopes was blended with the character of Sarty and renamed Ben Quick. Ben's problem is that everyone accuses him of being a barn burner although he is, as the film makes clear, nothing of the kind. Years of false accusations have hardened him, however, and taught him to put his faith in money, his charm, and his good looks. The film opens with a shot of a barn that suddenly is consumed in flames, followed by a cut to a trial scene, in which Ben is thrown out of town. He walks down the street before the credits begin to roll, over a shot of a barge heading down the Mississippi River. Ben then steps off the barge into the river, wades to dry land, and trudges through a forest and onto a road where he hitches a ride into Frenchman's Bend.

This opening bears comparison to that of *The Molly Maguires*, which also begins with a burning building. The dramatic construction and lyrical development of that image in the later film show how Ritt's craft developed in the twelve intervening years. They also demonstrate the differences of tone and texture between the two films. The fire in *Summer* clearly represents both the torrid climate and the characters' sexual passion, whereas the flames that set the stage in the later film suggest the combustive elements of social injustice and labor unrest that will provoke the rebel coal miners to action.

In Ritt's iconography, Ben's movement onto the river and then into the water signals his redemptive function, for his intervention will ultimately unify the Varner family. The abrupt transition from fire to water plainly signals the film's marked departure from Faulkner's darker, more incendiary work.

Ritt's Ben Quick manages to hitch a ride into Frenchman's Bend (here updated to the 1950s) with Clara Varner (Joanne Woodward) and her sister-in-law, Eula (Lee Remick); there he discovers that Will Varner owns practically everything. As in the novel, he starts out as Varner's tenant farmer, works his way up to clerking in his store, and ends up marrying the boss's daughter. This time, however, that daughter is Clara, a schoolteacher, not Eula, who has become the wife of Jody Varner.

Will Varner, played with gusto by Orson Welles, is an autocratic father to his two children. Jody, though slimmed down and handsome (he is played by Anthony Franciosa), is a weakling who is not good at business and a disappointment to his father—he is one of the many son figures in Ritt's work who are estranged from distant fathers. Jody's only desire is to make love to his wife, Eula, who bears no resemblance to the Faulkner character of the same name but, as portrayed by Lee Remick, is a lively, vibrant, and intelligent woman. In contrast, Clara is a sexually frustrated schoolteacher who has been courted for years by Alan Stewart, a weak, aristocratic landowner who remains under his mother's thumb—he is emblematic of the dying aristocracy now being replaced by the vulgar Varners. Realizing that this seeming suitor won't propose, Clara finally does it for him, but Alan can't bring himself to make a commitment.

A number of famous scenes from Faulkner are altered by Ravetch and Frank to serve the story they are telling. When Ben Quick goes to the Varner house to ask for work, he tracks dirt onto a valuable rug—as Ab Snopes does in "Barn Burning." In the film, however, Clara brings the rug to Ben's place and asks him to clean it, whereupon Ben taunts her by saying that he "riles" her more than the rug. No further mention is made of the rug, for the incident here has been used as merely an excuse to bring Clara and Ben together in a sexually charged situation.

Ravetch and Frank also utilize Faulkner's episode of a sale of wild horses, which in the novel results in significant destruction and injury to several townspeople. In the film Varner agrees to let Ben clerk in his store if he will auction off some wild horses, and he is impressed when Ben sells the horses at a nice profit. The corral is left open, allowing the horses to run through the town and into the lobby of the town's hotel, but here the incident is treated as a joke rather than a reflection of reckless destructiveness. Ben's defiant cunning convinces Varner that he is the man Clara should marry. Ravetch and Frank's Varner wants heirs, and having lost hope of getting them from Jody, he desperately wants some from Clara. He decides that Ben Quick will revitalize his bloodline and give him grandsons to carry on his name.

In reshaping the character of Will Varner, Ravetch and Frank (as they would in *The Sound and the Fury* as well) borrowed more from Tennessee Williams than from Faulkner. Faulkner's Varner—"thin as a rail"—is made a "huge man, powerful by virtue of his size and his immense energy, his gargantuan appetite for life" (Faulkner, *Hamlet* 20). His size, his extensive property holdings, and his recent extended hospital stay are reminiscent of Williams's Big Daddy in *Cat on Hot Tin Roof*, the film version of which was also released in 1958, the same year as *Summer*. Orson Welles's girth matches that of Burl Ives in the Williams film, and the arguments between Jody and his father echo those between Big Daddy and Brick (played by Paul Newman). In an interview in 1987, Ritt mistakenly stated that Williams had borrowed the character from Faulkner, when in fact Ravetch and Frank had borrowed from Williams.

Ritt's film resolves its various plot lines in hasty fashion. After a courting scene by a stream—the use of water as a procreative image is effective here—in which Ben declares his intentions to Clara, he is ambushed by Jody, who wants to kill him for stealing his place in business and in his father's affections. To save himself, Ben shows Jody examples of the "treasure" he found on the French-man's Place, which he now owns, and offers it to him. Delighted at the prospect of finding enough money to become independent of his father, Jody buys the property after unearthing a bag of coins that Ben has planted. Later Varner finds Jody digging for more, and he shows him that the coins were recently minted, proving that he had been duped.

After discovering that Alan Stewart and Clara are not engaged, Varner throws a tantrum at the Stewart home and then returns to his barn to check on a foaling mare, commenting that he is glad "*somethin'* around here is gettin' born." Jody locks him in the barn and sets fire to it, and then he suddenly changes his mind. This change of heart miraculously brings father and son closer together. A lynch mob in town, however, decides to go after Ben Quick. Clara picks him up in her car and drives him to the Varner house where Ben tells her how much he hates fires and how he once turned in his father. Clara, who has had a rocky relation-ship with her own father, finally responds to him. When the lynch mob arrives at the house, Varner intervenes, saying that he started the fire with a cigar, and then he invites everyone to a party on Sunday.

The story concludes in high comic style, as Ben lectures Will Varner on busi-ness ethics, dealing with people, and the sanctity of life. Jody and Eula are happy again, Clara and Ben seal their love with a kiss, and Varner even decides to marry Minnie (in the novel they are married to others). All decide to settle down for the night, and the film ends with a shot of the house as the lights go off.

The Long Hot Summer, like Ritt's other domestic films of this period, has a happy ending. The plot complications, caused by misunderstandings, are re-solved once everyone acknowledges his or her part in the problems. There is no social satire here; if Will Varner's business dealings are a bit crude, Ben Quick will make them more humane. In the process he gets the girl and some money, and he clears his name. All this has nothing to do with Faulkner, and in its endorsement of the status quo, little to do with the Ravetch-Ritt collaborations of the '60s and '70s, with their emphasis on social criticism and reform.

The Long Hot Summer might have little of Faulkner in it, but it is, except for its hurried and contrived ending, a well-observed, well-acted, well-paced, and entertaining film. It won Paul Newman the Best Actor award at the 1958 Cannes Film Festival. The following year Ritt, Wald, and Ravetch and Frank presented a far less successful version of Faulkner's *The Sound and the Fury*—a wooden, plodding, confused film that succeeds neither as an adaptation nor as a film in its own right. This is easily the most misguided of the Ritt-Ravetch collaborations.

The novel's plot revolves around the Compson family. Jason Compson, a dipsomaniac, and Caroline Compson, a faded remnant of southern gentility, have four children. The eldest son, Quentin, is a moody intellectual who drowns himself while a student at Harvard—his section of the narrative takes place on the day of his suicide. The daughter, Caddy, is restless and self-destructive but also compassionate and stouthearted. The younger Jason, like the Snopses, is an insensitive materialist. Benjy, the idiot son, is, like Quentin, extremely sensitive; his sensory impressions constitute the novel's first section. The family is taken care of by the maid, Dilsey, narrator of the fourth section, who embodies the enduring values of wisdom and compassion.

All three brothers are fixated on Caddy. Quentin seems incestuously attracted to her, and he tries to prevent her from sleeping with a local rake, Quentin Ames, even to the point of proposing a suicide pact. The central issue for Quentin is that the loss of his sister's virginity would destroy those verities in which he desperately wants to believe: family honor, chastity, and history, all of which Faulkner associates with rigidity and death. Caddy, however, does get pregnant by Ames, and this becomes the crucial event in the lives of the brothers. All this is foreshadowed by what Faulkner called the novel's central event: Caddy, age seven, is playing with her brothers by a creek and muddies her drawers; when she takes off her dress to change, Quentin slaps her. She then violates another rule by climbing a tree to look in on her grandmother's wake.

Eventually Quentin drowns himself in the Charles River because he cannot deal with the concept of change. Caddy marries a banker, has a daughter whom she names Quentin after her brother, divorces, and leaves the baby to be raised by the Compsons. At this point Jason suffers a major setback, being denied a promised position at the bank, and he takes out his resentment on Quentin II. After his father's death, Jason becomes head of the family, and when Caddy sends him money for Quentin II's support, he embezzles most of it.

Various other incidents from Jason's and Dilsey's narratives are utilized in the film. Jason tells of his discovery of Quentin II's flirtation with a man in a red tie who has come to town with a carnival, of his having Benjy castrated, and of his plans to send him to an asylum. Dilsey then reveals that Quentin II has run away with the carnival man and has taken the money Jason embezzled. Jason gives chase but can't find her.

Ravetch and Frank again substantially revised and refashioned Faulkner in bringing this complex novel to the screen. Despite its intricate manipulation of time, the novel seems cinematic in its use of "montage" techniques, intercutting past and present so that events collide with one another to evoke character and theme. The screenwriters scrapped this technical artistry altogether, however, choosing instead to present the story in present time and in chronological order. As in *The Long Hot Summer*, the action of the film is placed in the 1950s. Unlike the earlier film, however, Wald decided to shoot the film in the studio. Wald had lost thirteen days of shooting on location to overcast skies in Louisiana and he didn't want to repeat that. This decision seriously handicapped Ritt, who had to sacrifice the atmosphere and texture that real locations contributed to his best work.

The film revolves around the maturation of its heroine, Quentin II (Joanne Woodward), and the shape and theme of this coming-of-age story is closer to Ravetch, Frank, and Ritt than to Faulkner. Its presentation remains confused whether one focuses on Faulkner or on Ritt. The story now chronicles Quentin II's rebellion against her step-uncle Jason (a hopelessly miscast Yul Brynner), who insists that she be respectable while she demands to be left alone. By the end of the film, she has decided not to run away with Charlie Busch, the carnival man (Stuart Whitman), but to seduce Jason, whose wisdom and sensitivity she has come to appreciate.

Ravetch and Frank keep the character of Quentin in the film by turning him into Uncle Howard, an alcoholic who lives in the Compson house and is dependent on Jason. Caddy (Margaret Leighton) returns from her travels to see Quentin II, and she, too, moves back into the house. Here Ravetch and Frank are again borrowing from Tennessee Williams, this time modeling Caddy on Blanche Dubois, an image of ravaged southern womanhood. The film's Caddy seduces Jason's boss, à la Blanche, by walking into his store and saying, "A sweet little boy offered to drive me home." The music is even reminiscent of Elia Kazan's film of *A Streetcar Named Desire*. To make it possible for Quentin II to contemplate marrying Jason, it is revealed that his mother was Mr. Compson's second wife, whose Cajun ancestry justifies the casting of the swarthy Brynner. Benjy (Jack Warden) is presented as silent, expressionless, and occasionally menacing, but no insight is provided into his character.

Faulkner's pivotal moment, in which Caddy muddies her drawers, is recalled in a ludicrous scene as Caddy and Uncle Howard sit by a brook. Howard, still anguished by his sister's promiscuous behavior, cries out, "How many were there?" The vignette, providing no thematic resolution, is one of many scenes about a troubled family that add up to little effect.

The film ultimately concerns only the maturation of a rebellious girl. Like *The Long Hot Summer*, it offers a portrait of a decaying aristocratic South that is being taken over by the more modern, aggressive likes of Jason Compson. Eventually, however, it becomes clear that Jason, like Ben Quick, is a sensitive and worthy fellow and the right man for the feisty heroine embodied by Joanne Woodward. When the film's Jason, unlike his literary prototype, finds Quentin II with Charlie Busch and the money, he tells her that she can keep it because he had intended to spend it on her anyway. All then ends happily with the prospect of romance and marriage between these two now sympathetic characters. Faulkner's themes of the destruction of a family and a way of life are not even hinted at here, leaving the film with neither Faulkner's potentially cinematic technique nor his richly evocative story. What is substituted remains superficial and unconvincing melodrama.

Jerry Wald was, however, most impressed with the film; his memos to Ritt during shooting are full of enthusiastic praise. In a letter to John Einfeld at Fox, he wrote: "*The Sound and the Fury* is a different kind of motion picture. It makes no compromises with tradition. It is daring and will appeal to our long lost audience who have come to regard Hollywood as a western factory. . . . from the beginning of this project we were assured of great and instant acceptance. When we made *The Long Hot Summer* last year we were actually doing rehearsal on film for *The Sound and the Fury. The Long Hot Summer* was an experiment, and a very successful one. It was the first time the public had been given Faulkner in heroic doses—and they went for it" (RC 1-22-59).

The studio executives, however, did not share Wald's enthusiasm. The film was not released as a prestige product, and that irked Ritt at the time. In a letter to Buddy Adler, he wrote, "I just heard about the release date for *The Sound and the Fury.* I can't think of a better way to put a knife into the heart of this picture." He went on, "This picture represents a lot of sweat and hard work. I broke my back to help organize it and brought it in four days under schedule, apparently so that the brass could then use it as a cheap picture" (RC 2-6-59). Ritt's enthusiasm for the film apparently dampened over the years, however, for he rarely discussed it.

Jerry Wald was an active and dynamic producer, hated by some—he is supposedly the model for Sammy Glick in Bud Schulberg's *What Makes Sammy Run*—but respected by others, including Clifford Odets, who wrote the screenplay for Wald's *Humoresque, The Story on Page One,* and *Wild in the Country.* Wald also produced the film version of Odets's *Clash by Night.* Wald thought seriously about film as an art form and he tried to bring serious films based on literary works to the screen; but he was torn between his ambitions for his films and the dictates of commercial success. In addition to the films discussed here,

Wald produced numerous literary adaptations, including *Mildred Pierce, Key Largo, The Glass Menagerie, The Breaking Point,* and *Sons and Lovers.*

Wald also wrote about adapting literary works for the screen. The year *The Sound and the Fury* was released, Wald published two essays, "Faulkner in Hollywood" in *Films in Review* and "From Faulkner to Film" in the *Saturday Review.* In 1954 he wrote "Screen Adaptation," also for *Films in Review.* In that essay Wald declares that film is an art form and that many screenwriters "have mastered film writing technique with the same degree of skill and assurance as that which Thomas Mann and Somerset Maugham [Wald produced *Miss Sadie Thompson*] mastered theirs."

Wald goes on to argue that in adapting a work of literature to the screen, a writer has two primary tasks. The first is length—if a story cannot be told in 120 minutes, it is not worth telling. The other key problem is what to cut: "Only the most gifted of screenwriters can keep the intent, the flavor, the theme, and the spirit of the original."

Wald was able to adhere to his own dictates in a number of his literary productions, including *The Long Hot Summer.* By his standards, however, *The Sound and the Fury* must be considered a failure. In shifting the dark, tragic tone of the film from a story of two women who are damned to the story of a woman who is saved by returning to her family, Wald and Ritt violate both Faulkner's intent and his theme. The film remains among each man's least successful efforts.

CHAPTER 4

Lost in Europe: *Five Branded Women* and *Paris Blues*

After *The Sound and the Fury*, Ritt accepted an offer from Dino De Laurentis to go to northern Italy, near Turin, to direct *Jovanka E L'Altri*, which was released in English as *Five Branded Women* in 1960. Ritt would always despise this film, never listing it among credits. When his papers were donated to the Motion Picture Academy Library after his death, nothing from that film was included. Years after making it, he told a reporter that if he had had enough money in 1960, he would have bought up all copies of the film. In an interview with Bruce Cook, he commented: "Never made a bad picture? You bet I have—*Five Branded Women*, the only one I'm ashamed of. Maybe you missed that one, it was hardly released in this country, and I keep it off my list. I did it for Dino De Laurentis and it was just for the money. I found out then what I should have known before—that you can never work just for money and expect to do anything good" (Cook 52).

The story takes place in Yugoslavia during the German occupation of World War II. Five women are exiled from their town and forced to shave their heads for fraternizing with German officers. One of the officers, named Keller (Steve Forrest), is castrated by members of the Yugoslav resistance movement in a scene early in the film. The women (Silvana Mangano, Jean Moreau, Barbara Bel Geddes, Vera Miles, and Carla Gravino) wander the countryside, eventually deciding to join the resistance movement and commit to group action.

While *Five Branded Women* is a flat, stodgy, awkwardly dubbed film, it is significant among Ritt's early work as the only film before *Hud* that focuses on a group rather than on the isolated individual. Like many of the early films, *Five Branded Women* remains interesting primarily as a forerunner of an important later film, in this case *The Molly Maguires*, which grapples with similar issues.

The five women are thrown together as exiles, despised by their own people and by the enemy. The partisans cut their hair and the Germans then decide to expatriate them. Jovanka (Mangano) becomes their leader by virtue of her stubbornness and strength. She is vocal in her hatred of war and blames both sides for the brutality inflicted on innocent people. She makes love with Keller merely to experience some warmth and tenderness, although Keller, a predatory nihilist who is representative of war's savagery, tries to disabuse her of any romantic feelings. Declaring that sex is no different if there is love, he insists that people shouldn't believe in anything except themselves. This cynical attitude confirms Jovanka's individualist tendencies, which in turn make her Ritt's focal point.

The women's status as partisans is confirmed when they witness an ambush of German troops and then proceed to take the boots and weapons off the dead soldiers. Jovanka's status as leader is firmly established when she shoots two soldiers who try to rape the women. Later, after the partisans have watched them ambush a German troop, they vote to integrate the women into their group. The same partisans who shaved their heads and caused their exile now welcome them as comrades.

The leader and spiritual center of the partisans is Velko (Van Heflin), who advocates discipline and obedience above all. In welcoming the women into the group, he warns everyone against forming a sexual or emotional relationship with another member, because it could lead to a breakdown of discipline and endanger the others. This savage, inhuman attitude angers Jovanka, but she agrees to put up with it for the remainder of the war. When Velko, who was responsible for cutting off Jovanka's hair, suggests that they should now become friends, she replies that it will be impossible until he comes to feel what shame or humiliation means—in short, to allow a human emotion to find its way into his battle-scarred will.

The personal antagonism between these two individualist leaders, an antagonism which is at the core of the film, finds its most dramatic and disturbing moment in the trial of one of the women, Danza (Vera Miles), and a partisan, Branco (Harry Guardino). Danza, ironically, should not have been exiled with the others because she had never had an affair with Keller. While on guard one evening, however, she agrees to have sex with Branco, who in his carnal appetites mirrors the German officer. While the couple are thus neglecting their duty, some Germans are able to infiltrate the camp. Although the invaders are killed by the partisans, Danza and Branco are tried for endangering the group, and they are sentenced to death.

The main advocate for the death penalty is Velko. Jovanka tries to defend the couple, stating that what they did was "human" and that the law is "inhuman." The majority vote for death, however, and Jovanka is selected to be a member of the firing squad.

Among the many ironic symmetries that dominate the film, Branco is executed for the same transgression for which he earlier castrated Keller, and Danza is finally punished for committing the same crime she was unjustly accused of earlier. The execution of Danza provides the most jarring moment in the film, dramatically confirming Jovanka's sense that the war has dehumanized even the forces of good. Jovanka cannot participate, and it is left to another member of the firing squad to shoot Danza.

The audience's growing ambivalence about the two sides is further complicated by the treatment of a German prisoner of war, Captain Reinhardt (Richard Basehart). The captain, a professor of philosophy before the war, is presented as one of the more humane characters in the film. Ljuba (Jeanne Moreau), one of the women who captures and guards him, is clearly attracted to him. When Ljuba must assist with the birth of Mira's (Carla Gravina) baby, Reinhardt clearly has an opportunity to take Ljuba's gun and escape, but he stays to help with the birth instead. Later, knowing that the Germans do not have any partisan prisoners to exchange for him, he makes a half-hearted escape attempt and Ljuba is forced to shoot him.

Ritt cuts between Velko and Jovanka kneeling over a dead comrade who was shot during a sabotage raid and a similar shot of Ljuba kneeling beside Reinhardt's body, as if to parallel the scenes and the dead men, linking them together. Jovanka tells Velko, "All we do is hate and kill. Are we any better than the Germans?" and he replies, "We have become savages. Isn't that what we had to do to survive? They made us into savages. . . . Later we may hope we can go back." She cries, "We will never go back," but Velko insists, "We must."

If Ritt's mature films concern themselves in large part with the dehumanization of modern society, *Five Branded Women* serves as an early, if wooden, effort to explore this theme. It is less a film about the good guys versus the bad guys—though Ritt clearly sympathizes with the partisans—than about the dehumanizing effects of war on individuals trapped in a predatory group structure that has become necessary for survival.

The film concludes with the remains of the partisan band retreating through the mountains as the Germans relentlessly pursue them. Realizing that the Germans will soon overtake them, Velko decides to sacrifice his life for his comrades by holding off the Germans with a machine gun to give the partisans time to escape. Jovanka, whose attitude toward Velko has softened, insists on staying with him—clearly it is a suicide mission for both.

While they wait for the Germans to advance into firing range, Jovanka again expresses her sense of hopelessness: "Will there never be peace because people will never change?" Velko insists that "people will change," but she remains skeptical, asking, "Am I to believe that?" Velko says, "We must." Ritt then cuts to a long shot of a snow-capped mountain peak and a horizon uncluttered by people.

This final sequence is at best ambiguous. Jovanka, Ritt's individualist, who has grudgingly accepted group discipline, remains to the end skeptical about human nature and the cause she fights for. Velko, however, appears to protest too much. Van Heflin portrays him as insistent in his point of view, as if he is afraid to think otherwise. Ritt's decision to focus his final shot on a landscape rather than on the retreating partisans makes one wonder about Ritt's own evolving belief in the human enterprise.

The conflict between Jovanka and Velko was to be replayed ten years later between the principal characters in one of Ritt's most compelling works, *The Molly Maguires*. In that film McParlan, a Pinkerton agent, infiltrates the band of rebels who kill and blow up mines in protest of the dire conditions of miners in nineteenth-century Pennsylvania. Like Jovanka, he is tormented because, although he clearly upholds his own values, he begins to sympathize with the rebels' point of view. Conflicts between the group and the individual, between violence and the law, were themes Ritt could not consider in a formulaic or simplistic way. Despite his later disdain, *Five Branded Women*, with all its technical lapses and Ritt's occasional loss of control over his material, remains an intriguing film in its dogged focus on a theme rarely considered at the time it was made.

When Ritt returned from Italy, he busied himself with various projects, among them Walter Bernstein's script originally called "the trolley car script" and then "The Greatest Ride in Town." This project, on Ritt's desk since 1956, had been revived intermittently. Ritt was also sent the tear sheets for the John Williams novel *Night Song*, a story of the New York jazz underworld and a self-destructive saxophonist, which an agent thought would be an ideal vehicle for Paul Newman and Sidney Poitier.

Ritt's next film did indeed star Newman and Poitier and it featured a jazz background, but the source was a tamer, less ambitious book than Williams's. *Paris Blues* was loosely adapted from Harold Flender's 1957 novel of the same name, which focuses on an American expatriate jazz saxophonist living in Paris. Eddie Cook is a successful black musician with his own band who has decided to remain in Europe after World War II. Disgusted and alienated by the racism of his native land, he finds Paris a congenial place where he is not judged by the color of his skin. Into his life comes Connie Mitchell, a schoolteacher from Chicago, who is in Paris on a group tour. They fall in love, but Connie insists that Eddie return to America where his roots are and confront the problems that exist there. Eddie's dilemma forms the crux of the novel's romantic story, as his conversations with Connie explicate its thematic concerns.

The film project developed primarily because Ritt had a commitment from the two stars. A story was to be built around them, but when work began on the film there was no script. Ritt's later evaluation of the film centered on this central problem: "[W]e had no script on that picture. We had the commitment from these actors, and everybody said, 'Jesus Christ, what a cast!' I said, 'We have no script!' We worked and potsked around on it; we had an eighty-five page script finally and I made it. It's no great shakes of a film, some people like it a lot. I always found it fairly entertaining, no more than that" (SMU 39).

Commenting on this project thirty years later, Walter Bernstein was able to recall very little about it; he does not really consider the script a work of his, despite the screen credit he received: "I did very little . . . really. I came in at the very end. I did some polishing as I remember." He remembers trying to persuade Ritt to "make it much tougher than it actually was." Bernstein recollected that he suggested pushing the relationship between Ram Bowen (Paul Newman) and Michel (Serge Reggiani), a guitar player in Ram's band and a drug addict, but he was unable to remember specific details (Bernstein, interview).

To accommodate the stars, Flender's plot about a single black musician was expanded and divided into two stories. Newman plays Ram Bowen, a white American trombone player and band leader who aspires to be a composer. During the course of the film he is working on a jazz piece, "Paris Blues," which he hopes to get published. Poitier plays Eddie Cook, who, like his counterpart in the novel, is living in Paris to escape the racism he experienced back home. Into their lives come two Americans on a two-week vacation, Lillian Corning (Joanne Woodward), a divorcee with two children—in the novel Lillian was a spinster in her sixties—and Connie Lampson (Diahann Carroll), a schoolteacher.

The film for the most part faithfully reproduces the novel's account of the affair of Eddie and Connie, who argues that the climate for blacks in America has improved and that Eddie needs to go back and confront his roots, his country, and its racial conflicts. At first Eddie balks, but at the end his love for Connie wins out and he decides to give America another chance.

The story of Ram and Lillian, created for the film, here eclipses Eddie's. Now Ram is the lead musician and central attraction at the Paris jazz club; in the novel Eddie was its main attraction. Eddie is Ram's best friend and a member of his band. Ram lives for music and has no time or inclination for other commitments. He enjoys a casual affair with Marie, who owns the club, but his is the life of the artist. Unlike Eddie, who has rejected his homeland on racial grounds, Ram merely considers it dull in comparison to Paris, which he feels is more conducive to the development of his art. When Lillian sets out to win his love and lure Ram back to America, he repeatedly warns her that he is the wrong man for a permanent attachment, but she persists. Falling for her in spite of himself, and in a fit of self-pity when France's leading music publisher tells him that his composition is "thin" and that he needs to study more seriously if he is to become a serious composer, Ram decides to go back with her.

The film concludes at the train station. Eddie is seeing Connie off, promising that he will join her in two weeks. Lillian also waits, until Ram finally appears to say that he can't go with her, that he must devote his life to his music. Lillian retorts that he will never forget her and that she is best thing that could have happened to him. Then the train departs, leaving behind the two musicians, who walk away together. Like so many Hollywood films, *Paris Blues* thus has it both ways, celebrating the artist's commitment in Ram's story and still offering us a romantic happy ending in Eddie's.

Unfortunately, the music publisher's assessment of Ram's score as "thin" can also be applied to the film, probably as a result of the script problems that Ritt would later recall. Although four writers are credited, the screenplay fails to bring any substance to the main characters, who simply meet and then spend time wandering around Paris and seeing the sights. Much of their conversation involves variations on the same themes: Connie tries to convince Eddie that he has roots in America and should go home, while Ram struggles to dissuade Lillian from falling in love with a musician. Their relationships, as a result, remain vague and superficial. Ritt achieves some atmospheric effect, but while the city comes alive, the characters and the story do not.

The film benefits most directly from Duke Ellington's music, and the scenes in the club are its most successful moments. When Ram plays "Mood Indigo" and "Sophisticated Lady," the weak story momentarily takes a back seat to the music. Ritt enjoyed his association with Ellington: "I went to see him many times, he lived at the Chateau Marmont or some other hotel. He got up late and had steak for breakfast. . . . Terrific guy" (SMU 40). Paul Newman had taken two months of trombone lessons to prepare for his role, becoming good enough, according to Ritt, "to get himself a $100 a week job in a night club" (Jackson

63). The most exuberant scene comes when Wild Man Moor, a somewhat unsavory character in the novel who is here transformed into Louis Armstrong, improvises a number with Ram and the club musicians. Excitement builds among the real Parisians Ritt chose for the audience as Armstrong's trumpet vies with Newman's trombone.

Ultimately, however, the musical numbers cannot compensate for an unfocused, aimless story that occasionally has the feel of a jazz improvisation but never really comes together. Ram Bowen resembles all of Ritt's early protagonists in his status as an outsider, but unlike many of these early characters (including Eddie Cook), he finally chooses to remain outside the mainstream. In that way, Ram prefigures Ritt's classic loners, who are never able to integrate themselves into society. Newman's characterization here has a harder edge than his Ben Quick in *The Long Hot Summer;* he would hone this character to perfection in *Hud* two years later.

CHAPTER 5

Ernest Hemingway and Jerry Wald: *Hemingway's Adventures of a Young Man*

In 1961 Ritt made one more film for Jerry Wald, a film based loosely on a series of Hemingway's short stories, mostly featuring Nick Adams. Wald, who remained committed to bringing literary properties to the screen, had produced in 1950 a remake of *To Have and Have Not* (renamed *The Breaking Point*), which was directed by Michael Curtiz and starred John Garfield and Patricia Neal.

The new project originated with the writer A. E. Hotchner, who had successfully adapted several Hemingway stories for television, pleasing (for the most part) Hemingway himself. The first of these was "The Battler," telecast in October 1956 for NBC's *Playwright's 56* series. This live performance was to star James Dean as Ad Francis, the half-crazy, punch-drunk prizefighter of the title, and Paul Newman as Nick. Two days before rehearsals were to begin, however, Dean was killed, so Newman ended up playing the title role, which he would reprise in Ritt's film.

The success of "The Battler" motivated Hotchner to dramatize five more Nick Adams stories for a television showcase series called *The Seven Lively Arts* in 1957. Entitled "The World of Nick Adams," the collection of short stories was directed by Robert Mulligan (who had directed the television version of *Edge of the City*) and scored by Aaron Copeland. Hemingway was sufficiently impressed to suggest that Hotchner add a few additional stories and turn his teleplay into a full-length film. Out of friendship for Hotchner, he even agreed to provide a voice-over prologue and an afterward adapted from his introduction to *Men at War*. But the production had not yet begun when, in July 1961, Hemingway killed himself.

"Hotchner and I were in Rome [scouting locations] when we got word that Hemingway was dead," Wald told the press. "That broke us up. Now we'll be just having an actor do the narration" (Laurence 270–71).

The sensational publicity occasioned by Hemingway's suicide gave the production an enormous boost of attention. All the magazine and newspaper articles and biographies that followed amounted to free publicity for the film. Wald even decided to premiere the film in Chicago, Hemingway's first city, in order to generate additional newspaper coverage, and he selected as the premiere date July 18, which was close to Hemingway's birthday. The working title for the script, "Young Man," was changed to "Ernest Hemingway's Young Man" on the revised final screenplay, but by the time of the film's premiere, the title had been expanded to *Hemingway's Adventures of a Young Man.*

In an attempt to blur the lines between Hemingway's fiction and his life, the title was purposely chosen to avoid reference to any one Hemingway story. Hemingway had expressed concern that he felt the public would confuse Nick Adam's life with his own, but in order to capitalize on the publicity resulting from his suicide, Wald decided to emphasize that confusion.[1] A disclaimer, written in small print, appeared in some newspaper ads: "This motion picture has a fictionalized story of a fictionalized character named Nick Adams and the story is not biographical in any way." The press kit, however, contained an ad that stated, above the title, "Nick Adams or Ernest Hemingway . . . One begins where the other leaves off." And, as a final tactic to enforce the association, the film opens with the famous Karsh image of Hemingway, which fades into the title sequence.

As he had done in shaping the Faulkner adaptations and other literary works he brought to the screen, Wald eliminated as much as possible any controversial material from the original stories to ensure that the film would appeal to the widest possible audience. Indeed, in this case he ended up excising almost everything that he thought might disturb his audience. For the most extended sequence in the film, recounting Nick's volunteer service as an ambulance driver for the Italian army, Hotchner utilized material from *A Farewell to Arms.* Like the novel's protagonist, Frederick Henry, Nick is wounded and falls in love with his nurse, here named Rosanna Griffi (Susan Strasberg). A scene was written and filmed of Rosanna coming to Nick's room at night, sitting on the edge of the bed and letting down her hair; the scene dissolves as they embrace. But this sexually suggestive vignette was later dropped, as was an extended scene in which Nick visits Signor Griffi to ask for his daughter's hand. During their talk, Signor Griffi asks Nick, "Are you . . . lovers?" and Nick replies, "Yes sir . . . we are."[2] With this explicit admission cut from the released film, Rosanna's death in a bombing is made more poignant by the implication that their love was pure.

Wald even wrote to church officials in Rome for advice on the script. In one sequence in a church, Nick, in a fit of grief after Rosanna's death, charges the altar and starts breaking things. A church official wrote Wald, "I deem that Nick's action of violence in the church should not involve any sacred objects on the altar. The same effect of revolt and despair could be achieved by having him knock off a set of candles lit in the front of St. Francis' statue" (RC 9-9-61). This suggestion was incorporated into the film.

One other example of Wald's meddling is characteristic. In Hemingway's story "Indian Camp," which provides the basis of an early episode in the film, Nick as a little boy goes with his father to the Indian camp across the lake, where an Indian woman is ill. Nick's father, a doctor, sees that he needs to perform a caesarian section, and having with him no anesthetic or proper instruments, he performs the surgery with a jackknife and sews the woman up with gut leader from his fishing tackle. Nick witnesses this primitive procedure and learns later that the woman's husband, unable to bear his wife's suffering, has cut his throat.

In the film, Nick is no longer a little boy but a youth of nineteen, which does not stop his overbearing mother (Jessica Tandy) from complaining about Nick's having witnessed a birth. The woman's husband, instead of killing himself, merely runs out of the house. Thus the story's powerful lesson that there is psychic pain more profound than physical pain is lost in the filmed sequence, which has been robbed of any real dramatic power. Wald had agreed to let stand Nick's father's suicide, which is reported at the end of the film, but he objected to having a second suicide in the film, explaining that suicide as a solution to screen problems "should be discouraged unless absolutely necessary."

Wald also left his mark on the film's casting, seriously compromising its effectiveness. Declaring that casting a star in the lead was not necessary for this film, he told *Newsweek*, "If you wait for Brando, you'll never get the picture done" (qtd. in Laurence 273). Hotchner agreed and recommended casting Keir Dullea, who had played the part of Nick on television. Wald, however, insisted on Richard Beymer, who was then starring in the film version of *West Side Story*, because he felt that Beymer would appeal to younger viewers. Unfortunately Beymer, even under Ritt's guidance, could not convincingly portray Nick's evolution into manhood. The film received mostly poor reviews, and many critics concentrated their harshest remarks on Beymer's performance. The young actor was reportedly so discouraged by these notices that he dropped out of acting for many years.

The war sequences were filmed in Verona. Wald claimed that this locale was selected out of respect for Hemingway, who had told Hotchner to stay away from Milan and recommended instead Verona and "the countryside around Caprino where Nick Adams fought his war and was wounded" (Phillips 87). Ritt was plagued with bad weather during the filming in Italy, but he used the overcast skies to good effect to create a sense of foreboding in the gray lighting of some of the scenes between Nick and Rosanna.

The film is at best uneven. Its virtues lie in the picaresque narrative energy of a young man striking out on his own, meeting adventures and absorbing lessons along the way, but this format, unfortunately, also contains the seeds of its undoing. Such a succession of loosely integrated episodes must be held together by the observable maturation of the protagonist, but again, Richard Beymer was not up to the task of portraying this growth process effectively. Still, Beymer must not bear all the blame for the film's shortcomings, for some episodes remain unfocused, belabored attempts to flesh out a bare and essentially episodic structure. As Hotchner observed, "The stories are connected only by the fact that Nick appears in all of them; other than that they are isolated experiences of fear, disillusionment, courage, love, war, and loneliness. . . . But to fuse them and embellish them for the screen without disturbing their impact was a particularly difficult assignment" (Phillips 82). The finished film suffers from Hotchner's and Ritt's inability to fuse these discrete episodes into a dramatically viable and meaningful whole.

Hemingway's Adventures of a Young Man was, however, an interesting transitional film for Ritt in its break from the imposed Hollywood happy ending and in the in-depth exploration of its themes, through the adapted vision of a modern writer who had been central in defining the modern sensibility. The plight of the individual within a disintegrating culture and his response to the dislocation this causes was Hemingway's characteristic subject, and it would become Ritt's focus for the remainder of the decade as he shifted his directorial efforts toward an unsparing depiction of the American psychic landscape. Ritt's Hemingway film is a coming-of-age story that leads to disillusionment; it presents Nick with a series of broken father surrogates who, like his own father, embody the heritage of a shattered culture. When Nick leaves Italy for home, he is schooled in nihilism: "They don't let you know what it's all about. They don't give you time to learn. They throw you in and tell you the rules and the first time they catch you off base they kill you. They kill you ugly, like poor Manera in the trench, or they kill you gracefully like they did Rosanna. But they kill you in the end."

This is the philosophy that is to shape the major Ritt protagonists for the next decade. In Nick Adams, Ritt develops the nihilist persona in its most concentrated form.

The film opens with a lyrical evocation of the natural world; it was to remain

Ritt's most vivid homage to the concept of a pastoral America until twenty years later, when these images would reemerge as the controlling motif of *Cross Creek*. Here the opening shots, many of them portraying Nick and his father fishing, hunting, and camping together in the Michigan lake country, are remarkable in that Ritt's camera stays far enough away from his characters to make them almost unrecognizable. (In similar scenes in *Cross Creek* there would be no human forms at all impinging on the landscape.)

Next comes a sequence wherein a camera mounted on a helicopter moves down into the heart of the Michigan wilderness. Ritt rarely drew attention to his camera, but he does so here to spectacular effect. The feeling is almost vertiginous, as Ritt moves abruptly from the natural world that is soon to be destroyed into a human world overwhelmed by disillusionment. The sensation of falling creates a physical rendering of the Romantic concept of man's fall from paradise into a world that will challenge and test him.

This dynamic opening sequence shot is followed by a voice-over narration: "In the place where you are born and where you grow up, you begin to learn the things that all men must know. They are the simplest things, the basic things and they will shape your entire life." Remarking that the story we are about to see is to center on the education of a writer, the narrator continues, "And if you are to be a writer, the stories that you make up will be true in proportion to the amount of this knowledge of life that you have."

The film's major weakness is that the events Nick experiences do not come across ultimately as a life lived but as scenes arranged for dramatic effect. Most seem artificial and wooden, and taken together, they do not add up to much of an adventure. Until Nick goes off to Italy as a volunteer, the action is made up of a series of episodes involving Nick at home and then on the road once he runs away. In each of these successive vignettes he learns, first from his father and then from a variety of father surrogates, that life beats you down.

The beginning of the film, where they are seen fishing, hunting, and camping together, establishes Nick's close relationship with his father (Arthur Kennedy). This opening tableau is followed by a scene in which the boy Nick watches his father back away from a fight with Joe Boulton, a half-breed handyman who has accused him of stealing logs. At home, then, Nick watches as his father is again intimidated, this time by his wife (Jessica Tandy). Jealous of her son's attachment to her husband, Mrs. Adams demands that Nick practice his viola before going out hunting with his father. When Dr. Adams yields to his wife, postponing the hunting trip, Nick realizes that he can't fight for his father, who is already a broken man.

Dr. Adams is partially redeemed in a scene shortly afterward, when he heroically delivers Mrs. Boulton's baby by performing a caesarian section under adverse circumstances. Returning home, however, he is again humiliated by his wife. Prior to that scene, Nick has broken up with his girlfriend, Carolin (Diane Baker), complaining only that the relationship "isn't fun anymore"—he is obviously at loose ends and can't explain himself. When Nick tells his father of the breakup, Dr. Adams tries to convince him to stay with Carolin. But Nick's view of marriage, no doubt a reflection of his own parents' unhappiness, is one of empty routine: "There I'll be in her old man's hardware store and her mother around the house all the time and going to Sunday dinners at their house, and having them over for dinner and her telling Carolin all the time what to do and how to act and the old man giving me advice on how to get ahead."

All Dr. Adams can manage in return is: "That's marriage boy. You'll cope with it." During this dialogue Ritt frames a "Home Sweet Home" embroidery on the wall between father and son; the film is weakened throughout by such clumsy devices for underlining a scene's intended message.

Nick leaves home to hitchhike his way to New York. On the way he meets "the Battler" and his friend Bugs. Nick enjoys their company until Battler's schizophrenic personality asserts itself and he tries to fight Nick; Bugs then tells Nick to leave. Although the exact nature of the relationship between Bugs and the Battler puzzles Nick, the despair on which their mutual dependence is based is not lost on him, but again, the film does not convey his perceptions effectively. Bugs advises Nick to get a buddy because "a man alone ain't got no damn chance" and finally warns him to go home because the road is not the place for him. Realizing that he doesn't "belong" with these two, Nick moves on.

This pattern of friendship and disillusionment is replicated when Nick meets Billy Campbell (Dan Dailey), an advance man for a touring burlesque show.[3] Billy is a drunk and a drug addict, whose boss, Mr. Turner (Fred Clark), wants him to take "the cure." Billy refuses, telling Nick that he drinks to fill an emotional thirst. Billy, like the Battler and Dr. Adams, is a spiritual cripple who has been beaten down by life. Mr. Turner, who is known as "Sliding Billy," is different, as he makes clear when explaining his nickname: "Now, there are those who just stand there and get knocked down and bleed and get up and get knocked down again. And there are those who roll with the punch and slide."

When Nick finally gets to Manhattan, he makes the rounds of newspaper offices and is told that he needs to gain some experience before he can become a newspaperman. He takes a job as a waiter, and then one night at a war rally held at the restaurant, an Italian countess asks for heroic young men to volunteer for the ambulance service, and Nick signs on. Returning to his apartment, he finds his father waiting for him in the lobby. Dr. Adams has plans of spending time with his son, and he is upset by Nick's decision, declaring, "I'd hate like hell to donate you to a war that has nothing to do with us. It's bad enough to die for your own country." He confesses to Nick that he needs him.

This confrontation is the film's dramatic highlight, primarily because of Arthur Kennedy's fine acting. Ritt's mis-en-scène is very effective here: as father and son argue over going to war, Ritt places between them an oval portrait of a woman, a symbolic substitute for mother. As Dr. Adams moves dejectedly toward the door, a small picture of a country house is seen between him and Nick's shadow. As he exits, remarking that Nick is "the best thing that ever happened to [him]," Nick's shadow precedes him to the door and then Ritt's camera frames Nick's anguished face. Nick will never see his father again.

If it had maintained this level of drama, emotion, and visual expressiveness, *Hemingway's Adventures of a Young Man* would have been a powerful film. Unfortunately, its longest section, chronicling Nick's experiences in Italy, is more representative. Ritt seems unable to bring any dramatic power to the war or to Nick's romance with Rosanna Griffi, who, as portrayed by Susan Strasberg, is almost as lifeless as Beymer. Her death serves more as a relief than a catharsis for the audience.

Nick proves his sense of duty and heroism when he risks his life to save Major Padula (Ricardo Montalban). Shortly thereafter, Nick is wounded, and while recuperating from an operation on his legs, he meets Rosanna, the nurse who cares for him. He declares his intention to marry her in a church, and then, after visiting her father to ask his permission, finds her dying in that same church, the victim of a bombing raid. While a marriage ceremony is hurriedly performed, Rosanna dies, and Ritt films the ceremony and her death in front of a crucifix. As elsewhere in his work, Ritt conveys a palpable impression of the uselessness of religion, here emphasizing with a heavy hand the irony of the images and Nick's breaking the candleholder on the altar near a statue of St. Francis. The clumsiness of this sequence is especially noteworthy in that it follows an affecting scene with Rosanna's father. Like the scene in which Nick said good-bye to his own father, this confrontation carries a sense of foreboding: he will lose Rosanna as well as his father; both fathers will lose their children. The sense of loss permeates the film.

Nick then returns home to learn from his mother that his father has committed suicide. Looking around his father's office, Nick faces his parents' wedding portrait. Hotchner's script called for voice-over narration, but Ritt wisely eliminated it. As he stares at the portrait, Mrs. Adams enters and Ritt's framing recalls the earlier scene between Nick and his father, except that now Nick occupies his father's place on the left side of the frame and Mrs. Adams is to the right with the "Home Sweet Home" embroidery between them. When his mother gives

Nick a letter left to him by his father, he objects that she has opened it; she retorts bitterly that her husband left her nothing. As she leaves the room, the door blocks the embroidered motto. Ritt then cuts to a shot of Nick fishing alone, and this is followed by a long shot of the lake with Nick in the canoe. The dwarfing of Nick in these shots suggests that nature offers him little solace. He leaves home for New York shortly thereafter.

Hotchner's original script ended with a quote from Hemingway's introduction to *Men at War:* "When you go to war as a boy, you have a great illusion of immortality. Other people get killed; not you. Then when you are badly wounded the first time, you lose that illusion and you have a bad time until you figure it out that nothing could happen to you that had not happened to all men before you. Whatever you had to do men had always done. If they had done it, then you could do it too."[4]

In the film this passage is cut to the final two lines, thereby eliminating Hemingway's rumination about mortality and the certainty of death, as well as the foreshadowing of Hemingway's own suicide the previous year. Again, morbidity such as this was not a suitable message, according to Wald, who preferred to focus on the life-affirming notion that a young man has to leave home in order to forge a future: every man has done it and so Nick will do it, too. In a memo to Hotchner, Wald wrote, "The audience must be made to feel that Nick's final decision to leave is the right one and its upbeat quality should be brought about by the thought that he will thereby make a better life for himself" (RC 9-23-61). This watered-down message is sadly indicative of a final product, from which most of the vitality has been drained out.

This was the last time that Ritt would make a film under terms dictated by a producer. Shortly after completing *Hemingway's Adventures of a Young Man,* Ritt entered a three-picture deal with Paul Newman and Paramount, a joint venture called Salem Pictures. At the time of the agreement Ritt said, "I suppose the production association of an actor and a director is unprecedented. I can think of no other independent company formed by this combination. Paul and I simply found that we had something in common, a philosophy about making motion pictures. We agreed that every American motion picture should be a reflection of our American way of life, just as vital a motive in movie-making as entertaining people and making money."[5]

This philosophy, so diametrically opposed to Wald's, would inaugurate Ritt's career as a director with some clout, one who could create projects to reflect his own views. The first project undertaken by the partners was to be a very loose adaptation of the first work of a young American writer named Larry McMurtry. The film, released in 1963 as *Hud,* would establish Ritt as one of America's most important filmmakers.

CHAPTER 6

The Death of the Western Hero:
Hud and *Hombre*

Hud (1963) and *Hombre* (1967) both written by Ravetch and Frank and starring Paul Newman, belong to a series of films from the sixties in which Ritt tackled major film genres, often shaping their traditional motifs to fit his evolving cultural vision. Undertaken after his extensive apprentice period, they are the work of a director in firm command of his material and craft; his skill evidences a sharp take on the American landscape.

In the 1960s and the 1970s, under the influence of modernist European films, the American Western began to change. One of the most profound manifestations of this evolution was the demythologizing of the basic tenets of some generic conventions. Some films of the era dismissed the formula altogether, depicting a corrupt society represented by dishonest and mendacious agents. The heroes who emerge from these communities also differ from the classic champions of traditional Western society, champions such as Shane or the Wyatt Earp of John Ford's *My Darling Clementine*.

Two of the earliest (and best) films to demythologize the Western in this way were *Hud* and *Hombre*. Released a year later than three films that had effectively employed the generic formula to evoke nostalgia over the passing of the West—*Ride the High Country*, *The Man Who Shot Liberty Valence*, and *Lonely Are the Brave*—*Hud* betrays no feelings of regret in deconstructing the Western hero, exposing his macho persona as empty and amoral, his mythic culture as bankrupt.

Interestingly, *Hud* appeared in the same year as *How the West Was Won*, the first Cinerama Western and Hollywood's last mighty effort to glamorize the genre. Thereafter, beginning with John Ford's last Western, *Cheyenne Autumn*, the films of this genre regularly tended to look with a jaundiced eye upon those same conceptions. The ten-year period that followed delivered John Sturges's *Hour of the Gun*, Sam Peckinpah's *The Wild Bunch*, Robert Altman's *McCabe and Mrs. Miller*, and Arthur Penn's *Little Big Man*.

More corrosive even than *Hud*, *Hombre* introduces a totally alienated antihero whose one positive act on behalf of his society is to be revealed as meaningless. Both of these Ritt films display their modernist influences in deliberate echoes of "classic" Westerns that validate society and romanticize its ideals. *Hud* develops much of its thematic texture by self-consciously recalling *Shane*, and, less obviously, Howard Hawks's *Red River* (1948), while *Hombre* purposely invokes the idealism of John Ford's *Stagecoach*, only to undercut it savagely.

When Irving Ravetch and Harriet Frank first brought Larry McMurtry's novel *Horseman Pass By* to Ritt's attention, it seemed that there was no part for Paul Newman, so Ravetch and Frank decided to expand the secondary role of Hud and make him the central character. The novel's Hud is a ruthless, egotistical hedonist, and the filmmakers saw that in centering their story around such a character, they had found a powerful theme. Ravetch and Frank felt that *Hud* dealt with "the greed and materialism that was beginning to take over America" (McGilligan, *Backstory 2* 287). Ritt, too, liked the idea of filming the story of a man "addicted to appetite . . . a classic American heel" (AFI 15, 21).

Newman jumped at the opportunity to play the role, and Ritt found this decision commendable: "It was a courageous change and it calls for an actor with Paul's kind of courage. Many name stars fear to play parts that are less than heroic." This praise was in part publicity hype, for Newman had already played an impressive range of antiheroes in *The Hustler*, *From the Terrace*, *Cat on a Hot Tin Roof*, and *Sweet Bird of Youth*. None of those characters, however, compared with Hud, who was described in the film's publicity as "the man with the barbed wire soul."

Horseman Pass By is a coming-of-age story filtered through the consciousness of Lonnie Bannon, a teenager who has lost both parents and now lives on a ranch with his grandfather, Homer Bannon, Homer's second wife, and his stepson, Hud. In adapting the novel, Ravetch and Frank made several key changes to tighten the relationships and sharpen the thematic focus: Hud becomes Homer Bannon's son rather than his stepson, and thus becomes Lonnie's uncle as well, and Homer has not remarried. These few modifications serve to highlight the relationship between three generations of Bannons. Another important character is the Bannon's cook, in the novel a black woman named Halmea: she is called Alma in the film and is played by a white actress, Patricia Neal. Ritt did not feel that he could make the relationship between Hud and a black woman work at that time. Other secondary characters who play important roles in developing the character of Lonnie in the novel are simply dropped from the film.

Hud self-consciously echoes the classic Western Shane (1953), and in so doing draws attention to its use of generic conventions to comment on the modern American West. An overt reference is made in the casting of Brandon de Wilde as the teenager Lonnie Bannon; as a child actor De Wilde had played Joey Starret in *Shane*. Both films deal with the youngster's education as he observes the deeds of the protagonist. Shane, of course, is the classic Western hero, first seen through Joey's eyes as an idealized figure in buckskin, astride a horse. George Stevens's mis-en-scène even suggests that Joey's view may be a boy's romantic vision: Shane and his horse, moving toward the Starret ranch, seem to glide across a stream without causing so much as a ripple in the water.

Shane presents its hero as a messianic figure, lightning fast with his pearl-handled guns, who descends from the mountains to save an emerging town from lawlessness. Although he had hoped to abandon his life of violence and adopt the peaceful ways of the plains homesteaders, fate intervenes and Shane accepts it with grace. Forced to kill in order to protect the settlers, he must then return to the isolation of the mountains. Before leaving, he instructs Joey in the use of the gun, which, as he has shown, can speak for the forces of society and law. He has, in effect, passed on the tenets of the hero to a disciple who will live by the code of the West.

After the credits, *Hud* opens with Lonnie in town looking for his uncle. His first clue comes from the owner of a bar who is sweeping up the broken glass in front of his place, the result of a fight started by Hud. The boy then finds his uncle's Cadillac parked in front of the house of a married woman. When Lonnie honks the car's horn, Hud emerges from the house, tucking in his shirt, boots in hand. This introduction immediately announces a break from the classic Western and the mythic hero.

Hud is identified by and associated with his flashy car. Unlike the horse, which establishes the Western hero's connection with nature, Hud's pink Cadillac represents a connection to the mechanized modern world. The illicit affair implied in his emergence from a married woman's house is foreign to the classic hero's code; apparently, it is central to Hud's way of life. His next action elaborates further on this impression of amorality: when the woman's husband drives up moments later, Hud implies that it is his nephew who is to blame. The gentlemanly code that Joey Starret learned from Shane is clearly not shared by Hud.

The West of the 1960s is not a place for heroes, but a wasteland where Hud's code of selfishness and materialism prevails.

Ritt's film thus openly breaks with tradition, yet it seems a logical extension of the classic Western, for it deals with the same thematic contradiction between wilderness and civilization by posing a protagonist who belongs to neither extreme. Set almost a hundred years after *Shane*, *Hud*'s West is now fully settled, but the tensions remain. Its atmosphere of unease recalls another film released seven years earlier, John Ford's *The Searchers*, whose hero, Ethan Edwards (John Wayne), seems ambivalent and alienated, more closely related to Hud than to Shane. Ethan demonstrates the strength, individualism, authority, and leadership expected of the Western hero, but unlike Shane, he is unable to fit in at all with the rituals of society: in one scene he breaks up a family funeral, and in another he interrupts a wedding.

Ritt, while quoting from these earlier films and maintaining the thematic paradigm, makes two significant departures. In the character of Hud he explores the characteristics of isolation and individualism, and he finds selfishness and immorality. Here the macho individualist, rather than remaining apart, is fully in tune with modern Western society which is seen to be as greedy and corrupt as its "hero" himself. If the classic film refused to choose between the loner and the settler's community, awkwardly attempting to embrace both, Ritt's protagonist Lonnie Bannon learns to reject both at the end of his film.

Hud, like most Westerns, opens with a shot of the landscape. The screenplay calls for a "full panoramic vista. The plains of Texas . . . are spread under a clear sky already beginning to shimmer with early morning heat. It is a vast, lonely land, dwarfing animal and man."[1] The shot is devoid of man or any sign of civilization. Jane Tomkins points out that the negations of the setting are also its draw: "Be brave, be strong enough to endure this, it says, and you will become like this—hard, austere, sublime"(Tomkins 71). The cinematographer James Wong Howe explained that he wanted to emphasize the "harsh skies and flat glare"; he even decided to filter out the clouds (Higham 94).

This standard opening shot, beautifully rendered in black and white accented by a ray of sunlight, is quickly undercut, however, by the sight of a truck pulling an open horse trailer. Ritt is calling attention to the disjunction of a world where horse and rider are no longer a graceful unit in movement through the natural landscape but are separated and subsumed by the mechanical motion of the truck. This image is followed by a shot of the highway that cuts through the plains, again emphasizing the transition from the world of nature to a West that has been claimed by modern technology.

Standing in contrast to this automechanical world and to Hud, whose Cadillac embodies it, is his father, Homer, who represents the old West. The generational and ethical conflict between father and son forms the basis of Lonnie's education.

Homer's name suggests his epic status. The owner of the cattle ranch where Hud and Lonnie live and work, he is in love with the land and feels a strong connection with nature and the wild. If Hud is linked with his car, Homer is associated with his two Texas longhorns, symbols of the pioneer lifestyle. These animals, whose monetary value makes them consistent with the modernist underpinnings of the film, directly invoke Hawks's *Red River*, the story of the founding of a cattle empire by Tom Dunson (John Wayne), who starts his ranch with two longhorns.

Despite the tendency of some critics to draw bold good-evil distinctions between father and son in Ritt's film, however, the contrast is not so simple. In a famous essay on *Hud*, Pauline Kael claims that the film runs counter to its creators' intentions, that what was supposed to be a condemnation of materialism becomes instead a celebration of it through glorification of Hud's character and some undercutting of Homer, the ethical spokesman. Kael is correct in pointing out the tensions in the film, but she overstates Hud's appeal. When Homer is shown to be partly responsible for the dilapidated condition of his ranch and wholly responsible for allowing Hud to take it away from him, some sympathy naturally accrues to the son of so hapless a father. The ruthless drive that makes Tom Dunson a truly epic founder and invests Hud with a potentially redemptive energy is wholly missing in Homer.

Dunson's success in *Red River* is predicated on his ambition, and although Hawks's film is critical of Dunson's ruthless treatment of people, this Western hero does manage to carve out an empire from the wilderness; his boisterous creative drive is instrumental in helping settlements to flower in the West. Homer Bannon, in contrast, despite his name and his unyielding moral righteousness, is shown to be weak and ineffectual. His principles having overwhelmed his ability to act, he stands helplessly by as the government destroys his diseased cattle. As his inaction also allows Hud to take over the ranch, it becomes clear that his vision of the future has been clouded by nostalgia for the past. The ambition that energized a true hero like Dunson to found an empire has deteriorated into the impotence of Homer Bannon.

Kael's comment that audiences identify with Hud because he "wants the good things in life and doesn't give a damn for the general welfare" is an oversimplification (Kael 79). What is attractive about Hud is precisely what audiences admire in classic Western heroes, their individualistic bravado. Hud exemplifies this glamorous American persona in his dislike of the government and the law. His code is the situational ethic of the frontier: "I always say the law was meant to be interpreted in a lenient manner, and that's what I try to do. Sometimes I lean to one side of it, sometimes I lean to the other. . . . This is our land and I don't want any government men on it anytime, anyplace, anywhere" (Ravetch and Frank 116).

Tom Dunson would have approved. Early in *Red River* when he chooses the land to claim for his ranch, he kills a representative of the owner. Dunson is a law unto himself; it is his strength and his flaw. Hud shares this disdain for authority, but he has no larger vision, no wilderness to conquer, no empires to build. His rebellious strength is not turned to any creative effort, and his independence seems to have become an end in itself.

The casting of Paul Newman as Hud subtly tempers the unpleasantness of this selfish persona. The twinkle in his eye, his offhand sweetness and sudden frankness remain attractive despite the character's unheroic behavior. Unlike the more inarticulate rebels of the 1950s, Newman's alienated misfits are typically garrulous, ironic, and witty. Ritt's film accentuates this unexpected charm, and even attempts to capitalize on Newman's air of emotional vulnerability, suggesting that Hud's harshness may have resulted from the trauma of the death of his older brother (Lonnie's father), for which Hud was in part responsible.

Another factor mitigating the iniquity of Hud is the overwhelming aura of death that permeates the film. It seems to locate the character in an environment that requires rebellion as a necessary condition for survival. The mood is established at the very beginning by Elmer Bernstein's haunting, elegiac score. When Truman Peters comes upon Lonnie and Hud at his house and threatens to fight, Hud dissuades him by making reference to his diabetic condition. Then, when Hud returns home, Homer tells him about a dead heifer, and they drive out to the range to examine it.

Ritt cuts to a shot of buzzards in a tree that fills the right side of the frame: the birds look down on a ranch hand who appears diminished in the center. The buzzards hold dominion over the scene, just as their image will hover over the rest of the film. Ritt slowly pulls his camera back to bring the Bannons' truck into view, and the tree with the buzzards seems to cut the frame in half, visually foreshadowing the schism between father and son that will hasten the death of Homer Bannon. The buzzards are also the harbingers of the disease that will destroy Homer's cattle and the way of life he represents.

Against Hud's advice, Homer brings in a government veterinarian who, after performing tests, concludes that the heifer has died of hoof-and-mouth disease and that all the Bannons' cattle must be destroyed. Much of the film's action is taken up with waiting for the vet's report and implementing the decision to kill the cattle once the verdict comes in.

The slaughter of the cattle is a brutal, horrifying scene. The passive beasts are rounded up and herded into a large pit, where they are surrounded by ranch hands who shoot at them until all are dead. The sounds of the frightened and dying cattle and the rifle fire are all that is to be heard as the scene plays out. Finally, lime is poured on the carcasses, and bulldozers cover the pit. This gory episode is the film's central scene and its most graphic image, vividly evoking the twentieth century's many incidents of mass human bloodshed.

In her study of the Western, Jane Tomkins examines the ways animals are utilized, particularly the horses and cattle that are emblematic of the genre. Cattle, according to Tompkins, are generally less visible in Westerns than the horse, "for cattle . . . are not broken and ridden, they are raised exclusively to be killed for food" (113). This is their function in *Red River*, where they are driven a thousand miles to Abilene to be butchered for the Midwest market.

In *Hud*, the horse, though still useful around the ranch, has been replaced elsewhere by the car and the truck. Here cattle are the more visible livestock, but they are seen only to be killed. In the end they are of no economic utility; though raised for that purpose, their narrative purpose is only to die out, to make way for the digging of oil wells, the next phase in the evolution of the West. After the slaughter of the herd, Homer shoots his two longhorns and then soon dies himself.

Tompkins argues that, symbolically, cattle represent natural physical and emotional urges, which the Western hero must subdue in order to survive. Hud, however, is a Westerner who makes no effort to subdue his physical and emotional urges, instead giving free rein to them, which only makes him more attractive to Lonnie, Alma, and the women in town. This same unbridled excess disgusts his father, in part because it led to the death of Hud's brother, but also because it is a selfish and amoral indulgence:

> You don't care for people. You don't give a damn about them. You live just for yourself—and that makes you not fit to live with. . . .
>
> You got all that charm going for you, and it makes the youngsters want to be like you. That's the shame of it, 'cause you don't value nothin', you don't respect nothin', you keep no check on your appetites at all. Men of your sort have come to be the heroes of our age. (Ravetch and Frank 163–64)

Ritt is fond of exploring the human psyche through doubles, making this theme a narrative strategy in many of his films. In *Hud* the extremes of character are represented by the defiant hedonism of Hud and the repressive moralism of Homer. Hud wants to save the cattle although it is morally wrong, while Homer is willing to destroy them without even putting up a fight. He dies without making provision for the distribution of his land, and Hud takes it over at the film's end.

Despite the apparent intent to damn Hud's character and through him the modern American persona—Homer remarks, "Little by little, the look of the country changes, because of the men we admire"—Hud is partially redeemed. Retaining the human vitality that seems to have been hardened out of his rigidly moralistic father, he struggles in vigorous rebellion against the decayed and dying landscape overseen by the buzzards. The very energy of his defiance sets him apart from the lifeless world around him.

Ritt wants also to imply, however, that this lifelessness is itself the result of the rapacious selfishness in the American character that Hud represents. Retaining the last vestiges of the frontier daring that once brought civilization to the wilds, he faces no ennobling challenge. A loner at the end of the frontier, Hud has nowhere to go. Like many modern artists, Ritt is concerned about what happens when the wilderness no longer threatens and the settler's descendants inherit the land without the need to work to tame it. Each generation has earned its way on the frontier by building on the work of its ancestors. If continuity is part of the heritage of the settlers, so must be industry and expansion.

When Hud inherits the ranch at the film's end, having plotted even earlier to take the land from his father, it seems probable that he will simply turn it over for oil drilling and make a lot of money, which his father had steadfastly refused to do. His actions have hastened his father's death; indeed, in the novel he actually shoots his dying father. In *Shane* the departing hero explains to his young protégé that there is no living with a killing. But Hud has no frontier, no mountain to exile himself to, and he feels no need to do so, anyway. Easily accommodating himself to the death of the father he has at least symbolically killed, he turns his attention to the looming oil deals that will consolidate his new position of power. Whereas in classic Westerns the acquisition of land was seen as an opportunity to build and to grow, in *Hud* Ritt has demonstrated the heartless exploitation that lies at the end of the western expansion.

The film ends more brutally than McMurtry's novel, where Lonnie, having rejected Hud, simply takes off for the open road. Catching a ride with a truck driver who remembers Homer, he seems to be returning in spirit to the grandfather as they talk. An early draft of the film script closed the same way, but Ritt ultimately chose to end with Hud rather than Lonnie. After Lonnie says goodbye and walks away, Hud returns to the house alone and the door slams shut after him. Again *The Searchers* is recalled, wherein Ethan Edwards's departing figure is framed by a doorway and then disappears as the door swings closed. Ethan is returning to the wilderness; Hud the amoral modern Westerner has instead taken over the ranch. Rejected by the youngster whose ethical sense seems to have been shaped on the example of his dead grandfather, this unromantic yet strangely sympathetic contemporary individualist is left alone, but in possession of the future.

Marty Rackin, head of Paramount, did not like Ritt's ending and asked him to change it. But Ritt loved the ending, as did Paul Newman, and they both stood firm against the studio's interference. Before Rackin was able to come up with an alternative ending, audience reaction and early critical notices convinced Paramount that they had a hit on their hands and the matter was dropped.

Hud created a furor at the Venice Film Festival, where it was widely acclaimed as the best film in the competition. It was passed over, however, by the festival jury, which aroused considerable antagonism from American film distributors as well as the international film community. Even the Italian press, declaring that "the Communists have taken over the Venice Festival," generally felt that *Hud* was treated unfairly. Though the film won the Catholic Film Office Award and the Eric Johnson Memorial Award, *Il Tempo* charged that "rarely has a festival finished so badly with verdicts so unjust and mistaken, so partisan and so debatable" and argued that that Paul Newman should have won the acting award, which went to Albert Finney for *Tom Jones* (*Hollywood Reporter*, September 16, 1963). *Il Messagero* lambasted the jury for brushing off Ritt and his film and asserted that Patricia Neal should have won the best actress award.

Hud netted Ritt his only Academy Award nomination for direction. (He lost to Tony Richardson for *Tom Jones*.) Paul Newman again lost out to Albert Finney, and Ravetch and Frank's screenplay lost out to John Osborne's for *Tom Jones*. However, Patricia Neal (Best Actress), Melvyn Douglas (Best Supporting Actor), and James Wong Howe (Best Cinematography) were all winners. Interestingly, despite all of those nominations, *Hud* did not receive a "Best Picture" nomination. The academy preferred *How the West Was Won*.

Hombre, like Hud, offers a contemplation of the modern Western hero, but its emphasis and its concerns are different. Hud's independence is portrayed as selfish and destructive, but it reflects the essential character of his society; John Russell, the protagonist of *Hombre*, is a man thoroughly estranged from his surroundings. In this film Ritt and screenwriters Ravetch and Frank take an unsparing look at perhaps the most alienated Westerner in the genre's history.

In *Hud*, Ritt examined the nature of the hero by contrasting a modern amoral hustler and a representative of an earlier generation of virtuous, hardworking pioneers. But John Russell carries within himself both sides of the dilemma explored in *Hombre*, making this a tighter and more unified work than its predecessor. Without the filter of the adolescent observer, Hud's cynicism and Homer's uprightness are now presented as facets of the same character, feeding off one another in unexpected ways.

Russell, again played by Paul Newman, is a white man raised by Apaches. As an Indian he has been shaped by the elements and the land, and he is a product of nature. He stands apart from civilization; he has the skills to survive in the wilderness. But he is also a white man, the adopted son of a boardinghouse proprietor who has recently died, leaving Russell his gold watch and the boardinghouse, symbols of the society he has been separated from.

Hombre opens not with a landscape shot but with an extreme close-up of the hero's face, establishing a personal focus that is unusual for a Western. This is followed by a point-of-view shot of a beautiful black stallion seen in the distance on top of a hill and then by a series of quick cuts: two Indian faces looking at the horse, a closer shot of the horse, another close-up of Russell, and then a close-up of the horse facing the camera and, by extension, Russell. These shots, uncommon for Ritt, who typically favors long takes, rapidly make the connection between the hero and the horse, with its natural connotations.

While Russell and his friends wait for the stallion to lead a wild herd toward a stream where they are to be trapped, Billy Lee Blake arrives and nearly disrupts the Indians' strategy. An emissary from the town, Blake has come to bring Russell down from the mountains and draw him into the white man's world. The spatial contrast of town and mountains recurs visually throughout the film to indicate that Russell remains separated from the other characters.

The opening shots also establish that the film's point of view is essentially Russell's own. This is a radical departure from Elmore Leonard's novel *Hombre*, which is narrated by Carl Allen, renamed Billy Lee Blake in the film. Like Lonnie Bannon, Carl is a young man, and the novel offers a coming-of-age story. The film's focus on Russell shifts its perspective from the representative of the town society to the character who remains outside it.[2]

The concentration on the outsider is important for the film's generic frame of reference as well. Like *Hud*, this film deliberately echoes another classic Western, drawing thematic substance from the earlier work; the intertextual relationship of the two films clarifies the meaning of Ritt's work. Much of *Hombre*'s story takes place on a stagecoach journey, thereby creating unmistakable parallels to John Ford's *Stagecoach* (1939). But there are sharp differences in the outcomes of the characters' travels and the two directors' attitudes toward the societies they portray.

Stagecoach is a celebration of community, following the adventures of a diverse group of travelers who must pass through extreme danger posed by intermittent Indian attacks before arriving at the appropriately named town of Lordsburg. Along the way they learn to act together to meet the travails of the journey, forming a unified society by recognizing and accepting their mutual dependence. A central event is the birth of a baby, which brings the characters together while neatly symbolizing the creative energy and endurance of the human race. At the end the good-hearted prostitute and the wrongly jailed prisoner are sent off to get married, presumably then to join society and perhaps change it for the better. One unredeemed sinner, a banker named Gatewood, is expelled from this community, apprehended in Lordsburg for embezzling bank funds and taken to jail.

Much of this action takes place against the backdrop of Monument Valley, which serves as a stunning reminder of the force and grandeur of nature. This superior force may be indifferent to humankind's struggles, but it is the stage on which we act out our dramas and pursue our dreams.

Hombre is a film with a very different feel and mood. After the introduction of Russell in the mountains, the action moves to the town of Sweetmary, which, unlike Lordsburg, is ironically named. The specter of death that hangs over the Bannon ranch is also to be felt in Sweetmary, itself a dying town. The railroad is coming but will bypass this town, and the stage line that serves it is soon to be out of business. The mud wagon, the privately hired conveyance on which much of the action takes place, is literally the last stagecoach out of town. The emptiness of existence here is emphasized visually in the literal emptiness of the town itself. No extras fill the background with the business of everyday life; the only life is provided by the characters who play significant roles in the story. In this lonely outpost these human beings are as isolated as if they were in the wilderness.

A disillusioned sheriff's bitter summation of his life serves equally well as a metaphor for the wasted promise of the dying town:

> I've been working since I was ten years old, cleaning out spittoons at a dime a day. And now it's thirty years later, and all I can see out the front door is a dirt road going nowhere. The only thing that ever changes the view is a spotted dog lifting his leg against the wall over there. Saturday nights I haul in the town drunks and get their twenty-five cent dinners and their rot-gut liquor heaved up all over my one good shirt. I wear five pounds of iron strapped to my leg, and that makes me fair game for any punk cowboy who's had one too many.
>
> Lady, I don't need a wife. I need *out.*

Unlike the benevolent lawman in *Stagecoach*, *Hombre*'s Sheriff Braden attempts to get out by joining the band of outlaws who rob the stagecoach. He is killed during the attempt, suggesting that the only way out is death.

The sheriff's cynicism pervades the film. Jessie (Diane Cilento), a middle-aged woman who has run the boardinghouse for Russell's father, becomes in essence the son's antagonist. When Russell comes to town, he decides to sell the boardinghouse, leaving Jessie without a job, so she joins the group leaving Sweetmary. A good woman like *Stagecoach*'s Dallas, Jessie is older, tougher, and without romantic illusions. She seems as tough as Russell himself, but she is still able to respond to others in ways that Russell, whose feelings are dead, cannot. Whereas she feels impelled to help those in need, Russell would just as soon abandon them.

Audra Favor (Barbara Rush), a younger woman and the wife of the Indian agent (Frederick March), who, like Gatewood, is revealed to be an embezzler, mourns the loss of romance from her life. Aristocratic in appearance, she is bored and sexually dissatisfied. Ironically acknowledging her husband's intellect, she notes, "He reads late into the night, which is just as well, because when he takes off his trousers and folds them neatly over the chair, that sharp keen intelligence of his doesn't count for very much."

The film's bleak atmosphere becomes strained when Mendez (Martin Balsam) speaks of being frightened by God when he was a child. Favor, the Indian agent, tells him not to be frightened because there is no God. When Mendez replies, "Not in either of us, perhaps," Favor responds, "Not anywhere." The conviction of meaninglessness reflects not only this character's cynicism, but the film's somber emotional exhaustion as well.

Attempting to escape the outlaws who have robbed the stagecoach, the passengers must journey on foot through wilderness, mountains, and desert, facing severe hardships with limited food and water. Feeling no responsibility for these people, Russell tries to take off on his own but is persuaded to lead the group to safety. On the stagecoach, he was treated as an outcast, forced to ride on top with the driver (more spatial distancing) because Audra Favor refused to ride with "an Indian"; but now his wilderness skills are needed, and he is called on to join the group.

Russell's continued indifference to this community in need distinguishes him from the classic Western hero, who willingly serves the communal welfare; this man's only noble impulse seems to be a desire to return the money stolen from the Apaches. He takes on the traditional hero's role, however, because of his competence in the natural setting. Away from the town and in the wilderness setting that defined him at in the film's opening, Russell becomes a dominant figure. But while his affinity for the land invests him with a mythic dimension, his harsh response to the weakness and the sufferings of the others makes him an uncomfortable and ambiguous hero.

This ambivalence is best illustrated when Favor, whose embezzled money has changed hands several times, tries to steal the gold again and, with it, the group's only water flask. Catching him in the act, Russell orders him into the desert without water. The others stand by passively and do not object. Although Russell's outrage is understandable and his decisiveness perhaps admirable, the ruthless tenor of his sense of justice is troubling. The next morning, as the group is resting in a deserted mine shaft, Favor comes into view parched and exhausted, but Russell remains pitiless, warning the others not to call out to him or they will reveal their location to the bandits. When Jessie protests this heartless treatment, Russell replies, "Yesterday you thought he would just go away, so it was all right?" It is one of the film's most dramatic moments, boldly contrasting Russell's cold determination against Jessie's belated compassion, which suddenly seems shallow in comparison.

This unresolved confrontation embodies the film's central thematic conflict. Both Russell and Jessie have been battered by life, but their differing responses to it indicate a dichotomy of human potential that seems irreconcilable. She is moved by the suffering of others, though her efforts may be misdirected and ineffectual. Much like *Hud*'s Alma, who is abused but still manages to elicit some sympathy from Hud, Jessie demonstrates a spirit of generosity that clearly affects Russell, but his alienation will not yet allow him to respond in kind.

Jessie's charitable gesture alerts the bandits, who quickly surround the group, now trapped in an abandoned mine building. Holding Mrs. Favor hostage, they tie her outside, where she is exposed to the torturous heat of the sun. When the leader of the outlaws offers to trade Mrs. Favor for the money, Russell warns the group that the bandits will likely shoot both Mrs. Favor and anyone who attempts to rescue her once they have the money. Even Mr. Favor refuses to help his wife, and Russell's cynicism is again confirmed by the behavior of the group.

Finally Jessie decides to make the attempt. Ritt handles this climactic moment with subtlety, understating the nobility of the gesture as Jessie walks quietly across the room to pick up the money bags, her eyes cast down at the floor. Challenged by the extremity of the situation, she acts with unwonted courage, as if prompted to an imperative expression of her character. Earlier, in an argument with Russell, she explained her philosophy: "We better deal with each other out of need and forget merit—because none of us have too much of that—not me, not you, not anybody!" Her self-sacrificing response to the need of the suffering woman is the basic impulse of human empathy that underlies the hope of community.

Russell appears to be powerfully affected by her example. Wounded by racism and separated from the group by the wilderness upbringing that encouraged in him a lonely independence, he has seen little good in society or "civilization." But Jessie's charitable impulse now seems to soften him, perhaps hinting that there is something to recommend the world he has shunned. Suddenly deciding to make the heroic gesture himself, he leaves the money to be returned to the Indians, fills the moneybags with paper and cloth, and sets out to rescue Mrs. Favor. It is not made clear whether Russell had intended to do this all along or has been truly moved by Jessie's compassion to sublimate his own nature, and this ambiguity saves the film from ending on what might have been a sentimental and simplistic note.

As Russell walks down the hill to cut Mrs. Favor loose, the movement repeats his descent from the mountains at the film's beginning. This cyclical patterning, echoed in the group's return to the abandoned mine, an early rest stop on the journey, confirms the film's air of existential despair and suggests, finally, that Russell's progress from nature to community was in fact a movement toward death.

Facing Russell at the bottom of the hill, the villain Grimes (Richard Boone) remarks, "I wonder what Hell looks like," and his last words are "We've all got to die, the only question is when." Such fatalism may have been part of the classic Western hero's makeup, but Ritt flatly deromanticizes it. This hero's death has no glamour, and the film's ending undercuts any sense of martyrdom. Managing to kill Grimes, Russell is himself fatally shot in the process. Billy Lee, who was supposed to cover him, has his view blocked by Mrs. Favor as she struggles up the hill toward the shack. As a result Russell is left to deal with the bandits alone.

Ritt handles Russell's death with subtle restraint, as in the portrayal of Jessie's attempt to make the heroic gesture. The sense of nostalgia and regret over the death of the hero that closes *Ride the High Country* and *Lonely Are the Brave* is entirely missing here. Russell is shot down in an act of self-sacrifice, but the nobility of his gesture is clouded by the ambiguity of his motives and the futility of the action, and this brutal death only seems to justify his earlier cynicism. Even the example of courage is undercut. When Russell stood apart he seemed heroic but unfeeling; when he acts for the group, he is quickly destroyed. The opposition between individualism and society is not resolved; Russell's death accomplishes nothing, for the people he died for were not worth saving. The Old West, which is yielding to the railroad and the modern world, seems now as empty and sterile as that which will replace it.

This suggestion of futility is accentuated in the film's closing moments. As Russell lies dead, his face, peaceful in death, dominates the right side of the frame; Jessie kneels beside him. But in the background Mrs. Favor is seen, still struggling up the hill, oblivious of the death of the man who has saved her life, as are the others who wait above. The film ends with a close-up of Russell's face in death, repeating the close-up that opened the film. Here, however, Russell is dressed as a white man, with his hair cut short. Clearly, his attempt to enter the "civilized" world has led only to death; the progression from wilderness to society has yielded nothing. At the time of its release, *Hombre* was, along with *Hud*, the most hopeless of modern Westerns.

The pessimism is confirmed again in Ritt's variation on the screenwriters' original ending. An earlier draft of the film script has Jessie and Mendez standing over Russell's grave in a cemetery, where he is only one of many who have died violently. As in *Hud*, Ritt chooses instead to close with his protagonist. While Hud is left alone to pursue his selfish ends, Russell is last seen in death, at last merged with the natural world, his only true home. Like Shane he has returned to the mountains, but unlike Shane, who would return as a savior in other guises, Ritt's Westerner is left literally dead, like the myth he has personified.

CHAPTER 7

Rashomon Redux: *The Outrage*

After the success of *Hud*, Ritt was offered many new projects, but none commanded his attention until, while vacationing with his wife, he received the first fifty pages of a script called "The Rape." Although at first ambivalent about the story, he soon became intrigued. "The Rape" (another working title was "Judgment in the Sun"), which would become *The Outrage*, was written by screenwriter/playwright Michael Kanin, who based his work on Akira Kurosawa's 1950 film *Rashomon* (released in the United States in 1951). Ritt, like most viewers, considered that film a masterpiece, and he was dubious about remaking it. He decided, finally, that if the remainder of the script was as powerful as the fifty pages he had just read, he would commit himself to the project: "The more I thought about doing the film, the more interested and excited I became. But I had to be careful and weigh my initial response. I had to make sure my reaction was valid, and not cluttered up with the emotional residue of *Rashomon*. The first thing I look for in any film property is emotion; or any genuine intellectual stimulation. And this I like to coordinate with strength and simplicity and visual style. *The Outrage* stimulated me more than any property I received" (Field 34).

In 1951 when Michael and Fay Kanin had seen Kurosawa's film, they felt they had seen a powerful play rendered as a superb film. Only three basic sets were needed for the story: the forest, the court, and the Rashomon Gate. The more they thought about it, the more excited the Kanins became about adapting the film for the Broadway stage. They negotiated for almost two years before obtaining the rights to the film and the two short stories, by Ryunosuke Akutagawa, on which it was based.

The Kanins' play, also entitled *Rashomon*, opened on Broadway on January 27, 1959. Produced by David Susskind (who had given Ritt his start in film) and Hardy Smith and directed by the distinguished theater and film director Peter Glenville, it also featured an outstanding cast, including Rod Steiger, Claire Bloom, Noel Willman, Oscar Homolka, and Akim Tamiroff. Well received by the critics, the Kanins' play enjoyed a respectable six-month run.

After the play's opening, a number of people expressed interest in making a film of it. The heads at one studio were concerned that the idea of telling four different stories about the same event might be too difficult for American audiences, and they were not enthusiastic about presenting a film that questioned the basic principle of truth. They offered to buy the film rights, however, if the concept were changed to a who-done-it, a guessing game in which one of the stories was eventually revealed to be true. Naturally, the Kanins turned them down.

One producer who was genuinely excited by the play was A. Ronald Lubin, a former agent who had packaged *Spartacus* and *Paths of Glory* for Kirk Douglas. (His earlier work as a producer included *Billy Budd* [1962], an adaptation of Melville's novella, with Peter Ustinov [who also directed], Robert Ryan, Melvyn Douglas, and Terence Stamp; and *Convicts Four* [1962], an offbeat drama about a long-term prisoner who becomes a professional artist, starring Ben Gazzara and featuring a supporting cast that included Rod Steiger, Vincent Price, and Sammy Davis Jr.) Lubin felt that *Rashomon* was a "dramatic story, intellectually stimulating, and [he] felt it could be tailored to reach a very wide audience" (Field 18).

Wanting to produce the film himself, Michael Kanin at first resisted Lubin's offer, but eventually he relented. Then, when Lubin had a difficult time selling the film to a studio without a script, he managed to prevail on Kanin to write one. Recalling that a few years earlier an American envoy and his wife had been killed by a bandit while riding in a jeep somewhere in the Middle East, Kanin thought the film version could be set in that part of the world. This story might serve as a useful backdrop, he felt, because there had speculation at the time about the killer's motives: Was he just a lone bandit, a Communist, a guerrilla fighter? Nobody really knew.

His other idea was to set the film in the American West:

[T]he West transposed itself perfectly in every respect. It was a time of legends, of great heroes, that are vibrant to this day. The Mexican bandit comes right out of our own history: the Cisco Kid, Juan Murietta, Pancho Villa, all the Mexican bandits who roamed back and forth across the Texas border. It was easy to transpose the Samurai and his wife into fallen, Southern aristocrats. Thousands of Southerners migrated to the West after the Civil War. Their lives broken, their holdings lost, they came to seek out a new life. . . . In fact *Rashomon* might have been written originally as a Western. (Field 14–15)

The Outrage, of course, was not the first Kurosawa film to be turned into a Western. John Sturges had made *The Seven Samurai* (1954) into *The Magnificent Seven* in 1960, and Sergio Leone would later use *Yojimbo* as the basis for *A Fistful of Dollars* (which was made in 1964 but not released in the United States until 1966). Lubin liked the Western idea for more practical reasons, "[A] Western is more lucrative and it would be more readily acceptable" (Field 19).

Martin Ritt was Lubin's first choice as director. "I felt he could infuse the film with strength and vitality while still retaining the intellectual concepts" (Field 19). Ritt agreed that the Western setting would work best: "It's the nearest thing to myth we have, and it is the classic idiom. The West also has such a classic, almost formal beauty" (35).

With half a script and Ritt almost committed, Lubin at first pitched the idea to Columbia because he had an allegiance to the studio, but he was quickly turned down. He next went to Fox, where Ritt had a commitment, and was turned down again. Both studios felt that the material had been around too long and that it would be uncommercial. The situation rapidly changed when Paul Newman, who had originally turned down the lead role as the Mexican bandit Carrasco, suddenly decided to do it. Ritt had meanwhile offered the part to Marlon Brando, who also declined to do it. Newman then reconsidered, regarding the part as a great challenge: "If I'm going to get clobbered, I might as well do it with this film. . . . There's something vital and exciting about putting your head on the butcher's block" (Field 36). Newman was at the time the number one box office star in the world, and so Lubin soon had offers from MGM and Paramount. Lubin and Ritt chose MGM because the studio heads put in more money faster and gave them artistic control of the film. It was budgeted at $3.2 million, then a very respectable figure.

MGM wanted Sophia Loren to play the female lead, but Lubin and Ritt hesitated. They felt that Loren could provide the right persona for some of the stories, especially the harsh, sexual scenes, but that she lacked the fragility needed for the earlier sequences. They opted instead for Claire Bloom, whose performance in the starring role had much impressed Lubin in the Broadway production.

The husband's role was more difficult to cast. The filmmakers wanted a star, but they had trouble finding someone who would accept third billing to Newman and Bloom. The size of the part also caused problems, for throughout most of the film the husband is tied to a tree; the actor would not be able to employ many of the usual tools of his trade. According to Lubin, "Laurence Harvey was the only actor who had the integrity, the guts, and the belief in the film, to take a chance, and make something of the husband's part" (Field 20). The cast was then rounded out with the hiring of Edward G. Robinson, William Shatner, and Howard da Silva.

Rashomon had been a breakthrough film for Akira Kurosawa and the Japanese cinema. The great director's career was in the doldrums after the critical and commercial failure of *The Idiot*, which opened in Japan in 1951, the same year *Rashomon* was released and won first prize at the Venice Film Festival. The international recognition revived Kurosawa's career, and at the same time brought Japanese film to the attention of movie audiences in the West.

The power of *Rashomon* lies in its flamboyant pictorial style. Kurosawa's manipulation of light and shadow, fluid camera movement, and artistic visual compositions were repeatedly applauded by the critics. His thematic exploration of the relativity of truth, the impossibility of absolutes, remains effective, although it was not then (and certainly is not now) a startling idea. Pirandello had first harvested that theme for the modern stage, and Orson Welles had exploited it brilliantly in *Citizen Kane* in 1941. The critical excitement over the Kurosawa film's ideas was therefore largely the result of timing and its compatibility with the currently fashionable European mode of existential despair over the instability of value and truth.

Rashomon employs what has since become a well-worn convention: each member of a group of characters recalls the same events, the rape of a woman and the apparent murder of her husband, in a different way. To tell the story, Kurosawa intercuts a series of flashbacks to create a nonlinear narrative that insists on the subjectivity of memory and its distortion of the truth. While it influenced such films as Alain Resnais's *Hiroshima Mon Amour* (1960) and *Last Year at Marienbad* (1962) and Joseph Losey's *The Go-Between* (1971), in comparison to those films, *Rashomon's* temporal structure is not overly complex. There is never any question as to whose narrative is being presented at a given moment; the various narrative frames and voices are clearly distinguished, locating the audience firmly within them. In Kurosawa's work, it is not the form of presentation that creates the interpretive challenge, but rather what is being recalled.

Rashomon is set in the twelfth century, when the authority of the central government and the Japanese court were being subverted by the growth of autonomous political and military powers in the provinces. Earthquakes, fires, epidemics, and rebellions contributed to a pervasive sense of chaos, caused by the dissolution of what was once established order. In the film, three characters take refuge from a storm beneath the ruined Rashomon gate, which had once guarded the southern entrance to the capital city of Kyoto. As a priest, a woodcutter, and a commoner wait for the rain to stop, they tell each other the story of how a noblewoman was raped in the forest, her samurai husband killed, and a thief named Tajomaru (Toshiro Mifune) arrested for the crimes. Most of the film is taken up by flashbacks that present four versions of the crime, as told by Tajomaru, the woman, the spirit of the samurai (through a medium), and the woodcutter, who witnessed the events.

Ritt was obviously intrigued by *Rashomon*'s theme, and no doubt he felt inspired by the challenge of finding his own way of expressing its complexity. His basic strength as a director, however, lay in his ability to articulate social themes visually by projecting them onto a realistic and believable landscape. He was not comfortable with philosophic abstraction, which is, of course, the material of *Rashomon*. Making this film was a bold step for Ritt, and in the process he did manage to expand his scope as a filmmaker, but he was wading into what for him were unchartered waters.

Ritt's interest in the relativity of truth theme was no doubt fueled by the popular reception of *Hud;* he was flabbergasted to find that the country's youth embraced the character of Hud, whom the filmmakers thought they had presented as an amoral, irresponsible heel. Paul Newman felt confident that the realization that Hud "was basically rotten at the core" would negate the attractiveness of a character who was merely good with women and "wore his pants right" (Jackson 75). Both Newman and Ritt had to admit that they were wrong, that they had misjudged the mood of America's youth. The overwhelming success of *Hud* no doubt pleased Ritt, but what he considered the audience's misreading of the film must have pushed him toward *The Outrage.*

The need to transform for his audience what was considered a cinematic masterpiece certainly compounded the challenge. In this case Ritt was adapting not a masterpiece from another medium, as he had done earlier with Faulkner's fiction, but a classic of his own medium; and the audaciousness of the attempt was soon apparent to his cinematographer, James Wong Howe: "It was a beautiful film in every way. . . . How, I thought, were we going to make a picture that's better than this?" (Field 21).

Howe realized, of course, that the Kurosawa film's great strength was its visual style. The shooting script is full of instructions for camera movement, while the dialogue remains minimal (Ritchie). *The Outrage* is much talkier; excessive dependence on telling rather than showing severely hampers Ritt's exposition. *The*

Outrage is, in fact, more indebted to the Kanins' play than to Kurosawa's film, and its theatrical roots were in part its undoing.

In adapting the stage play for the screen, the Kanins made what amounted to minor alterations. They adhered to the Kurosawa film's structure in constructing the play, dividing it between the three locations of the gate, the courtyard where the audience serves as the unseen tribunal, and the forest. They expanded the roles of the priest, the woodcutter, and the commoner (who becomes a wig-maker). In the play these characters appear more often and discuss the implications of the trial more fully, emphasizing the play's themes. The Kanins also provided more of a past for the woman, even introducing her mother, who testifies at the trial. The mother was a servant in the samurai's home; her daughter has married into the noble family.

Michael Kanin's screen version makes some changes in the characters to facilitate its cultural move from twelfth-century Japan to the American West of the nineteenth century. The thief Tajomaru becomes Carrasco, a Mexican bandit, played by Paul Newman. The samurai and his wife become the Wakefields, a Southern couple whose former way of life has been destroyed by the Civil War and who are now seeking to start anew in the West. The samurai connection is tangentially maintained by making Wakefield (Laurence Harvey) a colonel in the Confederate army. His wife (Claire Bloom), like her counterpart in the play, was a servant in the Wakefield home before marrying the master. The mother character is dropped from the film.

The characters derived from the trio who discuss the events at the Rashomon Gate here gather instead at the rundown railway station at Silver Gulch, awaiting a train that rarely stops there anymore. The priest becomes a preacher (William Shatner), who has been so spiritually shattered by the trial that he has decided to leave the ministry and the town. The woodcutter has become a prospector (Howard da Silva), and the commoner a con man (Edward G. Robinson).

The Outrage was filmed largely on location in a national forest of cacti near Tucson. Ritt believed that this setting contained the "intrinsic core of the film. It was filled with symbolic overtones"(Field 35). Some scenes were filmed on top of Chatsworth Mountain, north of Los Angeles. The scenes at the railway station were shot on a soundstage because the crew could not wait for rain in Arizona, and, unfortunately, almost everything about the railway station set looks artificial. Departing from the example of *Rashomon*, Ritt films the trial scenes in front of a judge, with onlookers watching the trial. These scenes are filmed outdoors, in front of a ruined stone building with only its facade remaining. The key scenes of the rape and murder are enacted in a grove with a waterfall and pond.

The location and time changes were the central modifications that Michael Kanin made in fashioning his screenplay. The character types were already present in the play, so he merely made some of the dialogue more colloquially suited to the American West. This difference is mostly apparent in the speech of Carrasco, who had to be made to sound Mexican, and the con man, who needed to be more overtly American. These are simply cosmetic touches, however, because the characters, as in Kurosawa's film, are basically types rather than realistic personages. In all versions, the story's power lies in what is revealed about human nature, not in the personalities of the characters themselves.

Shifting the film to the nineteenth-century American West may have seemed a good idea in the abstract, but it turned out to be a major mistake. The western landscape raises certain generic expectations, chiefly the problematic relationship between the hero and the landscape, which *The Outrage* does not even address. Here the setting contributes little to the narrative development; this theme-oriented story could be set almost anywhere, except in a landscape that projects its own mythic dimension. Neither Kanin nor Ritt managed to shape the material so as to meld theme, character, and setting into a unified whole. Whereas in Kurosawa's *Rashomon* the movement deeper into the forest resonates with psychological overtones and a sense of mystery, the key scenes in Ritt's film, while glibly picturesque, add little to the story's meaning.

Also in contradiction to the generic Western formula, this film projects no hero. While each character presents himself/herself in a positive light, the others undercut these self-portraits, so the versions cancel out one another and no one emerges as an attractive, compelling figure. The lead characters never transcend their assigned identities as a bandit and a rather anonymous Southern couple.

Ritt explained that he was attracted to the Arizona location because of its symbolic overtones, but he failed to exploit its mythic potential. In the Western genre, the desert serves as the most extreme testing ground for the hero. It is where, in his struggle to survive, he must imitate the brutality of his surroundings. As Jane Tomkins points out, "The desert pushes the consciousness of the hero and the reader/viewer beyond itself and into another realm" (84).

Ritt utilizes the desert as an establishing location, but then inexplicably transfers the main action to a water hole, which undercuts the brutality of that larger setting; the rape and murder take place not in the wilderness but in the comparative comfort of an oasis. He fails even to make use of the eerie desert silence, but follows the dictates of the play's structure by moving back too often to the railroad station where the characters endlessly expound on the action.

The Western, as many critics have pointed out, is a genre conditioned by polarities. Common themes are the confrontation of primitive nature with an emerging society and the struggle of that society to transcend the savagery of human history. Brutal violence is a given in the Western, regarded not as a violation of the norm but as a part of it. In the context of medieval Japan, *Rashomon* presents the rape and murder as stunning violations of a moral code and then documents each participant's efforts to interpret them so as to vindicate his or her actions and redeem a degree of personal prestige. Ritt, however, cannot draw upon this sense of "outrage" because his Western setting belies the social order it requires. While the need to deny or to excuse forms part of each of the characters' motivations in Ritt's film, it goes against the audience's conditioned assumption that violence is no aberration in the Western setting; on the contrary, it is expected.

Because *The Outrage* is rooted in the Western genre, it is important, however, that the conflict between violent savagery and civilized order be reconciled. John Cawelti writes that the Western is "an artistic device for resolving problems rather than confronting their irreconcilable ambiguities" (Cawelti 37). But the thematic mode of *Rashomon* and *The Outrage* is ambiguity, which plays against the dictates of the Western genre, though both films employ a problematic ending that seems to undercut this thesis.

Rashomon ends with the discovery of an abandoned infant, and this development pushes the story in a new direction. The three characters who have been merely discussing the events suddenly become more active. The commoner, who believes that man is impulsive and selfish, strips the baby of its blanket and clothing in order to sell them. The priest and the woodcutter rush to protect the baby, hoping thereby to maintain their belief in man's essential goodness. The woodcutter accuses the commoner of being evil and selfish. Then the commoner accuses the woodcutter of stealing the samurai's sword after witnessing his death, and the woodcutter must embarrassedly acknowledge the truth of this charge.

The departure of the commoner with his booty coincides with the end of the storm, thus linking man's impulsive, naked self with the storm. Guilty over his actions in the forest, the woodcutter decides to take the child home, saying, "I have six children of my own. One more wouldn't make it any more difficult" (Ritchie 90). The priest apologizes for suspecting the woodcutter's motives: "Thanks to you, I think I will be able to keep my faith in men" (91). Some have seen in this ending the triumph of the priest's point of view.

Kurosawa's ending is rather more complex than that. In the final shots, the woodcutter moves toward the camera, stops, and bows toward the priest. As he turns and moves on, the camera tracking with him, a sunny sky is visible and then the priest is shown again, small and confined under the gate. The impression, created by these two camera shots, that the woodcutter is walking into shadow restores the ambiguity of the earlier scenes. Finally, nothing seems reconciled.

Ritt's ending, on the other hand, is simply confused. It is preceded, as in the original film, by the prospector's version (that of the woodcutter in *Rashomon*), which Ritt stages as a farce and which some critics, correctly, have roundly disparaged. The resort to farce was a clear miscalculation, seeming to endorse the con man's contention that mankind is made up of selfish, brutish liars. His thematic adversary, the preacher, has been unfortunately silent throughout most of the film, giving the upper hand to the con man, who speaks most often and most eloquently. It does not help that William Shatner portrays the preacher as a callow idealist, while the dynamic performance of Edward G. Robinson steals the show.

The prospector's story presents both Carrasco and the husband as cowardly, bumbling oafs who, when they finally decide to duel, can't shoot straight and must resort to slugging it out in the manner of silent film slapstick comedians. Ritt has them tripping, biting, and throwing things at each other, running around the ravine area, even falling into the stream and fighting there. The wife watches like an interested spectator at a prize fight, egging them on and seeming more involved in the spectacle than in the outcome. The fight ends when the husband, in the process of stabbing Carrasco, trips and accidentally falls on the knife. He rises, faces the camera, weakly declaring "I tripped," which reduces his fate to a pratfall, and finally dies. Laurence Harvey's inept delivery of the line further undercuts the gravity of the scene.

After the death of the husband, Ritt cuts back to the railway station. First the moon is shown reflected in a puddle of water; the image shimmers and then disappears; the rain has stopped. The camera moves to reveal the trio of witnesses from the rear, and then a reverse angle shot shows them from the front: the preacher in profile in the foreground, staring silently off into space, with the con man behind him to the left and the prospector to the right. The con man, as usual, dominates the conversation that follows, during which the preacher remains immobile, saying nothing. "You like to think people are big. Big heroes, big villains, big something. And now you see them the way they are, little pipsqueaks, cowardly, rotten. . . . There's your miracle, holy man. Alas, we got the truth by the tail. Never be afraid of the truth. . . . Sooner or later you fellahs got to stop kidding yourselves. . . . The truth is like that little ball under the three shells. Now you see it, now you don't."

The film seems to confirm this cynical view, underscoring it with the disappearing moon in the water and the preacher's silence. Then comes the sound of the baby. The con man finds the infant, and before handing it over to the preacher, takes a small bag of money from around the baby's neck. The prospector, appalled by the man's greed, fights the con man to get it back. The con man then announces that he knows that the prospector stole the jewel-handled knife that killed the husband. The prospector then backs off, ashamed to have been discovered in his own moment of greed.

When he asks to be given the baby, explaining that he already has five at home, the preacher is moved by the prospector's humanity and gives him the child. As the prospector speaks, the preacher's face is in shadows, but when the prospector justifies his taking the dagger in order to feed his family, the preacher lifts his head into the light. He now receives his revelation: men may be cowardly and selfish, but he must accept them as brothers with all their imperfections. While this is happening, the con man succeeds in flagging down the train, and then he asks the preacher, who is walking off with the prospector and the child, to join him. The preacher looks back at the con man, framed in a doorway with a lantern in his hand, turns back toward the prospector, and as he walks away with him, his face reflecting contentment, Ritt freezes the frame and ends the film.

Unlike Kurosawa, Ritt leaves the con man alone but shows his preacher joining the prospector and the baby, and thus making his final image a gesture of affirmation. Following the low comedy staging of the climactic scene between the principals, however, the con man's bitter cynicism about mankind and truth and his exposure of the prospector's greed ring false. The ending feels tagged on, as unconvincing as the staging of the preacher's personal epiphany.

The air of mystery that invests Kurosawa's film is entirely missing from *The Outrage*, dissipated by the repeated device of cutting back to the three men at the railway station for comment on what has happened in the desert. The roles of this bedraggled trio are more prominent than those of the three discussants in Rashomon, and the constant hammering home of the thematic development undercuts the story's effectiveness. The con man has all the best lines, and his too often reiterated cynicism is given unnecessary visual emphasis in the presentation of the various stories. When he tells the preacher, "You can't even look at the dirty face of the world you live in without wanting to run from it," the preacher has nothing to say. Nor does it help to present the preacher as a man in the act of abandoning his congregation; Kurosawa's priest may be baffled, but he has not forsaken his flock. Ritt's preacher never seems to have anything to say; the role is more effectively drawn in *Rashomon* and more effectively handled by the actor playing it.

In attempting to flesh out the characters, *The Outrage* manages to distract the audience from its exploration of the nature of truth. The con man's speech about the nature of crime, in which he charges that small-time crooks like him are punished while murderers like Carrasco are made into legends, has little relevance to the thematic development of the story. Talk about the Southern aristocracy and the element of class distinction, rendered most apparent in the unequal relationship of the husband and wife, is another diversion from what should be the main thrust of the film.

Although not a successful work in itself, *The Outrage* boasts some of Ritt's most powerful pictorial compositions. The scene in which Carrasco sees the carriage with the husband and wife riding through the desert, his vision at first broken by the cacti and then focused on a beautiful lady's face covered by a veil, offers an evocative image of the lure of beauty as it pulls a man away from his routine into an experience that will change his life. The effect is repeated when Carrasco comes looking for the woman after he has tied up the husband: Ritt's camera glides along as the veiled woman walks among the desert plants, Alex North's music becoming increasingly romantic. Ritt then concentrates on her veiled face before cutting to Carrasco and a point-of-view shot of the woman as she faces him. Ritt is more effective here even than Kurosawa in establishing the overwhelming power of beauty.

The medium close-up shots of her face as she appears before the judge are also effective, and they make the composition shot of her framed by the ruined building and seemingly entrapped by her life and testimony all the more dramatic. Ritt's close-up of the Indian medium's face, with its bandanna, a detail repeated in the husband's gag, also provides an effective visual link. The sun is employed as a dramatic force in various scenes, as the Indian looks upward into the sunshine as his narrative begins, and the husband looks toward the receding light as he is dying at the episode's end. In order to retain the supernatural mood during the Indian's narrative, James Wong Howe used a Panavision lens to heighten the distortion created around the edges of the frame by the tension between the wide field of vision and the depth of field.

As the dying husband speaks of darkness closing in, a hand comes into the frame and removes the dagger from his chest. Howe then pictures a mist blown through the trees at what seems a great distance away. The camera moves up through the mist to the clear sky and begins spinning around before cutting back to the Indian medium. It is a disorienting effect, an exceptionally expressive moment. Ritt, who is not noted for such effects, utilizes them here to great effect in a film that requires the camera to be itself a character in an abstract drama.

Despite some notable advances in his art, *The Outrage* was a setback for Ritt. *Hud* and, later, *Hombre* showed that Ritt understood the conventions of the Western and could utilize them to his advantage. Those films, however, were written by Irving Ravetch and Harriet Frank and based on novels by Larry McMurtry and Elmore Leonard. In both cases the source material and the adaptations were rich in these writers' understanding of the form itself, the character types, and the use of visual imagery to meld the effects of landscape, character, and situation.

While *The Outrage* pays homage to a great film, Ritt and Kanin stumbled badly in failing to understand that transferring Kurosawa's material to the American West would require more than merely exploiting a mythic setting. Neglecting to shape their screenplay to the dictates of the screen, to let image and gesture substitute for verbal exposition, these filmmakers only managed to demonstrate that piling the generic baggage of the Western onto a drama of philosophic inquiry could only lead to the collapse of the Rashomon Gate.

CHAPTER 8

Secret Agent Man: *The Spy Who Came in from the Cold*

After completing *The Outrage*, Ritt considered several film offers that he would eventually abandon. Among the projects that commanded his attention for a time were *The Liberation of Lord Byron Jones*, a grim tale of race relations set in the South and based on a 1965 novel by Jesse Hill Ford; *Gaily, Gaily*, based on Ben Hecht's memoir about his early days as a newspaperman in Chicago; John Hersey's *The Wall*; an antiwar novel by Richard Linakis, *The Spring the War Ended*; Saul Bellow's *The Adventures of Augie March*; and *The Autobiography of Malcolm X*, which was to star Cassius Clay. All were eventually declined by Ritt, for reasons ranging from lackluster material to his own unsuitability as director of a given project.

Instead, in 1966 Ritt wrote to Dale Wasserman, author of *Man of La Mancha*, that he would be interested in directing the film version of the hit musical. Although this would seem to have been an uncharacteristic undertaking for Ritt, a year later he expressed similar interest in doing *Fiddler on the Roof*. Perhaps after the failure of *The Outrage*, he felt he needed a box office success. As it turned out, much to his surprise, he already had one.

When he read the galley proofs of John le Carré's novel *The Spy Who Came in from the Cold*, Ritt bought them immediately. Le Carré was a little-known writer of two well-received but relatively unsuccessful novels, *Call for the Dead* and *A Murder of Quality*, and so Ritt was able to acquire the rights for the very modest sum of twenty-eight thousand dollars. Upon its publication in 1963, *The Spy Who Came in from the Cold* became a runaway bestseller that, by the time

Ritt started making the film, had already sold 5 million copies in the United States alone. The book's success baffled and delighted Ritt: "[P]eople have complimented me on how shrewd I was, smelling out a bestseller in advance. But I never dreamed it would be a big success. I just thought it would make a nice, little, uncommercial but good movie. I'm still amazed at how it sold" (Peper 14).

Ritt no doubt was also eager to direct an espionage tale that bucked the 1960s dominant trend of escapist-romance spy thrillers. That decade saw the rise of the James Bond film—*Dr. No, From Russia with Love, Goldfinger,* and *Thunderball* were released between 1962 and 1966—and popular imitations such as the Matt Helm films with Dean Martin and the Flint movies starring James Coburn. On television, *The Man From U.N.C.L.E.* ran from 1964 until 1968, spawning a spin-off series, *The Girl From U.N.C.L.E.* (1966–67), and several feature films.

Ritt decided not only to direct *The Spy Who Came in from the Cold,* but to produce it as well, making this his first solo producing credit. He asked the noted British playwright John Osborne to adapt the novel, but Osborne declined, explaining that he was attracted by the "superb bleak subject" but was distressed by Ritt's plan to cast Paul Newman in the lead role (RC undated). How serious Ritt was about casting Newman is unclear, but he soon chose Burt Lancaster instead. Then, when production was delayed, Lancaster had to bow out because of other commitments and was replaced by Richard Burton, who had starred in the film version of Osborne's *Look Back in Anger* in 1959 and who had just finished filming *The Sandpiper* with Elizabeth Taylor. Ritt had to work hard to persuade Paramount to accept Burton and his $750,000 salary.

That choice entailed some extra, unforeseen problems that complicated the filmmaker's work. Having selected a mega-star to play a faceless spy, Ritt confronted the monumental task of persuading Burton to deromanticize his portrayal. As Burton's biographer Melvyn Bragg observed, "It was very hard for an actor—especially an intelligent and powerful actor like Burton—to take on trust a demand which eradicates many of the characteristics on which he has built his reputation" (Bragg 201). Ritt, however, prevailed: "We worked hard to scale down his extraordinary voice, his cocky bearing, his romantic aura" (Bart). The effort ultimately produced one of Burton's most memorable film performances, as well as an Oscar nomination for Best Actor.

Ritt also disapproved of Burton's heavy drinking, which the actor resented, and more unsettling tension was created by Elizabeth Taylor's jealous attitude toward Burton's co-star, Claire Bloom. Aware of a previous affair between the two, Taylor would not allow Burton even to be friendly with Bloom on the set, acting, according to Bragg, "like a one-woman KGB": Burton "was under twenty-four hour surveillance. She monitored every wink." (Bragg 201) This rivalry poisoned the atmosphere on the set, adding greatly to the difficulty of making the film.

Spy was filmed on location in Europe during the winter to capture the somber "gray" mood Ritt wanted for the picture, which he chose to film in black-and-white to accentuate the grim nature of the subject matter. "None of the values in the story were black and white. I wanted rain or greyness in every scene—no sunlight" (qtd. in Jackson 83).

Ritt explained that he was attracted to the novel because "it takes a realistic blast at the espionage methods of both sides. It really says 'a plague on both your houses' " (Watts).

Another concern of le Carré's book that echoed a motif central to Ritt's work was that of individualism: the novel focuses on political systems and social constructs that either respect or deny the worth of the individual. This theme is developed in a symbolic passage that is invoked twice in the novel; Dehn incorporates it into the dialogue once. Midway through the story, while being driven into East Germany, the protagonist Leamas recalls an incident that occurred when he was speeding from Cologne to Karlsruhe to meet his agent, Riemeck. As he was driving, a car suddenly pulled out in front of him. He flashed his headlights, sounded his horn, and hit the breaks, barely avoiding a collision. As he drove past the car, he noticed children in the back seat "waving and laughing" and the "stupid, frightened face of their father at the wheel." He pulled off the road: "He had a vision of the little car caught among them [some heavy lorries described earlier], pounded and smashed, until there was nothing left, nothing but the frenetic whine of klaxons and the blue lights flashing; and the bodies of children, torn like murdered refugees on the road across the dunes" (102).

This vision returns at the end of le Carré's novel as Leamas stares in disbelief at the body of Liz Gold: "As he fell, Leamas saw a small car smashed between great lorries, and the children waving cheerfully through the window."(219) The image of inexorably approaching chaos represented by the lorries echoes a slightly different image recollected by Leamas early in the novel: "He saw the long road outside Rotterdam, the long straight road beside the dunes, and the stream of refugees moving along it; saw the little airplane miles away, the procession stop and look towards it; and the plane coming in, neatly over the dunes; saw the chaos, the meaningless hell as the bombs hit the road" (15). Leamas's mental projections are telling: he does not imagine that he will be the one to smash the car with the children; this will be done by the giant lorries. But in relation to the car he barely avoids hitting, he is like a lorry driver and may be in some sense responsible for the death of the children. In the same way, he recognizes his implication in the death of Liz, who, like the children and the refugees from the bombing, is an innocent victim of the war between giant powers. Leamas feels responsible for Liz's death because he allowed himself to care for her and love her.

These passages implicate Leamas in the death and destruction of innocents, in the unbearable tragedy of war. The giant lorries, like the powers conducting the cold war, have taken their toll on Liz and the children, who understood nothing of what Control planned and Leamas carried out. The image of anonymous destructiveness enforces the novel's neutrality: regardless of the identity of the killer, the effect is the same on the innocent victims. All are responsible.

Le Carré's novel insists on the inhumanity of actions undertaken by both sides ostensibly on behalf of humanity. Early in the novel Control states his philosophy about means and ends: "I would say that since the war, our methods—ours and those of the opposition—have become much the same. I mean you can't be less ruthless than the opposition simply because your government's *policy* is benevolent, can you now?" (15). Control's cynicism does not necessarily invalidate his argument, but the horrendous implications of his argument provide the novel's moral target. In the end, his is a lorry driver's view, which le Carré condemns as the central destructive rationale of war making. The plot of his novel, with its multiple deceptions, double- and triple-crosses, dramatizes a Machiavellian political order in which human sympathies have no place. Human values have been replaced by a horrifying cynicism.

Control's views are echoed later in the novel by Fiedler, Mundt's deputy, who remarks to Leamas, "We're all the same, you know, that's the joke"(156). Fiedler is right: in adopting the same murderous means, both sides betray their supposedly idealistic ends. Le Carré's point is that both sides eschew human sympathy and ignore human values in their destructive competition. Before they die, Leamas tells Liz, "[B]ut everywhere's the same, people cheated and misled, whole lives thrown away, people shot and in prison, whole groups and classes of men written off for nothing" (212). The novel consistently projects this tone of disgust, revulsion, and anger, capped by the sad and nauseating recognition that the squalid deaths of its central characters accomplish nothing.

These themes are natural Ritt territory. Ritt was fascinated by the book not only for what it revealed about espionage and spying, but for what it had to say about the cold war. "The book's statement was that the power struggle in the world was denuding the human spirit. . . . There is no concern except to win" (Bart).

This novel, however, clearly would be a difficult one to film. The story was, in le Carré's words, "too tight-packed for comfort," narrating events in an understated tone and supplying only sparse and cryptic dialogue (" 'The Spy' " 13).

A delicate balance would have to be struck in deciding how much information the audience should know at each stage: if too much were held back at the beginning, the filmmakers might simply lose the audience; if they revealed too much, they risked patronizing the audience. Too much revision for the screen could undermine the various plot twists, making the story either too difficult to follow or simply unexciting.

In le Carré's novel, Leamas, a spy for British Intelligence, undertakes to pass as a defector in order to get into East Germany. There he is to foil the enemy's espionage apparatus by incriminating a German agent named Mundt, who has been routinely executing spies planted and controlled by Leamas, who heads the British operation in Berlin. Once he gets to East Germany, Leamas finds himself enmeshed in a fantastic trap set by his own government and by Mundt, who turns out to be a double agent. The real aim of British Intelligence is to discredit Fiedler, a Jew and a high-ranking figure in the Abteilung, who is on to Mundt. Leamas and Liz Gold, the woman he falls in love with, become the pawns in this struggle. In the course of the story, Fiedler is exposed, Mundt is cleared, and Leamas and Liz are killed.

A preliminary script by Guy Trosper retained the basic outline of le Carré's story but took too many liberties with the plot development, attempting to solidify the novel's emblematic characters by providing background details that only fuzzed the clear political-moral implications of the story. Le Carré's tale was exciting enough; clearly it would be better to remain faithful to it.

Paul Dehn's extensive revision retained le Carré's plot but scrapped all this unnecessary detail and restored the taut structure of the novel. One major alteration remained, however. Le Carré's Liz Gold is both Jewish and a Communist, and these attributes link her with Fiedler, also a Jew and a Communist, who is hated by the rabid anti-Semite Mundt. Both are killed to protect Mundt's status as a double agent. Le Carré explained, "I used Jewish people because I felt that after Stalin and Hitler they should particularly engage our protective instincts" ("To Russia" 6).

Le Carré also emphasizes in a scene in his novel (not in the film) between Liz and the president of the tribunal, that the attitude of East Germans toward Jews has not changed since the war: "Jews are all the same. . . . Comrade Mundt knows what to do with Jews. We don't need their kind here"(201). The fact that these two Jewish characters serve as pawns in a struggle to protect Western interests adds power and poignance to the novel. Leamas, who comes to like Fiedler and to love Liz, becomes another unwitting pawn in a plot that destroys the only two people he cares about.

In the film Liz Gold becomes Nan Perry, and her Jewishness, though not her

Communist Party membership, is excised. Trosper first made this change, and Dehn retained it. The film also bypasses much of the evolution of the lovers' relationship, including her nursing Leamas through a fever. Most important, it omits Leamas's own sense of the growing importance of Liz in his life: "It was caring about little things—the faith in ordinary life; that simplicity that made you break up a bit of bread into a paper bag, walk down to the beach and throw it to the gulls. It was this respect for triviality which he had never been allowed to possess; whether it was bread for the sea gulls or love, whatever it was he would go back and find it; he would make Liz find it for him" (le Carré, *The Spy* 89). Similarly, Liz, who is politically naive in both book and film, discovers that her love for Leamas is deeper than her commitment to the party. Her experiences in East Germany, especially her meeting with the president of the tribunal, undermine her faith in Communist doctrine.

It is a mark of the film's artistry that the romantic relationship works effectively despite its transformation. Especially helpful is Dehn's (and Ritt's) decision to soften the character of Leamas, who emerges in the book as a cynic with a quick temper. The film's Leamas falls for Nan quickly and seems a more romantic sort, in large part because he is portrayed by Richard Burton. The progress of their relationship thereby becomes believable despite the brevity of the treatment. In addition to shortening the lovers' idyll, the film version is more sparing than the novel in the handling of action, which occasions some swift and at times elliptical changes of scene.

Ritt's version concentrates on the inhuman behavior of the superpowers and the isolated, existential loneliness of Leamas. In developing the character of Nan Perry, Ritt must have decided that the Jewishness of le Carré's character would distract from her function in the film as another lonely figure who gravitates naturally toward the protagonist. Her bond with Leamas is thus made more definite than her connection with Fiedler, who would only deflect attention from Leamas's growing awareness of his own culpability in the drama. Ritt and Dehn seem to have felt that following the plot intricacies of le Carré's political story would be taxing enough for the audience; introducing cultural complexities that a novelist has the leisure to explore would be too much for film viewers, especially those accustomed to the melodramatic escapades of James Bond and Matt Helm. It was necessary, then, to focus on one man's struggle against the tide of a political conflict that threatens to destroy the last vestiges of his humanity. In this way, Ritt was able to remain faithful to the central details of le Carré's novel and at the same time focus on the themes that commanded his attention as a filmmaker.

The novel's narrative is spare, taut, and fast-moving. There is little extraneous detail and little use of symbol or figurative language. Its pace might be described as cinematic, for it moves swiftly from scene to scene, locale to locale. Ritt's film is even more economical than the novel, its transitions brisk, its characterization achieved through look, gesture, and plot function.

Oswald Morris's superb black-and-white cinematography captures the dreariness of the novel's landscape, matching the climate and geography of the film to the emotional weariness of characters who move through rainy streets in bleak, fog-bound cities. In one sequence, after leaving prison, Leamas sits on a park bench by a lake, feeding birds. This scene, which in almost any other Ritt film would be set apart visually as an encounter with natural beauty, is rendered here as merely another washed-out, gray-looking scene, during which Leamas is first contacted by an enemy agent.

Later, walking through wooded hills, he debates philosophy with Fiedler. In *The Molly Maguires*, Ritt would place his characters in a similar setting to allow them a moment of happy serenity and to emphasize how they have distanced themselves from the beauty of their surroundings. Here, moving through a bleak country setting, the two figures remain rooted in the sunless world of spies and counterspies, where men are trained to be distrustful as they measure every word and gesture of their opponents.

Spy opens at night with a shot of the barbed wire that crowns the Berlin Wall. The camera dwells on it as the credits begin, providing not only a setting and a mood but also a visual reminder of the concentration camps, that ultimate image of the postwar world and the legacy of the Nazis. The camera then pans left to reveal the area between East and West, where troops patrol the border. Sol Kaplan's melancholy piano solo evokes the almost lifeless quality of the world we are about to enter.

Leamas is introduced as he looks out of a patrol hut, his back to the camera; it is hardly the standard entrance of a star performer. His back remains to the camera as an American agent, who has brought him coffee, tries to convince him to get some sleep. Leamas is waiting for his agent, Karl Riemek, who has been discovered by Leamas's nemesis, Mundt, and is to cross back to the West that evening.

Leamas pours whiskey into his coffee and takes a few sips before leaving the hut to walk alone toward the border. At one point he is framed in profile between two heavily barred windows; it is one of many expressive compositions Ritt uses to convey mood and theme. This one suggests that Leamas is trapped by his job, by his disposition, and by the politics of the cold war. Eventually he is alerted to the sight of a man walking a bicycle past the East German checkpoint. Ritt cuts to Leamas, from whose point of view we watch Riemek walk slowly with his bicycle toward the West. Leamas's expression is vacant, revealing nothing.

After a series of quick crosscuts, large light beams are illuminated and a siren breaks the stillness of the night. Riemek is ordered to halt. Instead, he gets on the bicycle and attempts to ride to freedom. The camera isolates Riemek as he struggles to ride past the guards, perfectly rendering his vulnerability and the pathos of his situation. There are to be no miraculous, Hollywood heroics here, however: a number of gunshots are heard, and Riemek falls to the ground. Ritt's camera lingers for a moment on Leamas's impassive face.

No hint is given of Leamas's reaction to the killing of Riemek, merely a quick cut from his face to an airplane in flight. Then a close-up of Leamas in profile in a car, already back in London, being driven to meet Control. This is Ritt's technique for moving the film, matching his sequences with medium close-ups or close-ups of Leamas as he moves from situation to situation.

The following scene with Control (Cyril Cusack) functions as one of the thematic centerpieces of both novel and film. The sequence begins as Leamas gets out of the car, the camera following his movement from a high angle as he enters the building. Again, the camera's positioning emphasizes Leamas's entrapment: although he thinks himself in control of his actions, Leamas is in fact being manipulated by Control, as will be revealed to him and to the audience later. Ritt's high-angle camera placement thus provides a subtle visual clue to his predicament. Prior to that shot, Leamas is shown talking to his driver, asking what fate Control has in store for him; the man's evasive reply is "Better let Control tell you that. It's not my job." Leamas remarks, "But he knows, of course." Ritt's cut to a shot of a leafless tree, followed shortly by the high-angle shot described above, answers the question.

As Leamas walks toward the door of the office building, there is a match cut showing a secretary enter Control's office with a teapot. This is followed by a shot of Control standing facing the door to greet Leamas. Control remains standing as he begins his speech: "The ethic of our work, as I understand it, is based on a single assumption. That is, we are never going to be aggressors." Control looms over the seated Leamas, whose insignificance is thus reemphasized visually. Control continues, "We do disagreeable things, but we are defensive." As he speaks he moves from behind the desk, always above the seated Leamas, until he stands before him, then crosses in front to stand on Leamas's other side. When he says, "[O]ur methods can't afford to be less ruthless than those of the opposition," his back is to the camera, which focuses on Leamas, holding him in its gaze. Obviously, Leamas is as much the object of Control's plans as he is of the camera's movements.

Continuing his purposeful motion, Control then moves left of Leamas, remarking that since the war, "our methods and those of the Communists have become very much the same." Control stays in profile, still towering over Leamas, whose position remains unchanged. Control's dominance has been very clearly established, and the unsettling suggestion has been planted that the actions of the two superpowers are interchangeable, that the smug Western belief that right is on our side may be misguided.

Shortly before this speech, Control has mentioned that he wants Leamas to "stay out in the Cold a little longer," thereby involving Leamas in his plan. After Control's veiled hint about the equivalence of the adversaries' methods, the scene ends abruptly, without explanation of what his plan is. (The novel makes it clearer that Leamas is to be involved in a scheme to implicate Mundt.)

The next scenes provide a rather mysterious image of Leamas walking on a London street, looking disheveled and unshaven. He is next seen entering the Labor Exchange looking for a job; he is sent to the Library for Psychic Research, where he meets Nan Perry. Ritt thereby plants in the audience's mind some questions about Leamas's behavior, questions that are to be answered later when Leamas meets with Control for the second and last time.

Leamas's first glimpse of Nan is a point-of-view shot, as he is being interviewed by Mrs. Crail: he sees her framed by library shelves as she collects and replaces books. This is reminiscent of the opening shots of Riemek, seen first from the perspective of a guard looking through binoculars and later from that of Leamas, who sighted him caught visually between the two gates. Passing through the second, and apparently free, he was shot. Now, the similar framing of Nan suggests that, like Riemek, she will fall victim to the conflict between East and West.

This suggestion is soon confirmed by another of Ritt's ominous compositions. Nan invites Leamas to dinner at her apartment; while serving tea after the meal, she asks Leamas what he believes in. The placement of the actors here reverses the setup between Leamas and Control. Whereas in that scene Leamas remained seated, with Control looming over him, now Leamas sits in a chair while Nan kneels on the floor. Here, the camera asserts Leamas's dominance, echoing his point-of-view shot in the library. When Leamas attempts to deflect her question by being cynical—"Well, I believe the number 11 bus will get me to Hammersmith; I do not believe it will be driven by Father Christmas"—Nan proceeds to tell him that she believes in history and freedom. This makes Leamas laugh as he says, "Nan, don't tell me you're a bloody Communist!"

To justify her beliefs, she shows him a picture of herself marching in a nuclear disarmament rally. Leamas then tells her the story about the children getting killed by the lorries, which le Carré had introduced as a memory in the novel. Leamas here concludes his story with the remark, ". . . Communists, capitalists. It's the innocent who get slaughtered." Ritt thus not only externalizes the image, but concretizes it by explaining it. The thematic significance of the moment is, once again, enforced visually, as Nan now stands over the seated Leamas, mirroring Control's position. Between them is the top of a poster showing the mushroom cloud from a nuclear explosion. In this composition—Ritt's visual equivalent to le Carré's powerful verbal metaphor of the lorries—both Nan's and Control's philosophic positions are exposed as contributors to destruction.

The film moves on swiftly and economically. Leamas is shown beating up a grocer to whom he owes money, then leaving prison and being picked up by Ashe (Michael Hordern), who poses as a member of a prisoner's aid society. Ashe will introduce him to Carlton (Kiever in the novel), who is to finalize the terms of Leamas's defection as they arrange to fly to The Hague. Before that encounter, however, Leamas meets with Control at the home of George Smiley.

This meeting with Control is more detailed than le Carré's version, as Ritt provides clear information about Control's plan for Leamas to go to seed and then defect. One of the film's great successes is in moving swiftly through Leamas's decline while keeping the audience slightly off balance. Having provided in the first scene with Control a vague suggestion that Leamas will be part of a plan to discredit Mundt, Ritt has carefully overlaid that hint with uncertainty and menace in the scenes that followed.

Now, in the second meeting with Control, the filmmakers clarify the situation, explaining Leamas's faked defection before he leaves England with Carlton. Control compliments Leamas on his "act" and his assault on the grocer. He tells him not to change anything "even by a brush stroke." He then informs Leamas that the plan to expose Mundt has been in preparation for some time and that an operation called "Rolling Stone" that Leamas once participated in was part of that plan.

Unlike the scene of their first meeting, Control spends most of this scene sitting, on the same visual plane with Leamas. They might almost be equals except that Leamas, as in the first scene, seems almost imprisoned in his chair, while Control is at ease, with his legs crossed. This attitude quickly shifts when he mentions "Miss Perry"; at this point he stands, assuming the menacing, superior air he maintained in the earlier interview. His knowledge of Leamas's love affair indicates his power, and his commanding position now emphasizes not only Leamas's vulnerability but Nan's as well.

The shift of scene that follows is again accomplished swiftly: Leamas is next seen in Holland, being driven to a house where he meets Peters (Sam Wanamaker), another contact in the Communist spy network. Their conversation moves from the house to a beach and back to the house, as Leamas speaks about his past and about operation Rolling Stone, which piques Peters's interest. While taking notes at the house, Peters is given a newspaper with a picture of Leamas and a story about his disappearance; he passes it to Leamas. This is another example of the film's creative compression of plot: in the novel, Leamas sees the newspaper story in an airport men's room; but here the revelation becomes more dramatic, as he is shown the story by a Communist agent. This revision both increases the surprise effect and thereby heightens the suspense, as both the audience, which, after the last scene with Control, felt that it was in on the plot, and Leamas himself suddenly realize that they are in the dark again.

In the novel, after Leamas sees his picture, le Carré writes, "For the first time since it all began, Leamas was frightened" (94). In the film Peters hands Leamas the newspaper and then leaves the room. Leamas stares at the paper and then gets up and walks toward a window as the camera looks back through the glass to capture the dazed and shocked look on his face in close-up. Ritt then cuts to a point-of-view shot of the scene outside the window, a field viewed through a barbed-wire fence. It is an eerily evocative and terrifying picture, summoning up the opening image of the Berlin Wall and its accompanying Holocaust associations. The shot, in washed-out black-and-white, creates a powerful image of desolation and emptiness, embodying Leamas's feelings; it is an elegant example of how a filmmaker's visual images can improve upon the aesthetic effects of the novelist's prose.

The rest of the film remains faithful to the novel, though accomplishing its action in a more economical way. Leamas is transported to East Germany, where Peters is to hand him over to Fiedler. The entrance of this pivotal character is rendered dramatically: while waiting in his spare white room with Peters, Leamas asks if Fiedler is good at his job, to which Peters replies, "For a Jew." At this point there is a cut to the door opening abruptly as Fiedler enters.

The scenes with Fiedler in East Germany are again more economical than those in the novel. Ritt downplays Leamas's growing affection for Fiedler, keeping the relationship on a professional plane. In one sequence Leamas and Fiedler debate "philosophy," and the dialogue varies from le Carré's in order to parallel Leamas's discussion with Nan Perry. Almost repeating his earlier words, he tells Fiedler, "I don't believe in Father Christmas, God, or Karl Marx. I don't believe in anything that rocks the world." When Fiedler insists that "you have to have a philosophy," Leamas bluntly replies, "I reserve the right to be ignorant. That's the Western way of life."

Fiedler concludes by saying, "[Y]our job and mine permit us to take human life. If I want to kill you and I can only do it by putting a bomb in a crowded restaurant, that's the way I'll kill you. . . . Innocent people die every day. They might as well do it for a reason." The reference to the death of innocents recalls Leamas's story of the giant lorries, and the bomb imagery echoes the picture of the mushroom cloud in Nan's apartment. In contrast to the earlier scenes in which one or another character's dominance was indicated by a superior physical position, the dialogue between Fiedler and Leamas is conducted on an equal visual plane. Nan's naiveté may be exposed by Fiedler's coldhearted attitude, but Leamas's apathy appears in no way superior. He can only claim to be "ignorant."

The details of operation Rolling Stone eventually provide Fiedler the proof he needs to charge Mundt with treason. When Mundt is brought before the tribunal, Leamas learns during the hearing that he has been a pawn, that Rolling Stone was not an operation to incriminate Mundt but part of a daring bluff to vindicate him so that he can continue to serve British interests. Leamas has played a part in this plan and so served the purposes of his manipulators. He has assumed that when things do not go as expected the plan is going wrong, when in fact it has been working perfectly.

Nan, too, has been used. Having become crucial to the operation, she is destined to be involved until she is killed. When she enters the courtroom, Ritt pulls his camera back to reveal the whole scene for the first time. As the room takes on the appearance of a cage, it becomes apparent that Nan is being led into a trap. Ritt repeats this pullback to emphasize Nan's helplessness several times during her interrogation as her testimony seals Fiedler's doom.

Ritt indicates Leamas's awareness of how he has been used by varying the sequence of movements from the scene in which Leamas was shown his picture in the newspaper by Peters. Now Leamas turns slowly toward the camera and, in close-up, looks at Mundt, whose sneering face meets his. As Ritt cuts back to a close-up of Leamas and a matching close-up of Mundt, the look on Leamas's face reveals his knowledge and his fear. Mundt's face seems the embodiment of the image of emptiness that Leamas saw earlier. Ritt then has Mundt, in extreme close-up, walk past the camera and Leamas, then out of the courtroom, as Leamas turns his head in a matched profile shot. As he watches Mundt, the matched close-ups link the two men as part of the same plan.

Mundt's status as London's man is confirmed when he arranges for Leamas and Nan to escape, instructing them to drive to the Berlin Wall, where they will receive help in getting over it. Leamas eventually has to explain to Nan their part in the plan, and when she criticizes him further about the killing of Fiedler, Leamas erupts, "What the hell do you think spies are? Moral philosophers measuring everything they do against the word of God or Karl Marx? They're just a bunch of silly, squalid bastards . . . civil servants playing cowboys and Indians to brighten their rotten, little lives." This view of spying, endorsed by both the novel and the film, is a far cry from the heroic image of James Bond.

Once Leamas and Nan have been given directions for reaching and climbing the wall, their flight is filmed as a journey through a tunnel of darkness; it has the look of a mythic escape to the upper reaches. Leamas climbs up the wall and holds out his hand as Nan makes her ascent. Here Ritt makes another departure from the novel by showing the face of Nan's executioner: he is the same man who gave them the escape instructions. He is Mundt's man and, by extension, London's. Nan is shot, and she falls from Leamas's grasp, but not before the lights shine on her, as Ritt repeats the images and sounds that opened the film. If at the beginning the wall seemed an image of the totalitarian East, by the end it has become merely a barrier between two evils.

On the other side, Smiley urges him to jump to safety, but Leamas stares into the camera for a long moment before climbing down to die willingly beside Nan. Leamas, the advocate of expediency, thus makes a morally courageous protest against expediency and in favor of love.

Ritt's final image reiterates the bleak isolation of the world portrayed throughout the film. As Leamas falls, the camera remains distant from both figures, who seem to disappear as the lights go off and darkness envelopes them. The final shot is of the white cloth marking the break in the wire through which Leamas and Nan could get to the wall. In the center of the frame its whiteness is ghostlike against the dark, marking a spot where two lovers lie barely noticed by the camera.

Unlike Shakespeare's Romeo and Juliet, whose deaths at least manage to reconcile warring families and thus serve a redemptive function, the deaths of Leamas and Nan accomplish nothing. Earlier in the film Fiedler remarked to Leamas that, as a traitor, he is the cheapest currency of the cold war, and if he were killed a peasant wouldn't stop what he was doing to notice. Ritt's film, like le Carré's novel, tragically confirms Fiedler's nihilism.

CHAPTER 9

"I Believe in America":
The Brotherhood

Having explored myths of the American West and its archetypal hero in two Westerns, and then bucked the trend of escapist spy films with the stark *The Spy Who Came in from the Cold*, Ritt began his first work in an urban setting since *Edge of the City*. He thereby concluded his five-year survey of classic film genres by offering his take on the gangster film in *The Brotherhood*.

The project originated with Kirk Douglas, who was to both produce and star in the film. Douglas was interested in developing a story that would examine the dichotomy between the Mafia's intense family values and the brutal violence of its business—a subject that was to be exploited with astounding success four years later in *The Godfather*. He asked John Lewis Carlino, whose parents had been born in Sicily, to contribute an original script. Ritt became involved with the project as early as 1964, when the *Los Angeles Times* reported that he had agreed to direct five pictures for Paramount, among them *Spy* and two films for Kirk Douglas and Edward Lewis: "Montezuma," which was never produced,[1] and "The Hoodlums," which was changed to "The Hoods" before being released as *The Brotherhood*.

"The Hoodlums" passed through some significant conceptual challenges—including Ritt's own abandonment of the project—before filming actually began on October 16, 1967. Douglas arranged to have the script rewritten at his own expense in January 1967, and the changes convinced Ritt to return to the project.

In the original conception Douglas was to play an aging Italian patriarch, Tony Ginetta (the name would survive as that of Douglas's dead father in the completed film), but Douglas did not consider the role suitable to his talents. A fresh idea for revisions came in a memo from Peter Bart, who enclosed an article from the *New York Times* that dealt, in part, with the fact that the younger generation of Mafia businessmen were college educated and sophisticated in matters of industry and finance. Bart suggested making the younger brother an "urbane Mafia type."[2] When Carlino rewrote the script, he focused on the relationship of two brothers rather than on the father-son conflict. Completed in forty-six days (one day over schedule), at a cost of slightly over $3.5 million, the film was shot mostly at the Biograph Studios in New York and in New Jersey, with three weeks on location in Palermo, Sicily.

Of his conception for the film, Carlino wrote:

> The idea was to examine the criminal ethic from within as it developed through the history of Sicily under ever changing foreign domination. The man who planned the vendettas for the transgressions of his enemies became a law unto himself. Once he became a master of this method, he saw he could feed, not only on those above him, but on his own kind as well.
>
> *The Brotherhood* is the story of such a man, Frank Ginetta, who makes a fatal mistake in thinking that he can deal with the world outside his door with one set of morals and with his family with another. He is a man who carries with him the sense of self as related to the mystical ways of the old country Mafia and who finds himself gradually being absorbed into the anonymity of the new world structure of organized crime. He is a man tied to a way of life, a culture, a set of values no longer practiced. He is a man who cannot change.[3]

The character of Frank Ginetta is thus closely related to other Ritt protagonists of this period. Like Homer Bannon he is a throwback to another generation, out of sync with the values of the modern world and unable to accommodate himself to a life ethic he despises. Like John Russell, who is at home in the natural world that is disappearing with the coming of the railroad, Ginetta is comfortable in the Mafia of the Old World (La Santa Mama), with its ties to Sicilian and Italian culture. He is unable, however, to make the transition, like his brother's generation in organized crime, to extralegal maneuverings in the corporate world. His inability to adapt is largely responsible for his fall.

The Brotherhood was released at a time when the gangster film, like other cinematic genres, was entering a boldly experimental stage, challenging some of the very conventions that had defined it, and in the process developing more sophisticated storytelling devices. In 1967, the year before the release of *The Brotherhood*, audience sensibilities had been assaulted by two of the genre's most revolutionary works, Arthur Penn's *Bonnie and Clyde* and John Boorman's *Point Blank*. Both films forced audiences to bring new aesthetic resources to bear on their involvement with the generic elements of setting and plot and to sort through increasingly complex reactions to the films' protagonists.

The Brotherhood is not, in this sense, a typical sixties' film. Ritt was never a daring stylist, and he did not believe in letting technique distract from the narrative flow. Most of Ritt's films, from the very beginning to the end of his career, reflect the classic Hollywood concept of invisible style—the subordination of all cinematic elements to the service of the story. *The Brotherhood* never attempted the kind of aesthetic assault leveled by the more celebrated films of the decade. In its reliance on generic conventions, it remained a relatively conservative work. Ritt's artistry, however, makes its own demands on the audience, clearly establishing its spirit of modernity in a serious and self-conscious exploration of some central gangster film motifs.

This film also marks a departure from Ritt's previous practice in the utilization of technical contrivances that deliberately draw attention to the storytelling process itself. Except *The Outrage*, where the use of a frame is dictated by the reliance on multiple narrators, *The Brotherhood* is Ritt's only film to project a linear story through a frame device. Here the tale's air of tragedy is intensified by a narration beginning *in medias res*, as the main plot, which takes place in the past, is framed by a story which takes place in the present. Ritt also occasionally employs abrupt cutting devices between scenes, underlining the transitions by a combination of Lalo Schiffrin's insistent but effective score (utilizing a Jew's harp and a recurrent tarantella) and slow zoom shots that punctuate the transitions dramatically.

It is a commonplace in criticism of the gangster film that its classic period, the thirties, developed the poetics of the genre. Protagonists such as Rico in *Little Caesar*, Tom Powers in *The Public Enemy*, and Tony Camonte in *Scarface* are the centerpieces of popular tragedy—strong, charismatic figures who succumb to their own hubris or to fate. They also function as fantasy figures for the audience, for they exercise absolute freedom and great bravado in carving out their destinies, which allow them to rise to the top only to fall and die alone in the gutter. The classic gangster figure is not, however, a figure of complete audience identification. A viewer may thrill to the spectacle of such a character's audacity, but always the gangster is portrayed as sufficiently removed from ordinary experience so that he can only be observed from a distance.

The classic gangster films also established clear-cut oppositions between the insider and the outsider, and between the underworld and the law. In the 1930s, crime was a social issue, and so the criminal was brought down eventually by representatives of the system whose conventions were being flouted. These films also strongly implied that during the depression the American dream itself was possible only in the criminal world, in the pursuit of illegal activities. The fate of the gangster taught that these dreams were not possible, but it was a lesson that had to be learned through the experience of the film. Still, although these over-reachers were ultimately to be defeated, an aura of heroism attached itself to their struggle against what was depicted as a devouring system.

These defiant characters changed through the decades. In the forties, the complex problems created by World War II and its aftermath affected both the look and the content of such films. The focus shifted to society itself, rather than the gangster, for the noir look that dominated these films reflected the real world, and the gangster was only a part of this world. He became less an exemplar than a victim, and the films became less critical of the outlaw than of the society and of the human condition itself. An existential aura permeates these films, making social problems seem minimal compared with an emptiness at the center of existence. *High Sierra*, one of the great films of the decade, uses the figure of the gangster, the classic outsider, to illustrate the death of the American dream.

Fifties' gangsters resembled their thirties' prototypes, but without the tragic overtones: they were presented simply as rapacious monsters of uncontrollable appetite. The ruthless, and essentially selfish, nature of the classic gangster was here revealed unadorned. The gangster became an exemplar of the corporate, industrial world that was beginning to blight both the American and global landscapes. Edward G. Robinson's Rocco in *Key Largo*, a more grotesque version of his Rico, seemed to anticipate the decade in his bottomless appetite for "more." The gangster wanted power and money at any cost; no longer in revolt against the system; he was the system. As it became increasingly difficult to tell the good guys from the bad, the relationship between the underworld and corporate America became as fixed as that between organized crime and politics.

The Brotherhood very consciously draws on the generic traditions of previous decades. Like its classic thirties' ancestors, Ritt and Carlino's work aims for popular tragedy in the presentation of an aging Mafioso who finds himself torn between family loyalty and business, between the Old World and the new corporate Mafia. The tragic focus here, however, is different from that of the thirties' films, where the gangster fell because he was an overreacher, aspiring to gain the "top of the world." Frank Ginetta, is not an overreacher, but an established businessman. In his youth, Frank worked his way up through the Mafia organization, but that progress is of no interest to Ritt or Carlino, for Frank's is not a success story. In fact, it is Frank's resistance to the ambitions of the new corporate Mafia, which could make him even more successful, that eventually leads to his downfall. Frank is essentially a modest man who prefers simple pleasures to the ostentatious material success that seduced his cinematic ancestors. Ritt emphasizes this difference in Frank's appearance: whereas his cinematic forebears flaunted their success by sporting fancy jewelry and expensive suits, Frank dresses in a shabby corduroy sports jacket that is in marked contrast to the natty suits worn by his corporate partners and his brother Vince.

Ritt also draws on the existential ethos of the forties' films in *The Brotherhood*, as in *Hud* and *Hombre*, employing genre to explore the American landscape. One of the distinguishing aspects of this film is that it presents to the viewer a self-contained world; the New York City of *The Brotherhood* is inhabited only by the Mafia and Frank's family. Even the establishing shots are curiously devoid of any reference to the metropolitan masses. The characters' complete absorption in their own activities forces the audience to focus on Frank's personal dilemma. The isolation in which he faces his crucial decisions is the characteristic that links him to the existential detachment of the forties' hero.

This narrowed focus also enforces Ritt's view that big business has become synonymous with organized crime and has taken over the lives of individuals in the same way. The film thus builds on forties' and fifties' gangster films, wherein the mob takes precedence over the individual gangster's life. In the vacuum left by the corruption of the American dream, there seems less and less potential for individual success; now the only hope lies in group effort. The head mobster of the early films now becomes a faceless corporation or syndicate, and the gangster a mere employee. Vince Ginetta becomes a valued member of just such an anonymous yet lethal corporate structure, and this membership requires that he kill the older brother, who chafes under its control and dares to assert his identity and individuality.

The film opens with a medium close-up of the face of Vince Ginetta (Alex Cord) in profile, an airplane window behind him. An opening shot of a single character is rare in Ritt's work; *Hombre*, which was his first film to feature such an opening, proved to be his most corrosive genre film. Vince, like John Russell (and Hud), is to be revealed as a thoroughly alienated character; but unlike Russell, whose alienation from white civilization was presented in a positive light, Vince is a contemporary figure so thoroughly corrupted by modern life that he is beyond redemption. Possessing no values beyond money and success and devoid of even the rakish charm of Hud, Vince is Ritt's definitive hollow man, the end product of postindustrial society. (His presentation is not helped by Alex Cord's wooden performance, the film's major flaw.[4]) Unlike Hud, who suffers deeply for having accidentally caused his brother's death, Vince willingly kills his brother (and surrogate father) in order to maintain his own standing in the corporation. Again like *Hombre*, *The Brotherhood* will end with a shot of this central character; but while Russell's final act has redeemed him at the expense of society, Vince, as society's representative, is damned—haunted, isolated, and alone.

After the introduction of Vince, the plane lands in Palermo. Ritt cuts quickly from scene to scene as Vince gets into a cab, then places a call to an old man in a tavern where large wine casks establish the Old World setting. Clearly Palermo is a world apart—where even the cars, the motorcycles, and the airport cannot disguise a distinct separateness from the familiar modern world. A cut to a disembodied foot starting a motorcycle announces that a message is about to be sent: the rider moves quickly through narrow, winding streets until the camera comes to an old church and a village square. There it focuses on a man drinking at a table, surrounded by friends—the man is Frank. When the messenger whispers something in his ear, Frank rises and excuses himself; he is driven away. This first view of Frank significantly introduces him in a jovial, social situation and thus distinguishes him from his brother, who was first presented as an isolated figure, separated even from his fellow passengers on the plane. Thereafter, Frank is generally seen surrounded by people, while Vince is invariably pictured alone. The point is made even more emphatic when Ritt cuts back to Vince's car as it passes a funeral procession.

Eventually the brothers' cars converge in a deserted area. Frank is already hidden in an ancient ruined structure, its medieval grandeur emphasized as Vince emerges from his car: he starts to climb the hill, and Ritt frames the ruin in a reverse shot, invoking the ritualistic aura of ancient tragedy. The symbolic tension is broken when Frank recognizes Vince and runs toward him, assuring his guards that this is his brother. Frank embraces Vince and immediately asks about the family. Frank's good-natured concern for family and his affection for his brother are immediately apparent; Vince is more guarded.

Ritt then cuts to Frank's house, where the brothers are having lunch; again Frank focuses on family, describing a plan for bringing his daughter Carmella to Sicily. When Vince excuses himself, Frank's wife (Irene Papas) remarks, "You know they are going to send someone." Frank gets angry and tells her to "cut it out." This cryptic exchange is ominous, and the sense of danger is emphasized when Ritt cuts to Vince's room, revealing a gun in his suitcase and then surveying the room's decorations—crucifixes and pictures that emphasize Christ's wounds. Vince looks out the window at Frank, who seems small and lost in a long shot. Ritt then cuts to Frank on the veranda: he looks to the left as the camera pulls back from him and the Sicilian landscape to dissolve into New York and the past.

The scenes from the past explain the relationship between Frank and Vince and the buildup to their confrontation in Sicily. These scenes also provide the heart of the film's narrative, for most of the story is devoted to the early days in America. This section opens—more typically for Ritt—with a shot of the New York City skyline. The camera then pulls back and pans right, moving toward Jersey City, across deserted swampland to a refuse dump and deserted shacks, finally settling on an open space. The camera remains distant and detached as a car arrives and three people scurry about. Voices are heard, but the words are unintelligible. Then the camera moves closer as one of the men fires three shots at another. The third man lifts the dead man and carries him to a chair. Finally, Ritt's camera closes in: the corpse is strapped to the chair, then one of the killers moves to face the dead man, opens his mouth and puts something in it. Then he dashes to the car, which speeds off. Ritt's camera returns to the dead man's face in close-up: there is a dead canary in his mouth, branding him as a "singer," an informer.

A cut to an opening door reveals a large banquet hall, where a wedding reception is taking place. The two assassins enter with their backs to the camera. Ritt then repeats a shot of the beaming faces of the wedding party being photographed, which provides a sharp contrast to the face of the murdered informer.

These opening segments bear an interesting resemblance to those in *The Godfather*, which employs a similar narrative strategy and was surely influenced by *The Brotherhood*. Francis Ford Coppola's film opens with a voice of a man who is detailing the violation of his daughter. The camera pulls back to reveal a room and then passes behind the head and shoulders of Don Corleone, as the supplicant asks the don to punish the men who raped and beat up his daughter. The camera then moves outside to revel in the wedding reception of Don Corleone's daughter.

The strategies of Ritt and Coppola are similar, as both directors juxtapose violent, troubling images—murder and rape—with scenes of family harmony and happiness in order to raise questions in the minds of their audiences: Who are these people? How do they conduct their business? Are they monsters? These characters seem very much like us, but what about the violence associated with them—what does it mean? Ritt and Carlino thus echo the famous banquet scene in *Macbeth*, in which Banquo's assassins appear to Macbeth, in effect bringing the usurper's two worlds together. Coppola's version of this juxtaposition is even more audacious than Ritt's: in *The Godfather* the two worlds are spatially linked, for both scenes take place simultaneously on the Corleone estate.

The early sequences of *The Brotherhood* establish the film's basic structure, which is built on a series of Ginetta family groupings—the outer world of wives and children, social gatherings and weddings, and an inner world composed of men who run the business, who kill. Frank's business world is further subdivided into the Old World Mafia and the new corporate Mafia. All is held together by the myth of the family—the concept, firmly held by the Ginettas, of an integrated group, protective of its members but secretive in its operations in order to protect its power.

Ritt's wedding reception sequence is a model of thematic clarity in editing and construction. It opens with images of family harmony: the action begins with the posing for a family picture, and then Frank dances with his daughter; shortly thereafter he greets the assassins, who are his corporate partners, the first of whom greets Frank with "mazel-tov" (immediately establishing that the new Mafia is ethnically mixed). Picturing the wedding reception, Ritt contrasts the two tables, separated spatially, at which are seated, on one side, the new Mafia, and on the other, Frank's friends, the old "soldiers" who speak Italian.

This sequence serves effectively to introduce the entire world of the film. The remainder of the action is to alternate between the Ginetta family and the two Mafias in separate sequences, but it never departs from the world established in the wedding scene. Although Ritt moves easily between indoors and outdoors, public and private, business and family, the film retains a closed-in, confined sensibility. This is deliberate, for the director wants to keep his characters in a visual vise in order to emphasize the oppressive sense of entrapment and inevitability that overhangs them and their world. Even the audience, safely at a distance from the family business, will come to feel trapped in this claustrophobic setting.

The plot follows the falling fortunes of Frank Ginetta, a proud second-generation Sicilian who occupies a seat on the board of the New York syndicate, control of which has fallen into the hands of Jewish and Irish leaders. The syndicate fronts for respectable corporations, operating through legal loopholes and union contacts to manipulate lucrative connections that extend even to electronic contracts with the federal government. Frank is increasingly at odds with the board, fearing trouble with the government, but he is accused of being old-fashioned.

Now Frank, whose father, a loyal soldier from the days of Murder, Inc., was slain in one of the purges that brought the new leadership to power, introduces his younger brother Vince, whom he raised after their father's death, into the syndicate. Vince, a college-educated accountant, is soon laundering dirty money with astounding skill; without Frank's knowledge, he is also making a secret deal with the leadership to further his own advancement, thereby distancing himself from his brother. Frank's longtime friend Bertolo (Luther Adler), who is also Vince's father-in-law, despairs of Frank's continued resistance to the new corporate style of the syndicate and takes the young man under his wing. Meanwhile, Frank is being pressured not only by his strained relationship with Vince but also by an impending Senate Crime Committee's investigation into his affairs.

Eventually Frank learns from the deposed Mafia copas that it was Bertolo who fingered the forty-one members of the brotherhood—including Frank's father—leading to their slaughter. Charged with satisfying the vendetta by killing Bertolo, Frank murders his old friend and then flees to Sicily. Vince, then, is required to prove his loyalty to the syndicate by performing the necessary "hit" on his own brother.

Like all of Ritt's sixties' work, *The Brotherhood* is structured around contrasts, particularly that between Frank and Vince. When first introduced, Frank has the look of a successful man: hosting his brother's wedding reception, he looks like a prosperous businessman, and although it is clear that he is a gangster, he appears to be a genial fellow and decidedly middle-class. It soon becomes apparent, however, that Frank is an outsider, unable to sustain an easy relationship with the members of the new syndicate. His outsider status invests him with a somewhat romantic air, as it creates for him the potential for heroic resistance.

Emotionally bound to the ways of the vanishing world of the old Mafia, and unable to accommodate himself to the faceless corporate world that has overtaken it, Frank tries to warn his brother against the impersonal, emasculating methods of the new syndicate: "Lousy thing is, Vinnie, you can't fight no more. You're a piece of furniture. Only thing now is the vote. . . . In Sicily when they want to make the bull fat, you take the knife and cut him, so he's no good no more. . . . He's no good for nothin'. He don't fight. Just gets fat. . . . That's the vote, Vinnie." Unlike *Hombre's* Russell, who mourns for the natural world of wide open spaces and the nobility of the horseman's physical closeness to it, Frank is the product of a competitive urban world and its immigrant code of honor, which teaches him to kill and to wield power through extortion. In a deceptively intimate scene in the back of a car before the killing of Bertolo, he reminisces about the good old days and his first "hit" as if he were talking about his first date—for Frank, murder was no more than a rite of passage. One of the most extraordinary aspects of *The Brotherhood* is its matter-of-fact presentation of this violent ethic, tamed and domesticated in Frank's nostalgic reminiscence, which subtly induces the viewer to accept it as normal and even romantic. Ritt and Carlino thus present Frank as no more threatening than the middle-class businessman he so nearly resembles, struggling merely to hold his own against the encroachment of corporate big business.

Frank is also shown to be a vibrant, loyal friend and a devoted family man. During the course of the film, mention is made of his sacrifices to send his brother to summer camp and then to college. Vince himself remarks that Frank put off getting married until he was older, so that he could devote himself to supporting his younger brother. He also remains loyal to his father's friends from the old days, drinking, playing boccie, and reminiscing with them. He even speaks with them in Italian, maintaining a link with the Old World. He seems genuinely to enjoy the camaraderie, the nearness of family, and his success.

Frank is also a man who understands and appreciates the limited scale of his achievements; satisfied with the human blessings of his lifestyle, he does not share the unbridled ambition of his syndicate partners. In a dispute with the Mafia board, he warns against defying the government. When he reiterates this caution to his brother—"Something's too big, the government for one"—Vince replies, "Not even the government." Unlike his brother and the members of the board, Frank is a simple, straightforward man. He even retains the appearance and the streetwise, colloquial speech of a blue-collar worker, suggesting that in spite of his success he has not forgotten his roots.

Vince more nearly resembles the Hud who emerges after Homer's land has been converted to oil fields, leaving nothing but an urban landscape and the success ethic. His personality may have also been shaped by his service in Vietnam, although the war is mentioned only briefly late in the film, at which point Frank remarks to Vince, "You got out just in time." During the wedding reception Vince is wearing his army uniform, like Michael Corleone at the beginning of *The Godfather*. Like Michael, Vince is more interested in business than in the old ways, eventually sacrificing family for profit and power. At last Vince even kills his brother, as Michael does at the end of *Godfather II*.

The contrast between the Ginetta brothers is enforced visually in the film's editing and in its mis-en-scène. One of its most effective moments is the one extended scene between Frank and his wife, Ida, beautifully acted by Kirk Douglas and Irene Papas.[5] After a heated argument with Vince, who declares, "Pop was nothing," Frank comes home drunk. There is no scene showing Frank drinking; Ritt simply cuts from the argument in Frank's office to the scene at his home. (Even the scenes in Frank's office involve family matters, not business.)

The homecoming scene opens with a static shot of the Ginettas' living room. Ritt's camera holds steady on the empty room for a few seconds, establishing the setting. This is most unusual in a film that regularly cuts swiftly from scene to scene, allowing no leisurely transitions. Ritt is deliberately slowing things down here in order to focus on Frank at his most endearing. As he wobbles in unsteadily and bows in a mock courtly way to Ida, she greets him in Italian, "Bona Serra, Signor." Frank returns the greeting in Italian, and then Ida helps him upstairs as they kiss. In the bedroom, as Ida helps him with his shoes and hangs up his jacket, Frank reminisces about seeing her for the first time at the convent, as they continue to kiss and hug. Ida gets undressed as a prelude to lovemaking, but Frank, after struggling unsuccessfully to take off his tie, falls asleep. Ida looks at him, her face full of affection. It is among the tenderest love scenes in all of Ritt's work.

Vince and his new bride, Emma (Susan Strasberg), are shown together only once, in a hotel room on their wedding night. Unlike the scene between Frank and Ida, who are together in the same frame most of time, here Ritt emphasizes the immediate distance between the newlyweds by filming them in shot–reverse shot sequences, keeping them isolated visually. They show no affection toward each other, spending their wedding night arguing about Vince's decision to join Frank's business.

The contrast between the brothers is emphasized visually in other ways: Frank is nearly always surrounded by family, friends, and associates, while Vince is invariably isolated in the frame. Frank's office is unpretentious, cluttered with family photographs and old-fashioned ledgers, while Vince's office is oak-paneled and bare, reflecting both his success and his personal emptiness. In one scene Vince goes to see his brother and finds him playing boccie with his friends; Vince is separated from the men by a chain-link fence. As he tries to speak to Frank through the fence, Ritt photographs him from behind, further emphasizing his isolation from his brother's world.

Vince's other visual association is with the world of the syndicate board, which meets in a stately mansion surrounded by greenery. The meeting room is elegant and beautifully furnished; the board members sit in tall, straight-backed chairs, formally discussing their agenda. When they vote, Ritt isolates them in separate shots, usually medium close-ups. Frank, however, is often pictured from a modified low angle that serves to enhance his moral stature; otherwise, he is shown leaning forward in his chair or seated to the side, unlike the others who sit up straight.

In the first syndicate scene, as the men enter the room, Frank plays a joke by remaining outside the door, which is a gate, and then pretending to lock them as if in jail; no one laughs. Then there is an abrupt cut to the Manhattan skyline, followed by a zoom to an empty alley and a long shot of someone getting out of a car. A closer shot reveals Bertolo, who opens another gate on his way to visit Vince in his office. The two gates function as a device linking the two worlds.

The most damning of these visual devices occurs toward the end of *The Brotherhood*, in two of the film's most dramatic sequences. The old Mafia soldiers gather in the basement of a fruit store, where they tell Frank that it was Bertolo who informed on his father and the forty others, leading to their murders. The names of the victims are seen on the walls of this dark room, stenciled in white on a black background—it is a mausoleum to the evil of the past. Frank at first denies that his friend, his brother's father-in-law, could have done such a thing, but he is finally convinced. When he rises to Bertolo's defense, he is again photographed from a low angle that emphasizes his stature.

This meeting scene, which opens with Ritt's camera circling slowly around the table, has a funereal quality, as the basement gloom is lit only by a single hanging light. The setting is in marked contrast to the syndicate's magnificent headquarters. This basement meeting is presided over by Don Peppino (Eduardo Cianneli), an almost vampirish presence who expresses his wish to serve nothing more than *l'honore* and to give La Santa Mama "what we owe." Hating the new syndicate with its Jews and Irish, he is devoted to keeping the blood "pure." When this ghoul instructs Frank that he must kill Bertolo, Ritt isolates Frank in medium close-up, separating him from the others in the room as he had the syndicate members earlier. Now it is made clear that although Frank may be tied to the group of old-timers by blood, a generational gulf yet separates them.

Dazed, Frank walks out of the meeting into a noisy, crowded fruit market. This is the only scene of street life in the film, but Frank remains oblivious to it and Ritt's camera remains on him. Shortly thereafter Frank invites Bertolo to lunch on the pretext that he wants to patch up their differences. The scene between the two men in the back of the car would stand comparison to a similar scene in *On the Waterfront*: it is beautifully written, and Douglas and Adler deliver a primer in naturalistic movie acting. Frank reminisces about the old days and shares a drink with Bertolo before accusing him of being a "fink," beating him, and tying his hands. The visual key here is that Frank is to the left of the frame and Bertolo to the right.

After Frank ties Bertolo's hands, Ritt cuts to a long shot of the car on an eerily deserted New York City highway. The car turns into an isolated area, where Bertolo is garroted while Frank reads the names of the dead. This sequence is followed quickly by a scene in which the syndicate votes to "hit" Frank, and then another scene in the back of a car, in which Egan (Murray Hamilton) tells Vince that he must kill his brother if the syndicate is to trust him. Significantly, this latter car scene is framed with Vince on the right side, his position linking him with Bertolo and thus irrevocably damning him.

The film's final movement reverts to Sicily, where it takes on the look and feel of ancient ritual. The air of tragedy fostered by the Old World setting brings the story full circle from the early scene in the ruins of an Arab-Norman castle. Frank now brings Vince to a family fiesta, set in a beautiful olive grove populated with hundreds of local residents. Introduced to his Sicilian relatives, Vince participates in the feast, eating grilled meats and drinking wine. In a lovely ritualistic moment, Frank stands heroically atop wine casks, breaks one open, and then leads a small band as the locals dance around an olive tree. Ritt intercuts shots of a black-clad Ida sitting alone under a tree, watching Frank, knowing what is about to happen.

The feast over, Frank tells Ida to go home; their parting is communicated primarily in gestures and eye contact. Then Frank walks with Vince through a grove of olive trees, reminiscing about his father and reiterating that he is "Mafioso." He sits on a rock to unwrap a small shotgun that belonged to his father and slowly puts two cartridges in it, explaining that the cartridges are called a la lupare, the wolf. He says that when "one of us gets it," it should come after food and wine, "first food, love, then a la lupare." He gives the gun to Vince and tells him to "make it quick." He kisses him, and then sits on the rock and looks away.

Ritt films the sequence primarily in a shot–reverse shot sequence, separating the brothers, so that the distance that has grown between them is contrasted sharply with the opening scenes, when they were filmed together in the same frame. Now only when Frank gives Vince the gun do they come together in the frame. The deadly contact is emphasized in close-up when Frank kisses Vince, just as Don Peppino had kissed Frank when charging him to kill Bertolo. Ritt then focuses only on Vince, in a medium long shot, as he fires both barrels at his brother; the sound of the gunshot recalls the sound of the airplane engine that opened the film. Finally, there is a medium close-up of Vince facing the camera, anguished and alone.

As in *Hud* and *Hombre*, Ritt modified the script's ending to increase the devastating finality of the conclusion. Carlino's script includes five additional scenes following the shooting. Scene 64 has Vince emerging from the trees, carrying the shotgun; Toto takes the gun and moves toward Frank's body. Scene 65 shows Vince in the car, followed by a shot of Ida sewing. Scene 68 returns to the car, with Toto driving and Vince in back starting to cry. The camera moves closer to Vince's hand as he rubs the cheek he scraped against his brother's face. "The tears stop. The camera moves in still closer until only Vince's eyes are in the frame. They are beyond any expression of sorrow or grief now. They are dead, completely lifeless. . . ." The final scene (69) calls for a high-angle shot of the car as it approaches the outskirts of Palermo. A voice is singing a Sicilian-Arab prayer. There is a shot of the sea "glistening with the last rays of sunlight, while the car, alone on the road, speeds into the darkness." The singing stops as the camera holds on the car.[6]

Ritt's decision to end the film with Frank's death leaves the audience with the full brutality of the killing, avoiding the distractions of the screenplay's final scenes. As in his decision to end Hud not with Lon but with Hud himself, Ritt is forcing his audience to deal with the deeds of these flawed characters, whose permanent isolation provides the final image.

Time magazine noted that Ritt had "fashioned a film like grappa, with a raw kick and a bitter aftertaste. Seldom has a movie so resembled its characters. Like them, it has a primitive volatility. . . . Like them it has aspects of a legend that has outlived its time.[7] This out-of-time quality derives in part from Ritt's careful attempt to emulate the tight, archaic rhythm of ancient tragedy.

The plot's circular structure and the emphasis on Old World settings are meant to move the action into the realm of ancient Greek and Christian modes of tragedy, which aimed to combine the concepts of fate and free will without attempting to reconcile the apparent contradictions. *The Brotherhood* is designed for a similar effect, pervaded from the beginning by a sense of inevitability. The element of fate is introduced when Vince tells Frank during his wedding reception that he wants to go into the business with him, remarking, "Frank, I'm in. I've always been in, haven't I?" Despite this sense of his own "fate," this young overreacher mistakenly thinks that he can fit in his "way." Although Emma tells him, "There's only one way . . . and its theirs," and his brother warns him about the fatted bull and the vote, Vince persists in believing in his freedom.

Of all of Ritt's major films, *The Brotherhood* has the leanest structure; conveying no extraneous detail, its scenes move along with a speed unusual in Ritt's work. Ritt's camera usually tends to linger to explore the world of a given film, creating a strong local flavor that enhances his themes, but this sense of place is not to be found in the tight, closed, ultimately suffocating world of the film.

Frank, however, is the one who is truly free. Despite his membership in the syndicate, he persists in doing things his way. He refuses to let others take care of "finks" despite admonitions from his partners. He refuses to support their money-laundering schemes, and he plans to kill Bertolo although he knows that he will in turn be killed. His ability to rise above the modern mob, the dignity with which he faces his death, and the sacrifice he makes for his family ennoble him. Unlike early gangster heroes who enacted the tragic pattern of a brilliant rise and sudden fall because of pride, greed, and ambition, Frank's *hamartia* does not come as a dying insight. This man foresees the result of his actions; he goes deliberately to his death. Like the heroes of sixties' Westerns, heroes who understand that there is no room for them in the modern world and so willingly embrace death, Frank knows that he has nowhere to go, that he is at the end of the road. Comprehending the larger reality, he accepts his fate with nobility.

Frank's sacrifice, nevertheless, merely leaves the world to Vince and the syndicate. His final words—"Ain't that funny. Me like pop, you like me. We're all the same guy."—suggest that the brothers are to be interpreted as aspects of a single character. Vince certainly represents the cold, brutal aspect of Frank's nature and his father's. Like Hud, Vince is the end product of the search for success, the modern corporate man; he is incapable of love or any kind of nobility, he can only calculate and kill. In killing Frank, he commits not only fratricide, but patricide as well. Ritt thrusts the final horror of his act upon the audience with no distracting denouement because he wants to make the point that this is the world we live in and this is what we have become.

The release of *The Brotherhood* drew protests from a group called Americans of Italian Descent (AID), who charged that the story dealt in ethnic stereotypes and tried to persuade Paramount to withdraw the film before its opening at New York's Radio City Music Hall. Joseph Jordan, executive director of the organization, wrote to James Gould, the president of Radio City that the film "denigrates, slurs, defames, and stigmatizes 22 million Americans of Italian descent" (RC undated). Neither Ritt nor Paramount was to be dissuaded, however, and the film eventually opened in hundreds of theaters nationwide.

It was not an overwhelming critical success, although *Variety* gave it an excellent review and predicted big box office returns. Reviewers in some of the national magazines were less friendly. Pauline Kael in the *New Yorker* declared that the movie did not work dramatically and gave the audience little insight into "the new business of crime" (Jan. 25, 1969). Vincent Canby of the *New York Times* faulted Ritt's direction as lacking "style" (Jan. 17, 1969).

Such critical indifference can perhaps be blamed on the film's style, which seemed too traditional for 1969. Appearing in the era of *Bonnie and Clyde, Point Blank, The Wild Bunch, Midnight Cowboy,* and *Easy Rider,* Ritt's gangster film could easily be dismissed as a throwback to another era. It looked too small; its approach too conservative. For a gangster film, it was not even especially violent, for Ritt seemed purposely to avoid bloodletting—although the garroting of Bertolo is terrifying, it is understated in comparison to the more audacious experiments in film violence by Arthur Penn, Sam Peckinpah, and Stanley Kubrick.

History, however, will likely be kinder to *The Brotherhood,* for it is a film of undeniable power, a pioneer among gangster films of the postwar era. It anticipates many of the deepest themes of *The Godfather*—the concentration on the family, the portrayal of the gangsters as typical characters, the compartmentalization of family and business affairs. Douglas considered the juxtaposition of the violent family business with the domesticity of family life to be *The Brotherhood's* central concern, and he recommended that publicity for the film emphasize this jarring contrast. His suggestion of an album of photographs alternating family pictures with violent scene was in fact adopted and realized by the publicity department.[8]

Ritt's film is also revolutionary in its focus on generational conflict and character. Pauline Kael's criticism that the film fails because it does not offer details of the business is therefore beside the point. Neither Carlino nor Ritt is interested so much in the workings of crime as in the dynamics of the relationships involved in this peculiar family setting. Again, Frank Ginetta is not a man driven toward ever greater success, and if Vince is in a hurry to succeed, the details of his business dealings are of less concern than his dealings with his brother.

Unlike many gangster films, *The Brotherhood* is less an urban drama than a tragic folktale, spare and lean in structure and rapid in pace. Its dramatic ambitions fall short in part because of a lack of balance between the family scenes and the business episodes and in part because of Alex Cord's inability to bring any real emotion to his role. Still, the film draws a primal power from its thematic complexity, its tight structure, and Kirk Douglas's masterful performance. In its exploration of the themes of the outsider and the decline of values and individuality in modern America, *The Brotherhood* ranks among Ritt's highest achievements as a director. As in *Hud, Hombre,* and *The Spy Who Came in from the Cold,* Ritt was able to transform the genre film into a serious vehicle for charting the decline of modern society.

CHAPTER 10

The Valley of Death:
The Molly Maguires

Ritt began developing what was to be his next film, *The Molly Maguires* (originally titled "Lament for the Molly Maguires"), in 1966, although the idea for it had taken hold of him years earlier. Walter Bernstein, who would write and coproduce the film, had discussed the story of a secret society of immigrant Irish miners with Ritt when both were working in television in the 1950s. Bernstein himself had become interested in this little known episode of American history while an undergraduate at Dartmouth in the late thirties.

Both Bernstein and Ritt felt that the miners' battle to improve the brutal conditions in the coal mines of northeastern Pennsylvania in the 1870s had a contemporary feel, and that it clearly paralleled the civil rights struggles and other social upheavals of the 1960s. Having decided to develop the story for the screen, Bernstein steeped himself in research, visiting the Library of Congress, university libraries, and newspaper archives in Pennsylvania to find out all he could about the Molly Maguires and coal-mining conditions during the latter part of the nineteenth century.

In 1968, while developing *The Molly Maguires*, Ritt was also working on *The Man Who Would Be King* for Warner Brothers. Announcing that project, Kenneth Hyman, executive vice president of worldwide production, stated that it would be the first of three pictures Ritt would make for the studio. The actual agreement called for Ritt to produce and direct two films and produce a third. It was also reported that Anthony Veiller, whose credits included *Stage Door*, *The Killers*, *Moulin Rouge*, and *Night of the Iguana*, would write the script. In a letter to Hyman in March, however, Ritt indicated his dissatisfaction with the script. He disliked using Rudyard Kipling as a character in a frame story, finding the device "heavy, old fashioned, soft, and sometimes even pretentious" (RC 3-27-68). Later, he asked Terrence Rattigan, who seems to have replaced Veiller, to look for a new framework, and he was still working on the film in June when he received a letter from John Bryan complimenting him on the idea of turning the two protagonists into GIs. Both this change and the frame device would be retained by John Huston, coauthor of the script and eventual director of the film that was released in 1975.

In December 1966, however, Bernstein had submitted to Ritt a treatment of *The Molly Maguires*, which he liked. In a letter to Harvey Orkin of CMA (Creative Management Associates) in London, Ritt was already planning the cast: "Ideally I would like to go with Finney and Connery. Finney playing McParlan and Connery playing Keogh. I think Stanley Baker would be fine for the head of the company police. However, I think the picture is going to cost in the area of a million dollars, and before I can move in any direction I have to get an o.k. from Paramount. Paramount might want me to go with Newman or McQueen and Burt Lancaster. There is no question in my mind which I prefer, and I am almost sure that I will have my own way" (RC 12-30-66).

A few months later Albert Finney declined the role, saying that the film "was full of promise" but he was "unsure of what he wanted to do in the future" (RC 3-22-67). Robert Evans, head of Paramount, had no such uncertainty. Despite a few minor reservations about the script, he told Ritt that he thought this would be a "big picture" (RC 7-11-67). Plans were set for full preproduction planning.

One of the main challenges was to find a location that resembled a coal-mining town of the 1870s, for Ritt was determined that the film should have an authentic look. He also informed James Wong Howe, who would again be the cinematographer, that he wanted the film photographed in black and white to suit the coal-mining story; he wanted it visually stark, like *The Spy Who Came in from the Cold*. Paramount executives balked, however, because the black-and-white format would diminish the film's value for television release (Lightman 308).

Ritt's art director Tambi Larson came across the ideal location while scouting in Pennsylvania. Eckley, midway between Scranton and Wilkes-Barre, was at the time of the Mollies a town of several thousand people; but by the late 1960s it had only eighty-six inhabitants, and it was the only town left in the coal belt that was entirely owned by a coal operator. A location scout, David Golden, wrote that Eckley "is the closest to an old company town we saw in the area. Since it is still run by George Huss, who owns both the adjacent strip mine, and the town itself, very little change has been made in the buildings since they were built" (RC 9-22-67).

Some changes had to be made, however, to prepare the town as a location site. The studio built twenty additional houses to supplement the forty already there and repainted the existing ones to duplicate the slate gray appearance caused by the settling of coal dust from the mines. Ritt used the courthouse in Jim Thorpe, Pennsylvania, then known as Mauch Chunk, where the actual Molly trials had been held. Only slight changes were needed to restore its 1876 appearance. Other scenes were filmed in the jail where the Mollies were hanged.

The location scouting trip had been made in winter, and Howe reminded Ritt that the leafless trees described by Larson would all be blooming when filming started. The crew removed some existing trees and replanted birches like those that had been there in the 1870s, but even so it was necessary to hire a dozen locals during filming to pick the buds off the remaining trees. Some of the larger trees, which could not be removed, were sprayed to give them a duller hue for the background. All modern signs had to be taken down and television aerials removed from roofs, and telephone and power lines were all buried underground, at a cost of $105,000. The Eckley recreation hall was turned into the Emerald House Saloon for the film, a paved highway was buried under tons of dirt, and a ninety-six-foot high coal-breaker unit was erected (at a cost of $200,000) to dominate the town skyline.[1]

Ritt managed to assemble a fine cast. After Albert Finney turned down the role of McParlan, it went to Richard Harris, another over-the-top Irish actor, from whom Ritt could expect a rich, understated performance like that of Richard Burton in *Spy*. Sean Connery accepted the role of Kehoe, leader of the Mollies, and Frank Finlay, who had played Iago opposite Laurence Olivier's Othello, was signed on for Davies, the head of the local police. For the role of Mary Raines, a character created for the film to serve as McParlan's love interest, Ritt selected Samantha Eggar.

Bernstein's story treatment was based on a historical incident involving characters whose actual names were retained. The Molly Maguires was one of several Irish secret societies formed to protest British rule in Ireland. While rooted in a distaste for the British, this society directed its fury mainly against landlords who evicted their tenants for nonpayment of rent. Taking their name from a legendary Irish heroine who led a revolt of peasant farmers against rent collectors in the 1600s, the society's members occasionally dressed in women's clothing to surprise their enemies. They first began to attract attention in the 1840s; and during the "potato famine" of 1845–49, when many Irish came to America, the traditions of these rebellious groups came with them.

After the Civil War many Irish gravitated to the Pennsylvania coal mines. There they faced many of the familiar Old World prejudices, as the most skilled jobs were held by the English and Welsh. Age-old tensions were ignited, and the Molly Maguires were reborn in America, where they instigated numerous conflicts against mine owners during the 1870s. They were accused not only of murdering mine bosses but of intimidating judges and law enforcement officers. They were also active in politics, and their headquarters were said to be in Pittsburgh and New York.

The influence of the Mollies grew so powerful in Pennsylvania in the 1870s that Franklin Gowen, president of the Philadelphia and Reading Railroad Company and its affiliated Coal and Mining Company, decided it was necessary to break the society. To do so he needed legal evidence of their crimes, and he asked the Pinkerton National Detective Agency to get it for him. The man selected for the job was Pinkerton agent James McParlan, who was born in County Armagh, Ireland, in 1844 and arrived in the Pennsylvania coalfields at the age of twenty-nine. For two and a half years McParlan led a double life as a miner and an operative/informer, eventually exposing the leaders of the secret society. McParlan served as the chief witness for the prosecution in the 1876–77 trials that sent more than a dozen Mollies to the gallows.

Bernstein's story features James McParlan and John Kehoe, a leader of the Mollies who was caught and executed in 1878. For Bernstein and Ritt, the character of McParlan was to be the film's focal point. The figure of the informer was rooted in the consciousness of both from the experience of being blacklisted in the fifties. The theme of informing plays an integral part in *The Brotherhood*, Frank Ginetta's heroic dilemma deriving, in part, from his need to avenge himself on Bertolo, the man who informed on his father and others; it also permeates the universe of *The Spy Who Came in from the Cold*, where personal loyalty means nothing in the face of a system of state-sponsored betrayal. To the Irish, the informer was the lowest of men, and the sentiment was shared by the victims of the Hollywood blacklist. John Ford's *The Informer* (1935) plays on this feeling, developing as a character study of a man plagued by guilt and remorse. Ritt's film, while centered on the character of McParlan does not attempt to explore the inner man.

In an interview, Bernstein described his concept of the film's theme: "This will be an American success story of an immigrant who wasn't making it, presented with an opportunity to get ahead, to make something of himself and to deal with what the price of that was to him" (Stone).

The price of success is an underlying theme of most Ritt films of this period; it is placed at the center of *Hud* and *The Brotherhood* and provides the psychological texture to *Hombre* and *Spy*. The immigrant theme and the motif of violence, of course, are also important components of *The Brotherhood*.

Ritt himself echoed Bernstein in discussing the film's thematic concerns. Noting that America was more wide open then, he added, "[T]here was an enormous reward for knavery. I'm not sure that this kind of man didn't help to make the country at that time. I can find less excuse for an informer in the McCarthy period than in those days. Fundamentally, I think McParlan was a sonofabitch, but we try to be as fair as we can" (Stone).

Bernstein elaborated: "We wanted to give him the full benefit of his position, make him charming, courageous, daring, handsome, imaginative and enormously likable and put that at the service of something quite iniquitous. Not just make him the usual anti-hero who is really a hero. The difficulty has been how to keep it hard and truthful and unsentimental and yet in some kind of balance" (Stone).

In this respect, *The Molly Maguires* rights the imbalance of *The Brotherhood* by equalizing the antagonists. The earlier film failed to provide a proper foil to Kirk Douglas's commanding Frank Ginetta, for Alex Cord's Vince was too one-dimensional to interest the audience or to elicit any emotional response. In *The Molly Maguires*, however, Ritt displays two charismatic protagonists to engage the audience's sympathies, as McParlan's status as an immigrant and an underdog lends him the sympathy that was lacking from Vince. Kehoe and McParlan are both attractive characters who make very different choices, and they are complex enough to keep the attention of the audience and enrich the film's thematic texture.

The Molly Maguires opens with Ritt's most visually stunning sequence. From a direct shot of the sun, the camera slowly pulls back and moves upward to reveal a cloudless horizon. It then pans slowly to the left to show the upper part of a mine shaft, discovering a light rail track with boxcars of coal moving up and down into the mine via cables. The camera next moves down the track toward a chimney emitting brown smoke, until a cable in the middle of the frame cuts off the view of the entrance to the mine. The camera then remains on the cable wire for a few seconds before beginning to move almost imperceptibly down the shaft. Next, an abrupt cut to the flames on the miners' helmets illuminates an otherwise black space. This artificial light contrasts to the sunlight that has been suddenly left behind, differentiating the world above from the one below.

Now in the mine itself, we see miners cutting anthracite from the walls. Ritt's camera movements shift here from the fluid pans of the opening to quick cuts between scenes as various miners (including Jack Kehoe) are shown doing different jobs. When the whistle blows, most of the miners depart. Lights are extin-

A moment of camaraderie, as a stiff and unsmiling Axel (John Cassavetes) is introduced to Ellen (Kathleen Maguire) by his friend, Tyler (Sidney Poitier).

Axel confronts Malick (Jack Warden), finally standing up for himself and his dead friend, Tyler.

David and Jean Martin (Jeffrey Hunter and Patricia Owens) are welcomed by their new neighbors at a barbeque hosted by Herman Kreitzer (Pat Hingle).

Ben Quick (Paul Newman) symbolically suggests his heroic status by jumping from a barge into the Mississippi River.

Clara Varner (Joanne Woodward) confronts her wealthy father, Will Varner (Orson Welles).

As the new extended family sits down to breakfast, Ritt emphasizes the physical similarities of Rose (Sophia Loren), Mary (Ina Balin, back to camera), Frank (Anthony Quinn), and Noble (Mark Richman).

Paul Newman and Joanne Woodward are again cast as lovers, but this time the romance will not work out, as Ram Bowen (Newman) opts for his music over personal commitment.

Nick Adams (Richard Beymer) learns of the brutality of war as an ambulance driver in Italy.

Nick Adams shares a pastoral moment with his father (Arthur Kennedy) in the Michigan woods before leaving home.

A rider on the range of the modern West, Hud (Paul Newman) flirts with the family cook, Alma (Patricia Neal).

Lonnie Bannon (Brandon de Wilde) rejects his uncle Hud's amoral lifestyle and leaves the ranch to strike out on his own.

Carrasco (Paul Newman) ravishes Mrs. Wakefield (Claire Bloom) in Ritt's remake of *Rashamon*.

As Leamas (Richard Burton) sees Nan Perry (Claire Bloom) for the first time, Ritt traps her in a frame within a frame, prefiguring her status as a victim in a deadly game.

The composition asserts Leamas's dominance, as he and Nan talk over dinner in her flat.

As Nan stands over Leamas before a poster of a nuclear mushroom cloud, her political position is revealed as fraudulent and destructive.

The Indian heritage of Russell (Paul Newman) is evoked as part of the natural (pastoral) order, which will be displaced by the railroad.

Russell defends a fellow Indian against the taunts of a cowboy.

Deciding to sacrifice himself to free the wife of a government agent, Russell discusses his plan with Mendez (Martin Balsam).

Frank Ginetta (Kirk Douglas) is reminded of the debt he owes La Santa Mama in a tomb-like setting presided over by the ghoulish Don Peppino (Eduardo Cianneli).

In a scene reminiscent of *On the Waterfront*, Frank charms Bertolo (Luther Adler) before executing him.

In Sicily, the pastoral alternative to the film's Manhattan setting, Frank's (Kirk Douglas) heroic stature is emphasized amid a ritualistic village party.

After the party, Frank instructs his brother Vince (Alex Cord), who has been sent by the new corporate Mafia to kill Frank, in how to perform the shooting.

MM-252-364-78

One of Ritt's most damning industrial scenes, of children working in the coal mines, prefigures the factories that Ritt later exposes in *Norma Rae*.

In a film dominated by gray, gloomy settings, Ritt allows McParlan (Richard Harris) and Mary Raines (Samantha Eggar) a quiet, romantic, pastoral moment.

The two antagonists, Kehoe (Sean Connery) and McParlan (Richard Harris), are momentarily united in a joyous moment as they destroy the company store.

As Jack Jefferson (James Earl Jones) celebrates becoming the World Heavyweight Champion, Ritt emphasizes the artificiality of the setting and minimizes Jefferson as part of the crowd.

In a scene cut from the film, Jefferson (James Earl Jones) enjoys a moment by the water with his girlfriend Ellie (Jane Alexander) before he is arrested on a trumped up Mann Act violation.

In one of Ritt's few panoramic long shots, Jefferson is clearly hemmed in by his notoriety.

A joyous communal moment as the Morgans (Paul Winfield, Cicely Tyson, and Kevin Hooks) make their way home, while their friend (Taj Mahal) serenades them.

David Lee (Kevin Hooks) and his dog Sounder witness the arrest of his father.

Conroy (Jon Voigt) celebrates a joyous moment with his students as they run along the beach.

Alfred Miller (Michael Murphy) tells his friend Howard Prince (Woody Allen) that he is black-listed and asks him to be his "front."

Hecky Brown (Zero Mostel) tries to maintain his comic persona in a hotel bar, while the owner (Joshua Shelly) cheats him out of his rightful fee.

Marsh Turner (Rip Torn) shows Marjorie (Mary Steenburgen) the beauties of Cross Creek.

Rain soaked and barely dressed, Marjorie finally discovers her true voice as a writer.

Despondent over the death of Marsh Turner, Marjorie loses herself in the creek and resolves to stay and become part of the community.

Norma Rae (Sally Field) is removed from the factory in handcuffs by a sheriff after leading workers in a work stoppage.

A pastoral contrast, as Norma Rae and Sonny (Beau Bridges), whom she will soon marry, enjoy a picnic.

Emma (Sally Field) and Murphy (James Garner) enjoy a dance in Ritt's homage to community and small-town life.

guished momentarily, leaving us again in a darkness that is dominated by the sounds of the miners coughing as they wait to board the boxcars for the ascent to the top. Only the group we will come to know as the Mollies remain, to quickly plant explosives. Ritt cuts swiftly from one member to another as they place cans of powder and wire them. Finally, as they board a boxcar and ascend, we see their faces and then only darkness broken by the flames from their helmets.

The sudden burst of sunlight is jarring as the group alight from the boxcar, and Ritt films the men in an extended take as they walk away from the mine toward the camera. They continue to approach as the camera moves backward, keeping them in the center of the frame until all but Kehoe move away. Kehoe then walks alone toward the camera as it moves back again to reveal more of the mine area behind him. When the camera stops, Kehoe walks almost up to it and then exits to the left. As he does so, an explosion and a fire nearly fill the frame, and the film's credits begin.

A combination of documentary-like realism and an almost lyric beauty, this opening sequence evokes in images without words both the promise of America and its postindustrial desecration. *The Molly Maguires* marks the transitional stage between the beginning of the New World's betrayal, depicted in *Hombre*, and its culmination, as portrayed in *The Brotherhood.* The opening sequence was Ritt's own creation, replacing Bernstein's strictly functional series of images: the coal breaker looming above the mine shaft and the blast of the whistle signaling the end of the shift, the Mollies setting the explosives and leaving the mine, followed by a cut to each of their homes where the men are engaged in domestic activities when the explosion comes. (Kehoe, for example, is eating dinner when he hears the blast.)[2] Ritt's poetic rendering of the same basic information enhances the opening with a dramatic visual suggestion of thematic motifs.

The next scene, which introduces McParlan, reinforces this evocative mood. A police officer, to the right of the frame, waits at a railway station at night. A locomotive enters, moving toward the camera so that its headlight momentarily fills up the screen, just as the sun did in the opening shot. The artificial light, breaking through the darkness of night, recalls the miners' lamps. The only passenger to disembark is McParlan, who glances at the officer, walks toward the camera, and then exits the frame to the right.

Ritt has thus visually connected the two principals and their worlds. McParlan, who embodies the industrial-capitalist world that Kehoe is striving to destroy, is here associated with both the locomotive (the symbol of destructive modernity in *Hombre*) and the artificial light of the mines, the underground world that McParlan must infiltrate in order to expose the Mollies. Like Kehoe,

McParlan walks directly toward the camera, but he exits to the opposite side of the frame. Through his mis-en-scène, Ritt has dramatically suggested both the similarity of their personalities and their divergent paths.

The next scene opens with a lantern light in the center of the sign for the Emerald House, the miners' saloon to which McParlan goes after getting off the train. Again he walks down the road in the center of the frame, but now he moves off to the left to enter the saloon, here reiterating the visual link to Kehoe's movements. In the saloon Kehoe sees McParlan, and, at his signal, McParlan is invited by Frazier and Dougherty to join them at cards. Soon he is accused of cheating, a brawl ensues, and the police break it up by knocking out McParlan. In the next scene McParlan confronts police chief Davies.

Bernstein's script for the film was not revised significantly, but the scenes introducing McParlan were changed to make him a more sympathetic figure. In Bernstein's original conception, the film was to open with an explosion, but not one set up from inside the mine. Instead, three men run down the street at night, knock out the watchman, and set the explosion. This is followed by a scene in which Franklin Gowen speaks to Pinkerton agents about the Molly Maguires, suggesting that the Pinkertons send an Irish agent to infiltrate the group. They choose James McParlan, whom Bernstein describes as having "the face of a larcenous altar boy" and as "trust[ing] no one and believ[ing] only in himself."[3]

In the following scene, Gowen and McParlan dine in an elegant restaurant, where McParlan, eating oysters, remarks that he has been in America for eight years; he describes the immigrant dream as "the wish to belong, to share in the riches that spill out all around him, to be finally an owner where he is now only a servant." Bernstein writes, "Gowen believes in nothing; what he must discover is what McParlan believes in" ("Treatment").

These scenes immediately establish McParlan as the enemy and link him with the cynical Gowen. Their meeting in a restaurant, which obviously only the wealthy could afford, is another overt alienating device. Ritt's decision to eliminate these scenes and to make McParlan a more mysterious figure allows the audience, like Kehoe, to withhold its judgment. Revealing McParlan's status as an agent in the scene with Davies, only after his beating, Ritt casts a more sympathetic light on the character, whose speech to Davies about his hard life is also made less aggressive than the original, and further emphasizes his humanity: "I've failed enough in this country, the streets haven't exactly been paved with gold for me. But I've had my fill of empty pockets, Captain. I'm tired of being at the bottom of the barrel. I'm tired of always looking up. I want to look down."

As McParlan speaks these words, Ritt focuses on him in medium close-up, his face bruised from the brawl and wet from dunking his head in water. He looks like the downtrodden workingman he claims to be, and the homely images of empty pockets and looking up from the bottom of the barrel make his ambitions much easier to accept than Bernstein's oyster-fueled monologue about the desire to "share the riches" and become an "owner." Richard Harris delivers his lament in an understated, weary manner that convinces us that McParlan is indeed a poor slob who has tried and found no way out other than the path he has now adopted. His making the speech in a jail rather than in a fancy restaurant further emphasizes the desperation of his plight.

Eliminating the mention of the Pinkertons had practical motivations as well as dramatic ones. In 1968, when the Pinkerton Agency heard about the film, it requested script approval. Ritt resisted, as did Paramount's lawyers. By April of that year the agency, fearing that its reputation might be compromised, was demanding to see the script, and Paramount's lawyers relented. By that time, however, Bernstein's script revision had eliminated any reference to the Pinkerton Agency anyway; and because the changes were more effective dramatically, the loss of the historical reference did not hurt the film.

While *The Molly Maguires* is full of rich naturalistic detail about life in the mines, Ritt's central theme remains the price of success in America. The conflict between loyalty and betrayal in this pursuit is most fully embodied in McParlan, who uses the name McKenna while posing as a miner. Kehoe is a less interesting character: a miner who has experienced the brutality of the worker's life, he opts for violent rebellion when all else fails. Ritt's film does not dwell on the personal conflict between his Catholicism, which opposes the violence of the secret societies, and his emotional commitment to the Molly Maguires.

Ritt brings his thematic threads together when McParlan begins his life as a miner. He first finds a room in the house where Mary Raines, who will become McParlan's love interest, lives with her father, forty-two years a miner and now dying of a lung disease. Focusing on the muddy streets of the town and the dreary drabness of the homes, Ritt portrays the Raines home as threadbare and gloomy. When Mary shows McParlan to his room, the camera emphasizes its claustrophobic dimensions, barely containing the boarder and providing a singularly cheerless alternative to the mine. This bleak settling in is followed by a montage of a day in the mine, once more without dialogue; only the sounds of pick axes, coal cars, and men coughing supplement the visual images. Again Ritt emphasizes the airless confinement, the grime, and the darkness. No other film matches *The Molly Maguires* in its heroic attention to detail in depicting life in the mines. Neither John Ford's *How Green Was My Valley* (1941) nor Carol Reed's *The Stars Look Down* (1940) evokes the sensory experience of the miner with the power and immediacy of Ritt's portrayal.

This day-in-the-life montage is followed by a sequence in which the miners line up to be paid. McParlan comes up for his pay as the superintendent reads off his productivity statistics: "Coal mined . . . fourteen cars at sixty-six cents a car. Total—nine dollars and twenty-four cents." McParlan starts to hold out his hand for the money, but Jenkins continues to read. "Deduct . . . two kegs of powder at two dollars and fifty cents a keg—five dollars. Two gallons of oil at ninety cents a gallon—one dollar eighty. Fixing two broken drills—thirty cents. Pickax, shovel, cap and lantern—one dollar ninety. Total—nine dollars. Total wages for the week—twenty four cents."

This scene is extraordinarily rich on a sociopolitical level but also for what it reveals about McParlan, whose first reactions are amazement and then anger as he looks down at his blistered hands and the few coins he has netted for his week's work. He is not playing James McKenna here, but a true workman who wants to lash out against the system. Regaining control of himself, he reassumes his role and leaves. Again the duality in the character, clearly apparent to the audience, maintains a measure of sympathy for the man and interest in his dilemma, because it seems possible that despite his role as an agent, McParlan may yet be tempted to change his allegiance.

Shortly afterward, there is a scene in church, where the priest, Father O'Connor (Philip Bourneuf), delivers a sermon. He begins by drawing attention to the upcoming celebration of America's one hundredth anniversary, noting that the nation was founded by exiles and immigrants looking for a better life. He goes on to say, "[W]e identify with them, for they too were far from the land of their birth. They too were scorned and exploited." He then remarks on the violence needed to create this country and the belief that maybe violence "is the way to change bad conditions into good conditions." Finally, however, he condemns the Molly Maguires and brands them as "sinners" who will be damned. During the sermon Ritt cuts between close-ups of the priest and the faces of Kehoe, Frazier (Art Lund), Dougherty (Anthony Zerbe), and McAndrew (Anthony Costello), who compose the Mollies, as well as close-ups of McParlan, which again links him to the miners.

In McParlan, Ritt once more focuses on an outsider. Feeling a kinship with the Irish miners and developing empathy for their plight, McParlan must nevertheless divorce himself from their struggle and maintain his allegiance to his employers. He appears to be appalled by the chasm between the haves and have-nots created by the American system, yet he is sufficiently attracted by the promise of America that he will do anything to embrace its rewards. He is one of the exiles Father O'Connor refers to, but he yearns to belong. Like Vince Ginetta, he is willing forget his status as an ethnic exile in his desire to embrace success.

In Kehoe, Ritt presents a man whose connection to the group supersedes all else, an individual who believes that the group claims his first loyalty. Thus he resembles Frank Ginetta and even John Russell, who sacrifices himself for others. Kehoe, however, must forsake the church and its teachings if his earthly goals are to be realized, adopting violent means to achieve his ends. Exploring this struggle within Kehoe might have made him a more poignant figure, but the film fails to exploit this dramatic tension in his character.

Ritt and Bernstein clearly sympathize with Kehoe's goals, although their attitude toward his violent means remains ambivalent. Ritt commented, "Certainly this picture is not an advocacy of violence, but there is an attitude in this country that doesn't realize that if you treat people in a certain way there will be violence. Understanding that does not mean your condoning violence, but you can't put the blame on the victims of oppression" (Stone).

This ethical dilemma is reflected throughout the film. While Ritt seems to pull back from endorsing Father O'Connor's vehement denunciation of violence in the sermon scene, other scenes implicitly support his viewpoint. After the brutal scenes that precede the sermon, the priest's words seem out of touch with the world he inhabits and the lives of the congregation he serves, but some later sequences complicate the issue. The first is a scene in which the Mollies vote to kill a supervisor in neighboring Shenandoah, leading to a shoot-out that leaves a number of people dead or wounded. Then in an act of retaliation, Frazier and his wife are killed in bed while their infant screams in the background. During the funeral scene that follows, O'Connor blames Frazier for bringing this grisly fate on himself, but he then goes on to say, "But his wife's dead too, and a child's been orphaned. Violence begets violence until the innocent perish with the guilty." It is a mark of the film's moral complexity that it presents this message of stoic piety with evenhanded respect.

Throughout most of the film, Ritt forces the audience to sympathize with McParlan, employing a stylistic device that he exploits in a number of films during this period—notably The Brotherhood—interchanging the position of his thematic doubles in the frame. Just as McParlan and Kehoe were originally introduced in visually similar movements toward a camera that retreats before each man's purposeful advance, the two are again shown walking toward the camera, McParlan on the left, Kehoe on the right, when McParlan tells Kehoe why he has come to work in the mines. McParlan explains that he has been passing counterfeit money, but Kehoe doesn't believe this cover story. Their dialogue is interrupted when McParlan stops to play soccer with some children; when he rejoins Kehoe, their positions are reversed in profile shots. Ritt thus indicates that at this point Kehoe comes to trust McParlan.

This emotional bond is reinforced when McParlan is initiated into the Ancient Order of Hibernians and then helps to beat up a policeman who slugged Dougherty. When McParlan meets Davies in the mine to report on the incident, he remarks that the officer "had it coming." Although McParlan is cooperating with the owners, he still seems to sympathize with the miners. Indeed, he seems closer to Kehoe than to Davies. Later he becomes part of the Mollies and votes to kill the policeman who has been brutalizing miners in Shenandoah. After they escape a police trap, Ritt repeats the doubling setup: again Kehoe and McParlan talk while walking toward the camera. This time, however, McParlan again occupies the place on the left while Kehoe is on the right. The scene concludes with the men, once more in a profile, maintaining the reversed left-right positioning.

One of the film's most eloquent scenes is the picnic shared by McParlan and Mary Raines. McParlan has already solidified his relationship with Mary by taking her out to Philadelphia for the day, where they window-shop and McParlan buys Mary a hat. Bernstein's original script had included a scene in which they eat at a fancy restaurant, but like the similar scene involving the early meeting of McParland and Gowen, it was cut. Instead, Ritt shows the couple walking together, framing them first through blackened, leafless trees; the landscape seems almost lunar in its desolation as they walk past the relics of some mine buildings near a lake. In the background, Henry Mancini's music is romantic and elegiac, seemingly out of place in this barren terrain. When the couple finally reach a hill that is lush and green, with a bright blue sky in the background, it is as if they had entered a different world.

Then, as they eat a picnic lunch, Mary talks about wanting a decent man to help her escape. McParlan's reply exposes his cynicism, though it rings true in the world of the film: "You want decency. And trust and honor and maybe a bit of security, and all smiled upon by the law. Do you think you get those free? You've been out there, you've seen for yourself. Decency's not for the poor. You pay for decency, you buy it. And you buy the law, too, like you buy a loaf of bread."

When Mary insists that there is "still right and wrong," McParlan replies, "There's what you want and what you'll pay to get it. Nothing more." This scene is reminiscent of the sequence on the hillside in *Spy* when Fiedler and Leamas exchange views on cold war morality. That scene, however, presents an exchange between two hardened cynics, both of whom hate what they have become. Like them, McParlan, while despising himself, accepts the heartless ethic he feels is necessary for survival, while Mary insists on the possibility of moral transcendence.

This scene is balanced by another in which McParlan meets Davies in the same spot to report on his progress. Here Davies occupies the same side of the frame that Mary had in the picnic scene, and Ritt thus again uses visual placement to evoke the two sides of McParlan's character. As McParlan confesses to Davies that he sincerely tried to talk the Mollies out of their last violent encounter, Ritt provides an ironic counterpoint—a bird singing in the background. Oblivious to the symbolic overtones, McParlan merely comments that he dislikes birds.

McParlan's final moment of kinship with the miners' community comes during the wake for Mary's father. Kehoe, who felt an abiding affection for the old man, drinks heavily, and for the first time in the film losing his self-control, he expresses anger at the corpse for dying quietly. He exhorts it to make a sound, recalling that Raines was an expert blaster who taught him how to use dynamite and lamenting bitterly that it was never used "for his own benefit . . . just to show them he was alive." Kehoe then decides to rob the company store so that Raines can be buried in a suit.

Inside the store, he gets carried away and starts throwing clothes and then other supplies to the miners waiting outside. When Ritt reverses the angle, shooting Kehoe's actions from inside the store, McParlan, standing outside, appears to the right, where he occupies Mary's and Davies' place in the frame. Then, in one last gesture of solidarity, he joins Kehoe in the store. He stares for a moment at a pick axe, then picks up a shovel and starts destroying the store. Kehoe joins in, and their destructive spree culminates in setting fire to the store. His back to the camera and his arm around McParland's shoulder, Kehoe yells, "We're not dead yet!" The fire blazing before them confirms that this is the emotional high point of the story for both men and for the film audience as well.

The film then moves toward conclusion, with the police arresting the Mollies as they attempt to sabotage the mine. McParlan testifies at the trial, and the Mollies are condemned to death by hanging. Afterwards, in the empty courthouse, Mary tells McParlan that she would have risked sin even if "you'd been outside the law," but that she can't go with him after what he has done. She used to think there was nothing she wouldn't do to get out, but she knows now that she does draw the line. Then she walks away.

The final scene takes place in the prison, where Kehoe awaits his execution. Visiting him there, McParlan asks, "Did you really think you could have won?" Kehoe replies, "You worked down there—can you see yourself not lifting a finger?" When McParlan answers that he wouldn't have stayed down there, Kehoe's reply echoes McParlan's cynical credo in the picnic scene: "And where would you find it different? There's them on top and them below. Push up or push down . . . who's got more push, that's all that counts."

Kehoe then remarks that he knows McParlan has really come for absolution: "You'd like to be set free from what you've done." But Kehoe "can't stand the sight of a man carrying a cross," and he jumps at McParlan and starts choking him. The police enter and subdue Kehoe, who from the floor snarls, "You'll never be free. There's no punishment this side of hell can free you from what you did." And McParlan replies, "See you in hell."

McParlan leaves, but Ritt's camera stays on Kehoe, who sits on the floor, his back to the wall; as the barred door closes on him, the condemned man is seen in a long shot through the bars. McParlan walks out to the courtyard, which is dominated by the gallows the workmen have almost finished constructing. In a repetition of the introductory shots, he walks toward the camera, passing the gallows without a glance. Behind him a workman is testing the trapdoor by dropping a weighted bag through it as McParlan exits to the left.

The film's ending differs significantly from Bernstein's initial treatment, in which, after McParlan's visit with Kehoe in prison, there is a cut to the prison courtyard where the gallows is being prepared. Next comes a scene in which Mary, who has apparently married McParlan, hangs curtains in their new apartment. A quick cut shows the Mollies standing on the gallows, then Mary asks McParlan (referring to the curtains), "Will you help me hang them?" Another quick cut shows the trapdoor being sprung and the men falling through, and this is followed by a cut back to Mary and McParlan looking at each other as they realize the implications of her remark.

Bernstein's heavy-handed ending shifts the emphasis away from McParlan's personal treachery to a more political statement about the price of success. The finished film's conclusion, however, like the endings of *Hud*, *Hombre*, and *The Brotherhood*, is more dramatically effective. The political dimension is still there, but by focusing on McParlan walking past the gallows (as he focused on Vince Ginetta's face), Ritt ensures that the personal betrayal remains in the forefront. The insistence on character heightens the political implications of the betrayer's desecration of friendship. The general/political and the private/personal are thus crystallized in one compelling image.

The brutal ending of the film, which damns McParlan while also revealing the imminent execution of the rebellious Mollies, no doubt contributed to the film's commercial failure. Audiences apparently found it too demanding a moral conundrum, too bleak a vision, and this failure always gnawed at Ritt, who later singled out *The Molly Maguires* as his favorite film. In an interview at the American Film Institute, he speculated on its box office failure: "It was a very sophisticated film, in fact, because the leading character, instead of being painted black or white, was painted gray, purposefully. For an audience—a movie audience—it was too complicated. They didn't know who the hero of the film was. And many of them didn't agree with what Sean Connery represented. I thought he was the hero of the film" (AFI 22).

Ritt, of course, had miscalculated his audience's reaction to the characters in *Hud* as well. In both cases, the protagonists provide complex character studies, weaving together so evenhanded a mixture of attractive and repellent traits that the films proved too challenging for the commercial American cinema.

Another possible reason for the film's lack of appeal was objections that it sought to capitalize on the civil rights struggle by too closely paralleling the experience of the Black Panthers, many of whom disliked the film because of its lack of an uplifting ending. Ritt rejected the suggestion that he had exploited the contemporary racial struggle, maintaining that he had developed the idea of the film before the Black Panthers became prominent and noting that serious themes relevant in 1870 would also be relevant in 1970. The film's release also coincided with the murder of Joseph Yablonski, a United Mine Workers official, and his wife, bringing the discord that still existed between labor and management back to the headlines. Perhaps audiences didn't care to seek out a reminder of this still bloody strife at the movie theater.

Also, Paramount essentially dumped the film in theaters without mounting any real publicity campaign. When the initial reviews were lukewarm, the studio pulled the film and later rereleased it as part of a double bill. In Chicago it was released with *Watermelon Man*, causing *Chicago Sun Times* critic Roger Ebert to comment in his very positive review about our "cruelly arbitrary film distribution system" (Nov. 20, 1970).

The Molly Maguires remains a remarkably fine social film and one of Ritt's premier achievements. It is a richly textured work, offering the strongest naturalistic depiction of the abuses of coal mining ever put on film, as well as a meticulous reconstruction of the workers' daily lives. In addition, Ritt and Bernstein wove into the material some astute observation of immigrant psychology, the nature of friendship, and the relationship of informing and betrayal to the concept of success. Its savage indictment of the pursuit of affluence and upward mobility as a poisoning of the American psyche echoes the themes of *Hud* and *Hombre*, but with a heightened realism and a tone of dispassionate detachment that underscores the menace.

In his mostly negative review of the film, Stanley Kauffmann wrote that its best moments were reminiscent of *How Green Was My Valley*, ignoring the fact that Ford's film has quite different aims and purposes from Ritt's.[4] *How Green Was My Valley* uses the mine setting only as a background device, focusing instead on the family. Ford's is a memory film, narrated by Huw Morgan (Roddy

McDowell), who recalls his idealized life before changes in mining conditions caused his family to break up. No attempt is made to present realistic mining conditions; indeed, the life of the Morgan family seems quite idyllic. They have a lovely house and, until the economy collapses, enough money for a comfortable lifestyle. Throughout the story of loss and suffering, the disintegration of the family is Ford's central theme.

Ford even shows his miners singing as they walk together to the mines, their wives and children watching and waving as their menfolk take off for what appears to be another routine day at the office. Parents think nothing of having their children follow them into what seems to be a stable, decent profession. The scene in *The Molly Maguires* in which the miners go off to work provides a measure of the distance between Ford and Ritt's worlds. Ritt's miners are not a unified singing group but a bunch of solitary workers who trudge silently to the mines, barely acknowledging the existence of their compatriots. There are no families in the background to see them off. These are beaten, defeated men who leave miserable homes owned by the mining company only to descend to an even more squalid existence below ground.

Warner Brothers' 1935 film *Black Fury*, directed by Michael Curtiz and starring Paul Muni, also deals with coal mining, but again the protagonist, Joe Radek (Muni), is a happy-go-lucky miner with a comfortable home and plenty to eat. Even the conditions in the mine seem comfortable. In his review of the film, Albert Maltz, whose play about coal mining, *Black Pit*, opened the same year, complained that the men worked "genially in a well lighted room 'ten feet high.'" Radek literally stumbles into union activism when his girlfriend deserts him for another man. He gets drunk and wanders into a union meeting, where he hears the men talking about whether or not to fight, and, thinking of his girl, he yells, "Fight!" Because the men respect him, they rally around him and decide to strike. But all the strike does is threaten the miners comfortable lifestyle. In the end Radek works to undo the harm done by the strike and restore the miners' original working conditions.

Ritt's film was therefore the first serious attempt to expose the brutal conditions of the miners and to integrate a personal story with the sociological-political material. In so doing, Ritt created a film that surpasses the others in its representation of real, as opposed to "reel," history. Placed alongside *Hud, Hombre,* and *The Brotherhood, The Molly Maguires* composes the final chapter in Ritt's exploration of the effects of industrialism and mechanization on modern America. Offering a unified and unsparing look at our national character, Ritt's singular sociological vision remains one of most sustained achievements in the history of American film.

CHAPTER 11

The African American Experience: *The Great White Hope, Sounder,* and *Conrack*

In some respects *The Great White Hope* (1970) is the last of Ritt's sixties' films. Its protagonist, Jack Jefferson, is a prototypical Ritt outsider who has rejected the values of a society that resents what he is and what he believes and that ultimately beats him down. Its style, insular and filled with close-ups and tight visual compositions, is more reminiscent of *The Brotherhood* than of the films that would follow. It is, however, the first of three films Ritt made in quick succession focusing on the African American experience. *The Great White Hope* was followed by *Sounder* in 1972 and *Conrack* in 1974.

All were released at a time when a certain kind of black film was enjoying a surge of unprecedented popularity. Black audiences, particularly urban ones, were flocking to theaters to see films with black casts, stories, and themes. Films such as *Shaft, Super Fly, The Final Countdown, A Cool Breeze,* and *Sweet Sweetback's Baadasssss Song* were big box office. These were violent films that showed blacks facing down whites in brutal confrontations that left piles of bodies behind. The black cinema made revenge profitable by offering audiences a catharsis of blood as black characters killed their white oppressors. The emphasis in these films was on romance and wish fulfillment, particularly for the male audience. The ads for *Super Fly* stated it quite boldly: "Never a dude like this one! He's got a plan to stick it to The Man!"

Ritt's trilogy of African American films were, like his genre films, out of step with cinematic fashion. None of them features much violence; even *The Great White Hope*, which deals with the career of a boxer, has only one extended fight sequence. *Sounder* and *Conrack* are essentially family films, described by Ritt himself as love stories. "*Sounder* was the love story of a family and *Conrack* is also a love story, but between a young white man and a group of black kids." They offer sober reflections on the subject of racism, and although some members of the black community were critical of their relative lack of anger or, in the case of *Conrack*, for a perceived element of condescension, Ritt regarded them as a barometer of his personal feelings. Of *Conrack* he said, "I'm going my own way with *Conrack*. I believe it's going to be lovely and human and warm and funny and meaningful and angry. All those things that are present in the black-white condition in this country."[1]

Two of the films—*The Great White Hope* and *Conrack*—are based on true stories, while *Sounder* originated as a children's book. Each of them expresses a different viewpoint on the status of black characters in film. *Sounder* was the most successful artistically and commercially. Presenting its protagonists as ordinary people who survive and prevail through love and hard work, it gave the struggle of the poor a measure of dignity and true heroism lacking from exploitative, violent films such as *Super Fly*, which glorified a drug dealer. *Conrack* offered romance and wish fulfillment like the violent black films, but, typically for Ritt, it was a romance of togetherness rather than destruction. If it was an artistic failure, it was nevertheless a bold attempt to buck the trend.

The Great White Hope was also a failure, for Ritt was unable to rise above the agit-prop, one-dimensional flavor of the stage play. Its simplistic characterization resembled that of the violent anti-white films, where it suited the headlong rush of the material. Ritt's failure to enrich this aspect of his much more ambitious film reflected an inability to overcome the original's stage conventions and shape the material effectively for the screen; it was the same problem that had plagued him in *The Outrage*.

The Great White Hope, like *The Molly Maguires*, draws on a historical source, and it thereby extends Ritt's exploration of the American cultural landscape. Its protagonist, Jack Jefferson, is based on Jack Johnson, the first black heavyweight champion of the world. The story opens in 1908, when Johnson beat Tommy Burns in Australia to win the championship, and it follows his career up to 1915, when he was defeated in Havana by Jess Willard. The immediate source was a play of the same name that was the sensation of the 1968–69 Broadway season, winning all three major theater prizes—the Antoinette Perry Award, the Drama Critics Prize, and the Pulitzer prize.

Ritt's first experience in transferring a theater piece to the screen, *The Outrage*, was less than successful, in large part because of a decision to remain faithful to the Kanins' play rather than to Kurosawa's classic film. Hiring the playwright to adapt his own work only ensured that, despite Ritt's efforts to open up the action, the action remains dependent on a theatrical structure and some overly theatrical dialogue. *The Great White Hope* suffers from similar problems, no doubt also compounded by the decision to hire the playwright, Howard Sackler, to write the screenplay.

In 1968, when Arthur Miller asked Ritt to film his play *The Price*, Ritt declined, explaining that "this play more than any of your others would simply look like a photographed evening in the theatre" (RC 11-4-68). He was at first not interested in filming *The Great White Hope* either, and his instinct was confirmed by going to New York to see the play. He let himself be persuaded to undertake it, however, by the producer Lawrence Turman, who was at the height of his power following the astounding success of *The Graduate* in 1967 and the critically acclaimed *Pretty Poison* in 1968. Ritt was given artistic control, and he coproduced the film as well.

Even after taking on the project, he remained skeptical. The agent Flora Roberts sent a letter to Ritt, criticizing the play as a "rather characterless uni-dimensional comforter for the nice white liberal audience whose nerve ends are kept prickling by the sound effects" (RC undated). Ritt replied, "Many of my friends feel as you do about *The Great White Hope*. However, I think of it not so much as a play, but as a show and I think I can make a very good popular entertainment of it" (RC 3-7-69).

Some years later, when answering a question about adapting plays for the screen, however, Ritt seemed to have absorbed the lessons of his two unsuccessful projects: "Don't do it. They're really a different medium. A good play is written in the immediacy of time and place. Film's a totally different kind of experience . . . actually I like them better when they're done as plays, because if you open them up so-called, you tend to vitiate the impact and force of the playwright and if he's a good one, you're ripping it apart" (AFI 41). Later at that same seminar he remarked, "I will never do another play. Never. I think it's too difficult again, because I think to do one you're violating the other" (AFI 49). Ritt would go back on that vow over a decade later when he agreed to take over *Nuts*, based on a play by Tom Topor, and again he would achieve only indifferent results.

The Great White Hope is a play of epic scope, Brechtian in methodology with an agit-prop bent. It is a throwback in form and theme to the plays presented by the Group Theatre in the thirties, and part of its appeal to Ritt, no doubt, was its clarion call to the idealism of his youth. Ritt's first play with the Group Theatre had been Clifford Odets's *Golden Boy*, whose protagonist was also a boxer. Joe Bonaparte, that play's idealistic protagonist, must choose between the violence of the ring (Odets's metaphor for the capitalist system) and a career as a concert violinist. His choice of the former is the tragic flaw that destroys him. Ironically, Odets's own protagonist had been transformed into a black character (played by Sammy Davis Jr.) for the musical version that opened in 1964 (after Odets's death), thus complicating Odets's themes by the addition of an interracial love story.

Sackler's play is a large, sprawling affair composed of nineteen scenes and divided into three acts. It begins in Ohio and moves on to San Francisco, Reno, and Chicago, and then to London, Paris, Berlin, Belgrade, and Budapest, before concluding in Juarez, Mexico, and Havana. The play's expanse is matched by its hero, who, like Joe Bonaparte, is larger than life—proud, articulate, and yet an exemplary fighter. Jack Jefferson is meant to be a tragic figure, a man of authentic physical and emotional stature who is felled by his pride and his stubborn persistence in doing everything his own way. Like Odets, Sackler wants to "shoot bullets" at his audience, punctuating each scene with an emotional or physical confrontation. In act 1, scene 2, for example, an informal talk with reporters at a gym is disrupted by Jefferson's mistress, who enters screaming accusations. A peaceful idyll in the country with his white mistress is interrupted as they lie in bed when the doors to their cabin are broken down by marshals.

The play moves inexorably downward in a series of highly stylized scenes, following Jefferson from the height of his success as a fighter through his subsequent persecution by white society and the government. Jefferson is presented as a victim both of racism and of his own pride, undone by the naive and romantic notion that his private life is his own. He contributes to his own downfall by flaunting his white mistress, compounding the insult to white America that is represented by his championship belt. Eventually convicted on a trumped-up Mann Act charge, he escapes to Europe rather than go to prison. But he is hounded even there by the American government, finally forced out of boxing and into performing music hall routines in European cafes. His most degrading moment comes when he plays Uncle Tom to his white mistress's Little Eva in a Budapest beer hall. Jefferson refuses, meanwhile, to capitulate to offers of reduced charges if he will return to defend his championship and throw the fight.

Jefferson's circumstances become more and more desperate until the climax in Juarez, where Jefferson spurns his mistress, who then commits suicide by throwing herself down a well. Her broken, muddied body is brought on stage in a tableau reminiscent of Greek tragedy. Tortured with grief as he cries over her body, Jefferson then agrees to the demands of the government and the boxing promoters, demands that he lose the title fight in Havana. To heighten the pathos, Sackler has Jefferson suddenly decide against the fix during the fight. Finally, after putting up a heroic struggle, he is beaten fairly and then carried off the stage like Oedipus, a beaten, bloodied shell of what he once was.

Despite its honors and awards, *The Great White Hope* is a deeply flawed play. Polemical and self-righteous in tone, it offers mostly stereotypical characters, none of whom, except Jefferson, commands any interest. Even Ellie Bachman, his white mistress, remains so bland and undeveloped a character that even her suicide fails to yield the emotional jolt that the playwright clearly intended.

Jefferson himself seems too noble and too good to be true. Aside from his pride, he has no imperfections, much less character faults. This saintliness becomes a problem, especially in the second act, when he is subjected to multiple degradations in Europe but always remains superior to his tormentors. The overwrought scenes of harassment grow repetitive, and the Christ-like behavior of the hero becomes increasingly cumbersome. As Sackler seems to be dragging him through the stations of the cross, Jefferson degenerates into a symbol and essentially ceases to be a character at all.

The size and scope of *The Great White Hope,* however, were built-in lures for movie adaptation. The play came equipped with surefire mechanisms for opening up the action. There were the multiple American and international settings, escapes from the law, a love idyll in the countryside, crowd scenes, and the possibility of exciting, choreographed boxing sequences.

It also presented many potential problems. In particular, Sackler's tendency to structure each scene around a single big moment offers thematic tableaux rather than building blocks toward the revelation of character or theme. There are clumsy theatrical devices such as groups of characters who function as choruses of either good or evil, and characters who break away from the group to speak in asides to the audience. At the height of Jefferson's success, a character named Scipio confronts him with melodramatic premonitions of doom. Most problematic are the static characters who fit neatly into Sackler's polemical scheme but are much too flat for the livelier milieu of film.

Ritt's basic strategy, unfortunately, was to remain faithful to the play. Little is changed; the scenes unfold in the same repetitive manner as in the play, and much of the original dialogue is preserved. Ritt even retained some of the original cast, notably James Earl Jones as Jefferson, Jane Alexander as Ellie, Marlene Warfield as Clara, and Lou Gilbert as Goldie, Jefferson's manager. His filmic design was to make the play look like a small film locked inside a proscenium, in order to give it the claustrophobic feel he wanted and to emphasize the hero's entrapment.

Ritt never found a way, however, to balance the stylized presentation of character and plot with a visually stimulating portrayal of the boxer's world. As in

The Molly Maguires, he had an opportunity to re-create an era of American history in vivid, realistic images, but he offers instead a world that looks like an elaborate set. Even scenes that venture beyond the set manage to look theatrical and provide no effective support for the thematic weight of this tragic morality play.

The film begins with a shot of the championship belt against a black background.[2] The credits begin and then in the lower half screen the legs of two fighters are seen moving around a ring. By the time the credits conclude, the white boxer falls, and there is an abrupt cut to a door slamming as Frank Brady, the retired champion, leaves his house, refusing to "fight no dinge." The sudden transition punctuated by sound is borrowed from the play, as is Ritt's handling of the white reporters and promoters who try to persuade Brady to come out of retirement to fight Jefferson. He owes it to his race, they insist, to reclaim the belt. The scene is staged by grouping these people like a chorus and punctuating their comments in a stage-like rhythm. Ritt shoots this outdoor scene in a series of medium and close-up shots, minimizing space to emphasize the constriction of their racist sentiments. The stylistic overstatement, which is marginally effective on stage, seems lifeless and contrived on the screen.

Ritt's visual strategy in presenting his protagonist, however, is more effective. Jefferson is first seen punching a bag, as the camera circles gracefully around him. This shot stands out in a film that otherwise remains visually static, the sense of movement magnifying the fighter and setting him apart from his lackluster surroundings. It also metaphorically prefigures the circular course of his journey; for this fluid image of Jefferson at his peak also suggests that his movements will remain circumscribed, that he is already entrapped in a process that will lead to his fall. The film will end in the ring, from which this extraordinary physical specimen, smiling and radiant when introduced here, will exit a spent and bloodied shell. Ritt's introductory image of the hero at his best thus deepens the pathos of Jefferson's fall.

This scene also introduces Ellie Bachman (Jane Alexander), who is watching Jefferson work out. Goldie (Lou Gilbert), who comes in to announce that the championship fight will take place in Reno on July 4, is upset at Jefferson's flaunting his white mistress, especially with reporters coming. Jefferson, however, sweeps aside his objections and faces the reporters, confidently predicting victory over Brady. The interview is suddenly interrupted by Jefferson's black former mistress, who attacks Ellie, throwing the scene into chaos. Ritt then concludes the scene by pulling back his camera to show Jefferson and Ellie sitting together, looking small and isolated. After this scene, he regularly confines Jefferson alone in the frame.

The action shifts to Reno, where the next scene is meant to portray the festive atmosphere preceding the fight, but despite the crowds and parades, it looks staged and confined. The claustrophobic feeling is interrupted briefly when Brady emerges to be weighed before the fight. Ritt pulls his camera back and sweeps around the roofs and balconies and then back to Brady. In a modified low angle shot, Brady is seen holding up the belt and speaking to the crowd. Jefferson's entrance is more subdued visually, as he enters in close-up to the side of the frame. When he speaks to the crowd, Ritt shows only his head.

When both fighters enter the stadium, Ritt again pans up and over the arena and focuses on the crowd, which fills the frame. This panning movement recalls the opening of *The Molly Maguires,* but Ritt is more abrupt here, allowing no pause for observing the space. Overwhelmed by the press of the crowd and then quick close-ups of Jefferson's smiling face as he jabs at Brady, the viewer is given no long shot of the fight to establish it as part of a larger spectacle. Ritt's cutting isolates Jefferson from the crowd.

He continues to emphasize this isolation even when Jefferson is at play. Abruptly shifting the scene to the streets of Chicago and the Cafe De Champion, Jefferson's new club, Ritt defines the nature of Jefferson's status within his society by presenting him in a very artificial-looking set, suggesting that his fame and stature may be only an illusion. Jefferson is celebrating his victory in a black neighborhood, but Ritt never offers even a momentary sense that there is a real crowd here, because, again, most shots are either medium or tight close-ups. Even when Jefferson dances in the street, he seems trapped in the frame. The camera is relentless in isolating and confining him.

The foreshadowing of doom grows overly emphatic when Ritt brings on Scipio, a soothsayer-like choral character from the play, to confront Jefferson about his white mistress and his absorption in success. In the play, this character appears during the funeral of Jefferson's mother, but this scene is dropped from the film. His appearance provides an awkward moment that Ritt could easily have dispensed with. The camera has already visually approximated Scipio's warning, making his prophetic diatribe sound even more heavy-handed in the film than it does in the play.

Several emblematic visual compositions near the end of the film deserve comment. The penultimate scene in Mexico recalls the earlier scene in the San Francisco gym. Again the scene opens upon Jefferson punching a bag. This time, however, Ritt does not circle his camera around his subject, but fixes it on Jefferson, who appears bloated and out of shape. Ellie, who comes in with his lunch, is no longer the elegantly dressed, beaming woman of scene 2; looking drawn, she wears sunglasses to cover her eyes, and her skin is blotched. As they argue,

Ritt employs the shot–reverse shot technique he utilized earlier in Ellie's scene with an underhanded district attorney who sought to entrap her. The repetition, linking Jefferson with the hostile interrogator, suggests how far apart they have grown. Leaving the gym, she walks toward the camera, which closes in on her face until it blurs. Her destruction is complete. In a few moments her lifeless, broken body will be carried back in.

As Ellie walks out, Ritt repeats the long shot from scene 2, showing Jefferson looking cornered by the wall. In that earlier moment, he sat with Ellie; now he is alone, forced to recognize all the forces, including his own pride, that have conspired to defeat him.

The final scene is the only boxing sequence in the film. Unlike the close-ups of the fight scene in Reno, Ritt's composition here brings the boxers and the crowd together in the frame. Jefferson has come, of course, to lose, but toward the end of the fight, disgusted by the smug expressions he sees on the faces of the promoters, he decides to fight to win. Despite his best efforts, however, he is not in good enough shape to defeat his opponent.

After the fight, the white victor is carried off by the crowd, the belt draped around his neck, his face bloodied and bruised, like the psyche of the nation that needs a "white hope." Ritt's final shot is of Jefferson, his back to the camera, being supported by Goldie and his trainer Tick as they walk away from the camera through a series of archways. Whereas Sackler concludes his play with the "Kid" in triumph on the shoulders of the crowd, Ritt ends with his beaten hero, who like Russell and Leamas, is defeated but ennobled; framed by the arches that give him a kind of epic grandeur, Jefferson is presented as an outsider who was better than the system that has destroyed him.

The Great White Hope portrays an America so rampantly racist that it will go to any lengths to defeat a supremely gifted and confident black champion. Ritt's film is well meaning, but in the absence of the complexity he brought to *The Molly Maguires*, its shallow self-righteousness elicits no more than a knee-jerk response. The playwright-screenwriter's stereotypical characters and the agit-prop rhythm of the plot rob both play and film of any emotional or intellectual charge. Ritt has not improved matters by turning the screen into an elaborate proscenium. He manages to make some interesting visual commentary through his mis-en-scène but ultimately he fails to free his material of the original's theatrical constraints, which he has all too willingly embraced.

Ritt does, however, succeed in giving James Earl Jones room to re-create his Broadway role on screen. Jones's Jefferson is indeed an epic, heroic character, and Ritt's theater-film style accommodates the actor's theatrical performance to the screen. Jefferson's rebellious stance, however, while heroic and sympathetic in the style of Russell, Leamas, and Kehoe, remains oddly remote from a recognizable world. Here Ritt's hero is surrounded by mouthpieces, not characters, and marooned in a cinematic world that seems to be defined only by its crowd scenes.

Ritt himself claimed to like the film, "because it was juicy and full of beans and full of life and full of appetite and full of America" (Jackson 113). His enthusiasm was rather disingenuous, however, for in 1987 when Boston University was planning to present him with a Lifetime Achievement Award, Ritt wrote to George Bluestone, who organized the affair, to say, " I have one reservation about the films chosen. I had too many bad memories of making *The Great White Hope*. I would like you to eliminate it from the perspective [sic]" (RC 10-8-87). While the subject matter was full of American history and culture, the film failed because Ritt did not make it "full of life or full of America." He would remedy that omission in *Sounder*, a film that introduces a bold new visual style and inaugurates a period in which Ritt's vision becomes reflective rather than dark and brooding. The constricted look of *The Great White Hope* disappears, replaced by a recognizable world that yields to the camera's shaping yet seems complex enough to extend beyond the confines of the frame. *Sounder* is lyrical rather than static, its mood open and exploratory rather than dark and confined.

William H. Armstrong's novel *Sounder* was published in 1969; the following year it won the American Library Association's John Newberry Medal as the year's "most distinguished contribution to children's literature." The book attracted the attention of Robert Radnitz, a former English professor at the University of Virginia, who had become a film producer. Having long been interested in children's literature, Radnitz brought to his new profession an ambition to produce films for children that were substantive and serious. "Children are capable of understanding much more than producers give them credit for. They want something besides treacle. They are hungry for sustenance. And one thing they don't want is dishonesty. They want to learn about life and the world, and they want the truth."[3]

Radnitz's films reflected his philosophy. His first work, *A Dog of Flanders* (1960), won the Grand Prix Golden Lion Award at the Venice Film Festival, and the honor was repeated in 1964 for *The Island of the Blue Dolphins*. None of Radnitz's films were made in Hollywood. A great believer, as was Ritt, in the value of location shooting, he produced all of his films in locations that lent authenticity and realism to the stories. This practice was repeated with *Sounder*.

Radnitz pitched *Sounder* to the Mattel Toy Company, which decided to co-produce the project and finance it for $1 million. He then sent the book to Ritt, who was deeply moved by the story and quickly agreed to direct it, although Radnitz told him, "I can't pay you anything" (AFI 42). Undeterred, Ritt took an 80 percent pay cut to make the film. Playwright (*Ceremonies in Dark Old Men*) and television writer (*N.Y.P.D.*) Lonne Elder III agreed to write the screenplay.

Ritt originally intended to shoot on location around Macon, Georgia, but he encountered so much racial hostility there that he moved the cast and crew to Clinton, Louisiana. A number of local residents appear in supporting roles. Teddy Airhart, who plays Mr. Perkins, was a Baton Rouge attorney, once the state's attorney general. The judge and his court clerk are played by Judge William Thomas Bennett and his real-life clerk Inez Durham, and their scene was filmed in Judge Bennett's actual courtroom. The Reverend Thomas Nathaniel Phillips, who portrays the black preacher, was the pastor of the New Hope Baptist Church.

Ritt's professional cast consisted of respected actors, although none had real box office recognition. Cicely Tyson (Rebecca Morgan) was known for her work on the stage, but with the exception of a featured role in *The Heart Is a Lonely Hunter* (1968), she had little film experience. Paul Winfield (Nathan Lee Morgan) was also a veteran of numerous stage and television productions, but he had not made a name in film. Both actors would receive Academy Award nominations for their performances, and Tyson would win the Best Actress Award from the National Society of Film Critics. The pivotal role of David Lee Morgan, their eldest son, was played by Kevin Hooks, who was then thirteen years old and the son of actor Robert Hooks (star of *N.Y.P.D.*).

Armstrong's novel is rather stark for a children's book, presenting the grim story of an unnamed boy who must learn to deal with the pain of loss and death. When the police come to arrest the boy's father, a poor black sharecropper, they shoot the family's coon dog Sounder, as he chases after them. The bulk of the narrative then centers on the boy's learning to cope with Sounder's disappearance—the dog has crawled off after the shooting, leaving the boy uncertain whether he is alive or dead—and his father's absence. Eventually Sounder comes home, but he is no longer a hunting dog, and when the father returns, he is likewise crippled from years on a chain gang. The novel concludes with the deaths of the father and Sounder and the boy's recognition that death is part of a continuum, articulated in a passage from Montaigne: "Only the unwise think that what has changed is dead."

Lonne Elder's script fleshes out this rather one-dimensional book with central characters, especially the mother and the father, who emerge as beautifully individualized, three-dimensional characters. The film's family is given the name Morgan, which immediately individualizes them, and Elder creates a vibrant community of strong characters for the film, among them Mrs. Boatwright, the white woman who employs Rebecca Morgan to wash her clothes but also befriends the family and gives books to David, Sheriff Young, and the Morgans' friend Ike (played by the musician Taj Mahal, who also wrote the music for the film). A pivotal figure is Camille (Janet MacLachlan), the schoolteacher who introduces David to the writings of W. E. B. DuBois—she replaces the novel's teacher, an older man who does not introduce the boy to black writers—thereby sparking David's hunger for an education and his intellectual coming of age. In the film, this personal and intellectual awakening takes precedence over David's love for Sounder, which remains the central relationship in the book. Elder's downplaying of the significance of the dog makes his decision to retain the novel's title seem questionable, but it gives the film a much wider scope in opening up the boy's world.

The film retains many of the book's major plot elements and preserves its simple, direct structure. The head of a family of sharecroppers in Louisiana in 1933, Nathan Morgan steals some meat from a white man's home in order to feed his family. When he is apprehended, tried, and sent to prison camp for one year, Mr. Perkins, the landowner, questions whether the family can harvest the crop in Nathan's absence. David, who sorely misses his father, walks for days with Sounder to find the prison camp, but he cannot find his father. On this journey he meets Camille, the mistress of an all black school. After staying with her for two days, the boy returns home. The family succeeds in harvesting the crop on time, and then Nathan, crippled, returns home and the family is reunited. Meanwhile, Camille has invited David to return to the school and to stay with her, and the film ends with Nathan driving him there.

The simplicity of this story frees Ritt to concentrate on textures and nuances in the everyday lives of his characters. It also allows his camera to linger on details, objects, and gestures that enrich the story line, giving a resonance to mundane scenes that creates the *illusion* of realism. Reviewing the film for *Ms.*, Toni Morrison praised its attention to detailing "the fabric of these lives," adding, "It relies, as almost no contemporary film does, on story line and acting ability for its power."[4] This was a technique that Ritt learned from his years in television, working with writers such as Paddy Chayefsky, whose naturalist dramas deeply influenced him. This naturalistic style would dominate later films such as *Norma Rae, Murphy's Romance,* and *Stanley and Iris,* which derive much of their power and complexity from Ritt's ability to derive significant emotional effects from the close observation of everyday life.

Ritt's visual style in *Sounder* is distinguished by his use of long takes and minimal use of cutting. For the first time, he relies primarily on long shots, creating a film that visually underscores spatial and temporal relations. *Sounder* is a work that gains power from its feeling for wholeness and continuity and its naturalistic sense of proportion.

This stylistic declaration is made in the opening sequence, a long shot that highlights a sunset behind a forest that occupies the foreground. The camera lingers on this scenic view until voices are heard off frame, and then the characters walk into the frame in silhouette. They are speaking as they walk through and then out of the frame; after a slight pan that seems to locate the characters in a different part of the forest, the camera never moves during this sequence. Unlike *The Great White Hope*, in which Ritt was laboriously creating a world suitable for his story, in Sounder he seems to be finding the one in which his story takes place.

One scene in *Sounder* is similar enough to one in *The Great White Hope* to demonstrate clearly the change in Ritt's approach. In the earlier film's penultimate scene in Juarez, as Ellie is trying to persuade Jack to give in to the government's demands and return to America, he tells her a story of fighting someone at a fair when he was young: "An Ah doin awright fo a youngster, when all it once he bulls me up gainss dat tent-side a de ring an SLAM, WHAM, somebody behine dere conks me, right through de canvas, musta use a two by four, an evy time Ah stans up he shove me back again, an SLAM, dere's anudder, down she come."

Jack is telling her that it doesn't matter what he does, the system is rigged against him. Ritt films this scene in extreme close-up, with Jack mostly in profile on the left and Ellie in profile to the right.

A much different effect is achieved in a parallel scene in *Sounder*, which opens with Nathan Lee and his son David Lee hunting for game. Frustrated by his inability to shoot a possum and provide meat for his family, Nathan is on edge when he gets home. His wife tries to comfort him, saying, "We've been through hard times before, Nathan Lee and we've made it." He replies, "And what we make it to, Rebecca? Another season of sharecropping for old man Perkins. Working from dawn till dusk so he can get richer and we can't even eat when cropping time is done."

This dialogue is filmed in a medium shot, with Rebecca to the left and Nathan to the right. As Nathan finishes speaking he walks away, leaving Rebecca alone in the frame. She then moves to the stove, picks up the coffee pot and pours a cup of coffee, and the camera remains on her until a reverse shot reveals Nathan, who simply stands near the table and then sits down. The emotional content of the scene is telling, but the characters' love and frustration, and the pain of poverty are made palpable strictly through minimal gesture and the camera's steady observation. Whereas in *The Great White Hope,* Ritt schematized the scene to emphasize the tragic weight of the story and the emotional distance between the characters, here the dialogue develops instead as part of the couple's domestic routine. Every aspect of the scene supports Nathan's bitterness, yet Rebecca concentrates on her chores, dramatically indicating that she will endure and prevail over her poverty.

This refusal to distort a situation with artificial camera maneuvers is most effective in the scenes leading to Nathan's arrest for stealing. The moment is preceded by a long-shot sequence as the characters return home after playing a baseball game. First a wagon and a group of people enter the frame from right to left; the Morgans and Ike follow, and they all turn and walk toward the camera. The progress is leisurely, the characters laughing, talking, and singing while Ike plays the guitar. The camera follows them, not singling out any of them, but content, as they are, to bask in the joy of the moment. A quick dissolve to a white church is followed by the movement of the characters into the frame, this time from left to right—again Ritt's strategy is to call attention to the world beyond the frame. As the characters continue their talk, the camera follows them; some move out of the frame, while Ike and the Morgans walk on. After Ike leaves them, the Morgans approach their home, and in a long shot it is revealed that there are people waiting for them.

Suddenly Sounder barks, signaling trouble, and the family runs toward the house. As the camera accompanies them, Ritt avoids the usual anticipatory cutting procedure, withholding any view of the deputies until Nathan sees them. This technique of restraint in presenting a pivotal incident actually heightens its dramatic impact. No dramatic cut is made until Nathan has been handcuffed and put on the wagon. Once he is seated, Ritt cuts to a close-up of Nathan's face, followed by a quick reverse to Rebecca. This standard Hollywood device for heightening the emotional charge of a dramatic parting here becomes doubly effective because Ritt has eschewed such artificial effects up to this point.

This stylistic method of understatement is consistent with Ritt's handling of the characters developed in Elder's script. The tendency in black films of the time was to caricature the white characters, but here the protagonists' white adversaries are presented not as larger-than-life "bad guys," but merely as average, mediocre, selfish people. The sequence in which Rebecca walks for miles to town to visit her husband offers a clear example. When she arrives at the jail the sweat on her face recalls earlier scenes, making it apparent that her walk has taken hours. The white sheriff, however, refuses to acknowledge her heroic effort, matter-of-factly telling Rebecca that she can't see her husband, that visiting days are restricted to Sundays and holidays and that women are never allowed.

The sheriff then excuses the callous inhumanity of his attitude by pointing out repeatedly that he only follows the rules; he even volunteers to drive out to the Morgan home to inform Rebecca of the date of the trial. Rebecca's mounting anger and frustration are plain, but her reaction is muted, allowing only an acid remark, "You got yourself a low-life job, sheriff." In the background to her right, a framed loyalty oath hangs on the wall—a blacklisted director's stark visual reminder of the personal and moral consequences of playing by the rules in a repressive system.

Rebecca's powers of restraint are again tested when she goes to Mr. Perkins's store for supplies. Perkins who also owns her land, rebukes her about Nathan's behavior, and once more she must harness her emotions because of her inability to talk back to the white landlord. In both scenes Ritt employs close-ups of Cicely Tyson's face as she listens, fiercely repressing the pain of the powerless.

The cumulative dramatic effect of these repeated incidents of banal, systematic oppression ultimately becomes more powerful than the exaggerated sadism of the exploitative films of the time. Both the sheriff and the storekeeper are granted some degree of humanity despite their bigotry, and this tolerant approach only underscores the humanity of the Morgans as it reflects the incremental, wearing effect of ingrained racism. Such incidents are presented not as spectacular or violent confrontations but as an oppressive shadow on the daily lives of the sharecroppers. In *Sounder* Ritt thus offers a deeper sense of the reality of racism than the dramatic lynchings and beatings that have served as the standard indicators of racial prejudice.

What comfort and pleasure the Morgans find in this marginal existence come from friends and from their love and devotion to each other. And if this modern society offers little, God offers even less. As in his other films, Ritt undercuts the clergy in *Sounder*, portraying the family's preacher as helpless and hollow, his words of comfort after Nathan's arrest as meaningless as those the minister offers Lonnie in *Hud*. Here a single scene shows the black community church, but Ritt's camera goes inside only briefly. Instead, the camera dwells on the horses tethered outside and then on a shot of the cemetery, while the congregation is heard singing hymns. This startling juxtaposition—horses (a metaphor here for the brutality of labor) and death—strongly suggests the nature of a reality that is more powerful than religion.

A central theme in Elder's script, although it receives only peripheral attention in the book, is the value of education. The film adds scenes depicting the six-mile walk David must make to attend a primarily white school. Elder also adds the character of Mrs. Boatwright, a white woman who encourages David's love of reading, even giving him a copy of *The Three Musketeers*, which David reads to his siblings. The key sequence in developing the education motif, however, is David's coming upon the school run by Camille Johnson while searching for his father.

David admires Camille's library, and, in an important departure from Armstrong's original narrative, she exposes him to books about and by African Americans. She shows him a books about Harriet Tubman and Crispus Attucks, and she reads to him from W. E. B. DuBois: "The longing of black men must have respect. The rich and bitter depths of their experience, the unknown treasures of their inner life, the strange renderings of nature they have seen, may give the world new points of view and make their loving, living and doing precious to all human hearts." Ritt's film thus both directly celebrates the African American culture and seeks to filter these lessons through David's consciousness. In Armstrong's book, David learns from Montaigne about the cycle of life; in the film he comes to an understanding of his personal heritage.

Shortly after David returns home, his father comes back from prison. Having suffered a leg injury in a dynamite blast, he now must walk with a cane. The reunion scene is justifiably famous for its emotional power. According to Radnitz, John Alonzo filmed the scene in one take with a handheld camera, and there were tears in his eyes when he finished.[5] Tyson's performance perfectly embodies the swelling tide of feelings suddenly unleashed, from her joyous yell when she recognizes Nathan approaching from afar, to the look of love rekindled as it slowly dawns on her that it is truly her husband she sees walking up the road. Ritt again handles the scene in a long shot, briefly withholding recognition and emotion before encompassing Rebecca sprinting toward her husband, the children individually recognizing the magnitude of the event and then running as well, and Nathan hobbling in frustration at not being able to move fast enough because of his cane.

The film's most deeply emotional scene, however, is that between David and his father. David has changed his mind about going to Camille's school because he wants to stay with his father, and when Nathan angrily insists that he must go to the school, the boy runs away. Finding him by a stream, Nathan tells his son that he loves him and, most important, that David needs to get an education in order "to beat the life they got laid out for you in this place." This father-son bonding scene is linked by the water motif to David's earlier discovery of Camille after bathing his hand in a stream. The water serves as a poetic image of rebirth and liberation through education.

The film then concludes with Nathan taking David to school. The educational journey that David is about to begin is one that will lead to knowledge of the world beyond the farm, a continuation of the movement outward that started when he went to look for his father. He will learn about his place in the world and, perhaps, how he can change that world. The film never attempts to specify what form such change might take, for such a prescriptive approach would falsify Ritt's insistence on the enormity and variety of life outside the frame. His camera throughout has recognized a spatial arena that cannot be contained within its necessarily limited narrative focus. It is this wider world that now opens before David. The ride to Camille's school is thus clearly only the first step on a long journey that promises to be difficult and torturous, yet also exciting and wondrous.

After the integral achievement of *Sounder*, *Conrack* (1974) comes as something of a disappointment. It, too, deals with racism, but unlike *The Great White Hope* and *Sounder*, which concentrate directly on the African American experience, *Conrack* divides its focus between the confrontation of its white outsider hero with the educational establishment and another realistic portrayal of the ingrained bigotry of the southern society. Unfortunately, the film's integration of these themes is not always successful.

This is Ritt's last film to confront the issue of racism, this time exploring it from a contemporary perspective (the story is set in 1969). The three films thus form a triptych, representing the subject at salient points throughout the century: *The Great White Hope*, dealing with the turn of the century; *Sounder*, taking place in 1933; and *Conrack*, in the late 1960s. Together they indicate that little progress has been made, that racism remains firmly embedded in American culture.

Like *The Great White Hope*, Conrack is based on a true story, Pat Conroy's autobiographical account (published as *The Water Is Wide* in 1972) of teaching nearly illiterate black children on Daufuskie Island, off the coast of South Carolina. Conroy recounts his thirteen months as a teacher in a two-room schoolhouse on the island, renamed Yamacraw, where he taught grades five through eight. The island, with its unpaved roads, oxcarts, and "glinting magnolias," is described as a place basically "ignored by the twentieth century"; its only brush with modernity is an industrial factory, near Savannah, Georgia, that spewed its waste into the ocean and eventually polluted the area's creeks and shoreline. Here Conroy met students who did not know the name of their country, that they lived on the Atlantic Ocean, or that the world was round. "I had stepped into the 19th century even though the 20th century was storming the beaches, and two cultures, Southern white and Southern black, were colliding."[6]

Conroy came to enjoy his work, but the combination of his unorthodox teaching methods and his disregard for school authorities eventually got him fired. He wrote the book as a way of coping with his anger at this dismissal, in the process addressing the complex experiences both of his time on the island and of the life's journey that led him to it. *The Water Is Wide* is thus basically a coming-of-age story, as Conroy's narrative moves from his "smooth watered" childhood in the fifties to the personal and political awakening in the sixties that led him to question his racist upbringing and motivated his desire to teach on the island. Conroy wrote—the line is repeated in the film—"At this time of my life a black man could probably have handed me a bucket of cow piss, commanded me to drink it in order that I might rid my soul of the stench of racism, and I would have only asked for a straw" (97–98).

Julian Bach, Conroy's agent, felt that Hollywood would be interested in the book, and he was right. Irving Ravetch and Harriet Frank Jr. found themselves laughing and crying while reading it. Along with Ritt, they successfully pitched the idea of a film to Twentieth Century–Fox.

Ritt, who coproduced the film with Ravetch and Frank, again decided to film on location. Jimmy Carter, embarrassed by the racist resistance Ritt had encountered while trying to film *Sounder* in Georgia, had invited him to give the state another chance, and Ritt took the governor up on his offer. Once the decision was made to film on St. Simon Island, just off the coast of New Brunswick, Carter made sure that all state agencies cooperated with Ritt and later attended the film's premiere. Ritt also contacted a local preacher to help find local children to play the students. Claiming to have cast them on an "educated guess," he succeeded, as he had in *Sounder*, in obtaining believable performances from them.

Ravetch and Frank made use of much of the book's dialogue, but streamlined it considerably by eliminating nearly all details of Conroy's life as well as his descriptions of life on the island and its more prominent inhabitants. Conroy takes his students on several trips, including one to Washington, D.C., but Ravetch and Frank focus on only one trip, to Beaufort on Halloween. This technique of compounding incidents and characters into a single representative episode or figure was applied also to Conroy's many confrontations with a variety of school administrators, all personified in the film's Mr. Skeffington (Hume Cronyn).

Condensation, focus, and emphasis are required of any film adaptation of a book, but some of the choices made by the screenwriters in this case oversimplified the story, turning characters and situations into stereotypes. Conroy's confrontation with the school board becomes a David and Goliath–like contest, eliminating the original narrative's shadings, detail, and complexity. The islanders are made uniformly noble and wise in their simplicity, contrasted flatly with their cynical, racist counterparts in town. Thus, while the film's honorable intentions render it moving at times, its simplistic characterizations and bare story remain too cartoonish to capture the experience the filmmakers wanted to portray. This is unusual for a Ravetch and Frank screenplay, which could usually be counted on to supply a variety of beautifully realized characters.

Conrack—the film's title is derived from the way the students pronounce Conroy's name—is structured along the lines of the archetypal Hollywood "education/social problem" film, recalling works such as *The Blackboard Jungle* (1955), *To Sir with Love* (1967), and *Up the Down Staircase* (1967). Nearly every film of this genre develops around the arrival of an idealistic teacher at a school plagued with antisocial students who exhibit behavioral problems of varying kinds. The teacher protagonists in such films usually find conventional pedagogical approaches to be a waste of time; they try different methods of presenting the standard curriculum and discover that nothing works. Once they opt for more unconventional approaches, however, their willingness to meet the students halfway eventually produces results. The students learn to accept and admire the teacher, and they gradually become receptive even to education. Other conventions of these films are the cynical teacher who is eventually won over by the new idealist and recommits himself to his calling, and one or two especially troublesome students who, by the end of the film, side with the teacher. These films also take place almost exclusively inside the school, picturing little of the world outside and revealing little about the protagonist's life outside the school.

Conrack, like earlier films in the genre, concerns an idealistic teacher who goes not to an inner-city school but to an isolated island, where he finds not delinquency but extreme ignorance. After his first day, he rages at the principal: "Three children cannot spell their names. Eighteen children do not know we're fighting a war in Southeast Asia. . . . One child thinks the earth is flat—and seventeen others agree with him. Two children don't know how old they are. Five children don't know their birth dates. Four children can't count to ten."

Like his cinematic predecessors, Conroy soon dispenses with traditional approaches to education. Trying to wake up his students and motivate them, he throws a hodgepodge of information at them: facts, jokes, stories, pictures. He performs for them, jokes with them, fights with them, and romances them. Displaying the soul of a performer, he does anything to make them learn, taking them for nature walks, teaching them how to brush their teeth, marching them along the beach while throwing out questions. He finds a projector and shows them movies; he plays records, shows them paintings, and introduces sex education.

Unlike his predecessors, however, Conroy runs into problems despite his success. In the earlier films, administrators were generally supportive of their innovative teachers, but *Conrack*'s protagonist is opposed by a principal who insists on traditional teaching and by the school superintendent. The principal, Mrs. Scott (Madge Sinclair), is a black teacher who understands that she must please the white hierarchy in order to succeed in her job. She insists that Conroy be a strict disciplinarian and use the whip. She calls the students lazy and stupid and refers to them as "babies." Conroy's reaction to her demands is defiance: "We're off the plantation, Mrs. Scott—and I'll be goddamned if you're gonna turn me into an overseer."

Mr. Skeffington, the superintendent, is a zealous reactionary—"I never in my heart accepted Appomattox"—whose intolerance is exacerbated by his hatred of the 1960s counterculture. In one scene he is shown with Conroy watching the Washington moratorium on television. Skeffington calls the marchers "hippies" and "freaks" and advocates stopping them with "flame-throwers and tanks." In Conroy's book this speech comes from a local businessman with racist attitudes; in attributing it to Skeffington, Ravetch and Frank magnify both his villainy and Conroy's righteousness, for Conroy, too, opposes the Vietnam War. As part of the film's strategy of consolidation, the screenwriters thus transferred the reactionary attitudes of several characters into a single individual, here creating something of a monster whose unbridled prejudice strains belief.

Conroy himself is another of Ritt's outsiders, a man who lives by his own set of principles, which are generally antithetical to those of the society at large. Ritt, Ravetch, and Frank handle the ethical conflict less effectively here than in *Hud* or *Hombre*, where there were other well-developed characters for the protagonist to react to or against, as well as a recognizable world that these characters inhabited. Ritt's manipulation and transformation of established generic conventions added complexity to these films, but such social and psychological texture is not be found in *Conrack*.

Unlike the earlier collaborations with Ravetch and Frank, or even Conroy's book, Ritt develops no sense of the film characters' world, as he did so effectively in *Sounder*. Only a few rather generic shots of the beach and marshlands of the island are offered to establish a sense of place. The film pictures no real island community either, only a number of characters who are introduced briefly, seemingly coming out of nowhere. Quickfellow (Antonio Fargas), who seems literally to appear from the air, does an eccentric turn and then is seen no more. The role of Mad Billy, another island character, is expanded for Paul Winfield, and it affords Conroy the opportunity to teach an adult, but again the character remains a cipher. The film's exclusive focus is on Conroy and the kids, reducing most other scenes to mere filler.

Nor is any real sense of conflict in the classroom developed here, as it is in

The Blackboard Jungle and other films of the genre. The children here are young, sweet, and passive; it doesn't take long for Conroy to connect with them and win them to his side. Conroy's personality, as portrayed in Jon Voigt's engaging performance, is so infectious that both the children and the audience quickly fall under his spell.

To provide a little conventional conflict, Ravetch and Frank invent one character, Mary, a thirteen year old who has dropped out of school, introducing her at the beginning of the story in an elaborate crosscutting sequence that creates a parallel between her world and Conroy's. Ritt cuts between scenes of Conroy getting up in his apartment in Beaufort and preparing for his trip to Yamacraw—he feeds his fish and a bird, tends his plants, packs his suitcase, and hitches a ride to the pier—and scenes of Mary waking up in Yamacraw and preparing to greet him at the opposite pier. The poverty of her surroundings and their rustic nature is carefully contrasted with the affluent modernity of Beaufort. This deliberate buildup promises more than it delivers, however, for with the exception of a few brief scenes in which Conroy asks Mary to cook and clean for him, teaches her how to make biscuits, and counsels her about marrying, little is made of the relationship. Although at first she refuses to go to school, Mary, too, falls quickly under Conroy's spell and soon is attending regularly.

Eventually, in spite of his dazzling success, Conroy is fired. In a marked departure from the plots of the earlier films of this genre, even from the gradual process in the book, this rejection is telescoped into one central incident in the film. Horrified to learn that his students have never even heard of Halloween, Conroy decides to take them to Beaufort to experience the holiday firsthand. In the book the planning and execution of this trip is accomplished without opposition; even Mrs. Brown (the Mrs. Scott of the film) goes along as a chaperon.

In the film, however, Skeffington is adamantly opposed to the trip, declaring, "Those children don't need trips. They need fundamentals. They need drill and more drill." When Conroy makes it an issue of principle—"These kids are my responsibility and it's up to me to decide how best to educate them"—he is testing Skeffington's power. Defiantly, he takes the children, who even "trick or treat" at Skeffington's house, and the trip is an unqualified success. The next day, however, Conroy is fired for insubordination, and neither his personal appeal to Skeffington nor a formal hearing in front of a judge works to reinstate him.

The film's ending is pure Hollywood. As Conroy arrives at the dock to leave the island, the children are there waiting for him. They sit at his feet in a semicircle as he conducts his patented rapid-fire question-and-answer session for the last time. The children respond with all the right answers, making it clear that this inspired teacher has made a difference, that Skeffington's exercise of power is a tragic abuse. As Conroy is carried away on the boat, Mary plays the opening of Beethoven's Fifth Symphony on a record player. Conroy has introduced them to this music, telling them that it was Beethoven's way of confronting death— "Death knockin' at the door"—and here it underscores the mood of a moment that is meant to be both triumphant and sad. The majesty of the music invests Conroy with added stature as the boat moves slowly away. But Ritt concentrates his attention on the children, leaving his camera focused on their backs for a long time as they watch the boat, which has moved out of the frame. The implication is that the children are now conscious of their own desolation. Mr. Skeffington, the embodiment of the business of education, may have triumphed over Conroy, the individualist, but he has left destruction in his wake.

Pat Conroy, who visited the set and watched the filming of the final scene, wrote about a very different ending: "I remember my own inability to say goodbye to the children of the island when I realized that my long fight with the school board was doomed to failure. Mine was not a single farewell but a series of unsatisfactory, embarrassed departures, and later a rising awareness that the children I had taught were very slowly becoming strangers to me again." He even put his own spin on the film's moment of apotheosis:

> Despite the scene's essentially triumphant nature, what they had captured was the dark sense of loss that is innate in the teaching experience. What they had managed to convey is that there is always going to be a farewell scene, that the students will always be looking back at teachers as they walk out of their lives forever. . . . the book and the movie were symbols of the gods smiling on me again, but how, on pained occasions, I would remember that the same gods would probably never smile on the kids I taught on Yamacraw Island. They might smirk. But smile? Never. Outside of the movies, some very harsh scripts are written.[7]

While the movie does emphasize Conroy's triumphs as a teacher, in Ritt's universe, the system does not reward those who live outside the rules, no matter how talented, brave, or wise. Like Jack Jefferson and Nathan Lee Morgan, Conroy is crushed by a society that has no use for him. In *The Great White Hope* and *Sounder,* the evils of racism grind relentlessly away at the characters, although *Sounder* presents a possibility that David's pursuit of an education may lead to a better lot than his father's.

Conroy finds himself defeated not so much by racism as by a society that is frightened by the cultural revolution of the sixties. Conroy butts his head up against the walls of ignorance and fear rather than against the forces of racism, which are present but muted by the filmmakers' distracted focus on the revolution generated by the young protesting the Vietnam War. The victims in the film, however, are ultimately the black children of Yamacraw Island, children who have been marginalized by the educational system and doomed to a life of ignorance and poverty. The audience may be assured that a person with the vitality of Conroy will survive his defeat, but Ritt's final image is of the children who have been given a glimpse of a better world only to have it cruelly snatched away from them.

Despite its shortcomings, *Conrack* generally received strong reviews, including a very favorable notice from Pauline Kael, who had also loved *Sounder.* Many critics were carried away by Voigt's strong presence and the film's potent sentiments and popular values. Having proved a strong family attraction, the film received the National Screen Council's Blue Ribbon Award for March, although its box office never matched the hopes of Twentieth Century–Fox.

On the other hand, the film was attacked by some black leaders as exploitative in its glorification of the white teacher at the expense of the black children. This attitude was effectively articulated by Ted Lange at an American Film Institute Seminar conducted by Ritt: "I think this is a white exploitation film for white people, to come see and feel very good about a white man who goes into the South to educate some black kids out of the kindness of his heart" (AFI 7–8). He goes on to say that the audience never sees the white Conroy learn from the island community; the relationship is completely one-sided. Ritt respected this criticism, but he also refuted it, telling Lange that the recommended point of view was fine but it was not the approach he took. Referring to Conroy, he argued: "He gave them love and he gave them understanding. And taught them that they could be loved by a white man, that a white man could commit himself to their cause, . . . aware all the time that there was an incipient paternalism in the relationship. I was aware of that. And yet, I decided to do the film, because I think it was better than not doing it" (AFI 8).

A personal appearance tour to promote the film was marred for Ritt and Ravetch and Frank by an interview that Pat Conroy gave to Jim Stingley of the *Los Angeles Times* (April 12, 1974) in which he dismissed the film as a "syrupy, fact-lacking affair that thrills pie-in-the-sky liberals with its fairy tale fight against bigotry." He went on to say that he took the job on the island not out of any sense of idealism but because he "was feeling a draft." Conroy soon sent an apologetic telegram to Ritt, calling himself "Conjerk." He also wrote a lengthy letter claiming that he had been quoted out of context and blaming the incident in part on people's being "confused by his sense of humor" (RC 4-24-74).

Ritt and Radnitz discussed plans to collaborate on another African American project. Radnitz had commissioned the noted African American playwright and novelist Alice Childress to adapt her novel, *A Hero Ain't Nothing but a Sandwich* for the screen. Ritt liked Childress's screenplay and was interested in doing the film, but he was deeply involved in cutting *The Front* and preparing for its opening: "[T]he importance of *The Front* to me, politically and philosophically is such that I will not leave it before it opens" (RC 3-22-76). In addition, Ritt fought with Radnitz over legal details and over the fact that the reduced salary he had taken for *Sounder* (and was prepared to take for this film) had been made public and this interfered with his negotiations on more commercial projects. Eventually, because Ritt and Radnitz were unable to iron out all of their problems, Ritt's agreement with Radnitz and Mattel, which again agreed to finance the film, was terminated. *A Hero Ain't Nothing but a Sandwich* was released in 1978, directed by Ralph Nelson (*Lilies of the Field*) and reuniting Ritt's stars from *Sounder*, Cicely Tyson and Paul Winfield.

CHAPTER 12

Suburban Interlude: *Pete 'n' Tillie*

In 1972, the same year he premiered *Sounder*, Ritt also released the most unusual film of the last two decades of his career, *Pete 'n' Tillie*. Based on Peter DeVries's novella "Witch's Milk" (1968), this is Ritt's only mature film set in the contemporary middle- and upper-middle-class world. His first Hollywood film, *No Down Payment*, featured a similar setting, but Ritt had shied away from such material for fifteen years since and would not return to it again. Of all his post-*Sounder* work, this is the darkest—a film from which the pastoral ideal is excluded and, as a result, the characters are allowed no hope of redemption.

Pete 'n' Tillie was produced and written by Julius J. Epstein, who, with his brother Philip, had written the screenplay for *Casablanca* (1943). The screenplay remains faithful to the novella in rendering the events of the story: Pete Seltzer (Walter Matthau) and Tillie Schlaine (Carol Burnett)—her name is Shilepsky in the novella—are two middle-aged "singles" who meet, have an affair, marry, and have a son whom they lose at the age of nine to leukemia. In the final act, the couple separate and Tillie checks herself into a rest home but then decides to reconcile with Pete. Basically a comedy that struggles to absorb the tragic, the film unfortunately never balances the two moods effectively. Although it moves along at a moderately interesting pace, controlled by Ritt's discriminating direction, the overall design feels tentative and confused.

Part of the problem lies in Epstein's decision to refashion the central characters. DeVries's Tillie is a hard-drinking, calculating woman who has few illusions about men and is able to size up Pete accurately, appreciating his good points while recognizing his faults. In the film, however, she becomes a humorless, milk-drinking, dutiful female who rarely exhibits any personality or emotion; and Carol Burnett delivers a subdued performance that borders on the school-marmish, as if to defuse her lively television persona by draining her character of all vitality. The attraction between this mismatched couple thereby becomes inexplicable. Pete is a witty punster who does motivational research; occasionally he shows a rakish charm, but the film's Tillie never responds to it. His jokes leave her stone-faced, and her lack of spontaneity is depressing.

The imbalance is inverted in Tillie's attraction to Pete. Devries has Tillie recognize and reflect on Pete's admirable qualities: he is fond of Tillie's mother, inviting her to live with them when they move to the suburbs (in the film, Tillie's mother is merely a photo on her mantle), and both more devoted to their son and more sensitive to Tillie's grief in the aftermath of the boy's death than his counterpart in the film.

The jokes and wisecracks offered by Epstein's Pete mask a cold, cynical, and essentially hollow man whose affairs, which seem motivated by insecurity in the novella, seem simply nihilistic in the film. Both book and film present Pete as "the last streetcar or the last available lug of a life preserver thrown to a woman past thirty"—"The Last Streetcar" was the film's original title—but DeVries's Tillie finds Pete to be, at least at the beginning, a "model husband," whereas both of the film characters' choices seem merely desperate (DeVries 226).

Ritt places these people in a setting that lacks any moral or social dimension. If, in *Sounder*, the Morgans lived in a world of poverty and racism, they were bound together by love and a sense of community. The world of Pete and Tillie offers no communal values and no real family feeling. Despite its air of affluence and comfort, the San Francisco of this film is as spiritually empty as the universe of *The Spy Who Came in from the Cold*.

The desolate atmosphere is reflected clearly in Ritt's negative portrayal of religion. In earlier films, such as *Hud* and *The Molly Maguires*, the clergy's words and efforts are treated cynically, shown to be ineffective and inadequate in the face of tragedy. Here they are a bankrupt extension of a society in whose empty contours they fit comfortably.

Ritt introduces a priest early in the film, which opens with a party at the expensive Mill Valley home of Tillie's best friend, Gertrude (Geraldine Page). As she enters the house, Tillie is greeted by Gertrude's husband, Bert (Barry Nelson), who invites her upstairs for sex. This interchange is half-joking, but Gertrude's reaction reveals that their marriage is loveless and empty, striking the opening note of the film's central theme. The only other guest who commands Ritt's camera is the priest, Father Keating (Kent Smith), who arrives shortly after

Tillie begins to talk to Pete. Ritt emphasizes the guests' discomfort at his arrival, and soon Pete (who is only one-quarter Jewish) becomes openly hostile, insisting on the appearance of a rabbi and then asking about fixed bingo games at the church.

Pete's antipathy to religion is not examined directly here but merges neatly into his defensive habit of dismissing or avoiding serious situations by means of jokes or puns. In the novella Pete's bitterness is in part explained by his father's desertion of the family when Pete was young, but the film never brings this subject up, instead simply presenting Pete as an alienated contemporary man. Leaving a game of charades as Father Keating is playing out "God's in his heaven, all's right with the world," Pete comments to Tillie, "I don't think all's right with the world, do you?" Tillie, too, averts a serious conversation by commenting on her efforts to be friendly to Gertrude's dog. Both characters prefer to dance around their malaise.

The next scene to touch on the subject of religion occurs after their marriage, when they are living in the suburbs. Tillie makes a surprise visit to Pete's office, catching him near the elevator with a young woman. When Pete returns home, Tillie broaches the subject by asking Pete what to put down for "religion" on their son's private-school application. Pete, obviously disgusted, answers "head hunter," but Tillie persists, remarking, "you're three-quarters Lutheran and one quarter Jewish." Pete replies, "Put down Jewtheran." Tillie then segues into asking about Pete's girlfriend.

The linkage of religion and infidelity that opened the film is thus repeated here, as is Pete's expression of distaste for religion. Ritt's staging of the scene is, as usual, significant: Tillie is seated in a chair in the rear of the frame, while Pete kneels on the floor in front of the bar in the foreground. This composition recalls the scene in *Spy* during Leamas and Nan's first date at her apartment, when she asks about his beliefs. There Nan is seated on the floor as Leamas sits above her, forcefully expressing his inability to believe in anything. Eventually, as Nan moves behind Leamas and dominates him, Ritt suggests that both of their views are questionable. The repetition of this dramatic positioning exposes the hollowness of the Seltzers' marriage and of their lives, and the expressions on their faces make it clear that both of them are aware of it as well.

The parallels to *Spy* extend to other scenes as well. After their initial meeting, Pete invites himself up to Tillie's apartment, where his insistent humor and unsolicited advice on how she should dress make a distinctly sour impression. When he leaves, Tillie looks out the window as he crosses the street, and Ritt films this movement from Tillie's point of view at a high angle; the angle is repeated when Pete arrives for his second date. This technique echoes the overhead shots of Leamas entering Control's office, signaling Leamas's entrapment as he is observed from the detached perspective of his superior; here it indicates both the watcher's emotional detachment and the eventual entrapment of both the watcher and the object of her gaze.

The courtship of Pete and Tillie proceeds as a series of short scenes in restaurants, where she seems totally bored by his jokes and puns. When Pete proposes that they go to his place for "a spot of heavy breathing," Tillie accepts matter-of-factly. Just before entering his bedroom, she turns to leave and picks up her coat, but when Pete calls to her, she changes her mind and enters his room with no indication of pleasure or passion. Ritt places them on opposite sides of the bed as Tillie undresses, again emphasizing the distance between them. Only after they have made love does Tillie smile, seemingly for the first time. Soon afterwards, she begins to suspect that Pete is having an affair with someone else and promptly announces that it is time to get married. After a quick cut to a moving train—for the seventies, an awkward sexual pun—they are shown honeymooning; then a series of vignettes portray Tillie as pregnant as they move to a house in the suburbs, the birth of their son, and Pete's affair with Lucy Lund.

The breakdown of the Seltzers' marriage parallels the deepening illness of their son, Robbie, who is eventually diagnosed as having leukemia. The first indication that Robbie is sick comes during a scene in which Bert is propositioning Tillie; she turns him down as the parking meter near her car changes to expired, which serves as a visual sign that the breezier, comedic tone of the story has also run its course. The film then switches gears for its final fifteen or twenty minutes, becoming decidedly maudlin.

During the plot's final movement, Pete and Tillie struggle to cope with Robbie's death, then with their separation, Tillie's time in a rest home, and finally a reconciliation. Throughout, the stations of the Seltzers' cross are marked by glancing references to religion and God.

One effective scene comes after the family's return from a vacation. Upstairs Pete and Robbie are joking around, listening to the Abbott and Costello "Who's on First" radio routine, which is heard in the background as Ritt focuses on the outside of the Seltzers' house and the light in Robbie's window. Inside, the camera frames the doorway for a moment and then Tillie walks through the door, cursing God as a "bastard," then a "bully" and a "butcher." In her grief over her son's affliction, she becomes more and more hysterical, and Ritt's camera draws gradually closer to her face as she vents her frustration, demanding, "What's all this crap about mercy and compassion . . . Suffer the little children." She concludes by shouting—presumably at an uncaring deity—"I spit on you," three times. Ritt handles this expressive moment with restraint, keeping the lighted room with its sounds of the comedy record and the laughter of father and son in the background. This tonal counterpoint, along with the mellow lighting and the fluid movement of Ritt's camera as it approaches her face, provides a subtly sympathetic backdrop for Burnett's most affecting scene.

Next, as Tillie's voice-over announces Robbie's death in "the dead of winter," Ritt's composition is again dramatic: Pete is shown alone, leaning helplessly against a hospital wall, with a white corridor looming in the background, while Tillie sits apart, at the foot of the child's bed.

Ritt then cuts to the couple in their car on their way home. Rain beats down on the windshield that frames their faces, the windshield wipers cutting across this frame within the frame. Again the mis-en-scène recalls a composition from *Spy*, wherein Leamas and Nan drive toward the Berlin Wall for their escape, Leamas denouncing the squalid world of politics and espionage, remarking on the slaughter of the innocent. Here Ritt cuts from face to face as Tillie talks about a funeral service, while Pete seems indifferent to the "church bit." Ritt cuts then to the windows of the church, where a minister is heard reading from Robert Louis Stevenson; the service is coldly secular.

Sometime later, again at a party in Gertrude's house, Father Keating is again shown with Tillie, who forces Pete to leave early. The scene in their home after the party offers their most dramatic confrontation. Once Pete has settled in front of the television to watch a football game and "wait for injuries," Tillie asks him what he would think if she saw Father Keating and "embraced Catholicism." Pete claims indifference, inquiring cynically why she would make a good Catholic when she was only a poor Congregationalist. Tillie answers that she needs some help in understanding why they have been punished. Pete's reply, further demonstrating his absurdist view, is that they are both basically "good people" and that their son has died not because of "retribution divine or otherwise" but because of a bug.

Tillie refuses to be satisfied with this cynicism, and demands that he express his feelings openly. In a medium close-up, Ritt focuses on Pete's face as he drops his jokester's mask, responding, "I've made a study of true feelings. Most of them deserve to be hidden." The naked despair in Pete's expression here echoes the emotions of pain and anger, unadorned by social bravado, that Ritt captured on his face when Pete first heard the diagnosis of his son's illness. This technique of focusing in on the moment of recognition in a sudden close-up thus recalls both the moment in *Spy* when Leamas first learns that he has been made a pawn in a double-cross and the instant at the conclusion of *The Brotherhood* when Vince Ginetta realizes that he has damned himself through fratricide.

Pete 'n' Tillie runs down from this point, as Tillie gradually loses her tight self-control, culminating in an episode in which she turns a hose on her friend Gertrude. Devastated, Tillie checks herself into a rest home. The film then ends limply with a visit from Pete, who has been living alone in an apartment. As they walk the grounds together, a boy running playfully from his mother darts between them. Pete sheds a tear, the gulf between them is suddenly bridged, and they decide to go home together.

Although Ritt told a reporter that he was attracted to the project because he wanted to do something "less heavy," he did acknowledge the sadness at its core: "Life is like that. Few escape heartache" (*New York Daily News*, Nov. 26, 1972). While he tried to stress the adult nature of the film and its upbeat message— "They stay together for years, separate and go back together. And that's how it should be."—*Pete 'n' Tillie* turned out to be one of Ritt's darkest films (*New York Daily News*, Nov. 26, 1972). If *Sounder* marked a break from the mood of his sixties' films and signaled a movement toward a more open vision of community and social redemption, *Pete 'n' Tillie* cast a harsh light on a modern society that had lost touch with the communal, human values that Ritt treasured.

Pete 'n' Tillie is not a successful film. As a director, Ritt was not comfortable with stories of mixed moods—this would become even more apparent in *Back Roads*—and the more Chekhovian tones of this piece eluded him. These characters were not the kind of individualists he empathized with—they were not outsiders but exemplars of their social milieu, pitted not against society or a social-political issue but against their own weakness. Like *The Outrage*, a work that dealt in abstractions, this story was alien to Ritt's sensibility, and the mismatch is apparent even in his direction of actors. Except in the scene of her emotional outburst, cursing God, Ritt was unable to coax a lifelike performance out of Carol Burnett, who had not been his first choice for the part. Instead, he offered it to Joanne Woodward, but she turned it down, saying, "I just want to stop playing parts that start out, 'She sits crying in her bathrobe' " (RC not dated). Walter Matthau's sour, wise-cracking performance also lacks dimension, leaving his character little more than a mouthpiece for Ritt's own bitter sense of alienation from the emptiness of modern, urban society. The director's discomfort is reflected in the awkward handling of much of the material.

CHAPTER 13

Exorcizing the Blacklist: *The Front* and *Casey's Shadow*

After the triumph of *Sounder* and the box office success of *Conrack*, Ritt again found himself busy fielding offers and sifting through potential projects. When Joyce Haber of the *Los Angeles Times* asked him to name a dream project, he replied, "My dream project would not be any one film, but rather to spend the next ten years of my life making films about my own country. It's what I know best, and where I've done my best work" (RC 3-22-73). The remainder of Ritt's work would indeed be devoted to explorations of the American landscape, particularly its back roads. His next project, however, would not only tackle American history but also reopen a chapter in his personal history.

Prior to the release of *Conrack*, Lew Wasserman of Universal had agreed to let Ritt develop "the blacklist story." In collaboration with Walter Bernstein, one of his closest friends, Ritt conceived *The Front*, which would be the first Hollywood film to confront the blacklist. It was the culmination of many years of thinking, talking, and planning; it was a project he doubted would ever come together. While making *The Molly Maguires* in Pennsylvania, Ritt and Walter Bernstein had spent numerous late night hours discussing such a film, but they were unable to come up with any good ideas about how to do it without preaching—"Neither of us wanted to do it head-on, or in a documentary-type fashion because we didn't want it to be a polemic." In its original conception it was, however, a serious work: "[T]he film was originally about Hecky, the Zero Mostel character. Halfway through, Walter and I decided it was going to be maudlin and sentimental, so together we came up with the notion of 'The Front'—we

152

remembered the story because it really happened—and decided that's what the film should be" (McGilligan, "Ritt Large" 44).

The project was turned down by several studios before David Begelman, now president of Columbia Pictures—he had once been Ritt's agent at MCI—decided to put up the money for a first draft. The studio wanted a big star—Robert Redford, Warren Beatty, and Jack Nicholson were mentioned—but Begelman was willing to finance the project before a star was secured. Ritt remembered, "I've been waiting a long time to make this film and I will be everlastingly grateful to David Begelman for making it possible, because at the time he said O.K. I did not have Woody Allen committed to the film" (from production information). When Allen agreed to play the lead, Columbia gave Ritt and Bernstein the go-ahead to make the film.

The Front deals with the television industry, not motion pictures, and is rooted in Walter Bernstein's own experience. After World War II Bernstein, who had been writing for the *New Yorker*, worked briefly in Hollywood before returning to New York in 1947 and finding work in the then emerging world of television. He soon became successful as a writer of live television drama, much in demand, to provide scripts for *Studio One, Philco Playhouse, Danger*, and *Robert Montgomery Presents*. Bernstein was writing for *The Somerset Maugham Theater* when he first met Ritt, but their relationship was cemented on the series *Danger*, where Ritt was producing numerous episodes with Yul Brynner as the director. Bernstein contributed an episode entitled "The Paper Box Kid" for that series, tailoring the lead role especially for Ritt. Bernstein later recalled that Ritt tended to "over intellectualize" his acting roles and that directors had a hard time curing him of that tendency, but that he was, in Bernstein's estimation, an "arresting physical presence" (Interview). "The Paper Box Kid" won enormous critical praise.

Bernstein was blacklisted in 1950 when his name appeared in *Red Channels*, a book sponsored by "Counterattack," a newsletter founded in 1947 by former FBI agents to fight Communism. *Red Channels* listed over one hundred actors, writers, producers, and directors, detailing their left-wing affiliations. The announced purpose of the book was to "show how Communists have been able to carry out their plan of infiltration of the radio and television industry" *(Red Channels)*. Bernstein was cited for having participated in the Scientific and Cultural Conference for World Peace and the Civil Rights Congress, and for marching in the 1947 May Day Parade in New York.

He would be unable to work under his own name until 1958, when producer Carlo Ponti and director Sidney Lumet hired him to write the screenplay for *That Kind of Woman*, which starred Sophia Loren and Tab Hunter. In the early

days of his professional ostracism, Bernstein wrote a few scripts under pseudonyms, "but the networks became wise so you had to produce a front" (Bernstein, Interview). The process of finding a front, however, produced its own
twists and turns:

> In finding a front, you had to get someone who legitimately could be accepted as a
> writer, who could participate in a story conference, etc. Most people wanted money
> for it, so you paid them 10 per cent or 15 per cent of your writer's fee.
>
> Other people fronted because they wanted to be writers and wanted the credits.
> The fellow who fronted for me the longest was a friend of my younger brother. He'd
> written for a trade magazine, had no ambitions, and fronted for me because he was a
> friend and he was against the blacklist and thought that what was happening was
> rotten. (*News*, a Columbia Pictures publicity packet, 3)

But Bernstein's recollections also included some humorous incidents:

> In retrospect the practice of getting fronts led to some absurdly funny situations. One
> front returned a script to me claiming it wasn't good enough. Another front stopped
> working for me because his analyst wouldn't let him. There was another case involving
> a man who's a rather well known writer-producer today. He offered to let me use his
> name, and for a couple of times it worked all right. Then one night we both had a
> show on the air, one of which was his, the other mine, both under his name. Mine got
> good reviews, his was panned, and that was the end of that. (*News*, a Columbia Pic-
> tures publicity packet, 2)

Bernstein was one of the lucky ones who survived the blacklist. The ultimate
irony was that he became well known in New York for writing under different
pseudonyms:

> Once the story editor of a prestigious program asked me to write a show for him. At
> the time I had no front and said I'd have to find somebody before I could do it. But I
> couldn't find anybody, and the story editor called me and said the producer thought I
> was stalling. And the editor replied, 'The producer *knows* you have a front because he
> was at MCA the other day and there was someone doing assignments for them who
> said he was Walter Bernstein's front.' I said, 'That's not true. I don't know anything
> about it.' But it was that *crazy*. I never found out who the person was. Obviously,
> somebody was getting work by saying he was fronting for me. (*News*, a Columbia
> Pictures publicity packet, 3)

A few years later, after he could write under his own name again, Bernstein
himself fronted for a friend who was still blacklisted but working on a film for
Ritt. Then called "The Greatest Ride in Town," the project proceeded under a
number of titles—"Trolley Car" was another title—and engaged Ritt's efforts
with several producers. At one time he was preparing it for John Garfield, an-

other victim of the blacklist who was named in *Red Channels*, and later with Paul Newman.

Bernstein incorporated these experiences and others into his script for *The Front*, which would eventually feature several other blacklisted performers: Zero Mostel, Herschel Bernardi, Lloyd Gough, and Joshua Shelley. In fashioning the script he highlighted the absurdist, Kafkaesque nature of the blacklist experience, but the laughs would eventually fade as the film became darker and the nightmarish aspects of the witch hunt eclipsed the humor. As Bernstein told the *New York Times*, "The point to be stressed about *The Front* is that while it has a good deal of comedy in it—at least I hope so—it is basically a very serious movie, a morality tale" (December 7, 1975). As in *The Molly Maguires*, he succeeded in fashioning an intricately structured, layered, and highly literate script that would serve as a platform on which Ritt could build one of his finest films.

The Front does not make the mistake of trying to tell the audience everything it needs to know about "the McCarthy years," but focuses instead on how the blacklist functioned and how people responded to its pressures. The film presents characters who cooperate with the House Committee on Un-American Activities (HUAC) to save their careers and others who refuse to cooperate, often at the price of their careers and sometimes of their lives. Despite the complaints of some critics, Ritt and Bernstein's decision to present this subject as a comedy was a sound one. Bernstein carefully attuned his script to the essential absurdity of the situation, introducing as a protagonist and audience-surrogate a sweet, bumbling everyman who just wants to get by but who nevertheless gets caught up in the horrific moral dilemma of his time.

The Front was the first Hollywood film to deal head-on with this subject. Charlie Chaplin confronts HUAC in *A King in New York* (1957), a mild and uneven comedy about America in the 1950s, but that film's primary concern is satirizing American commercialism, with occasional broad shots at targets such as wide-screen American movies and rock-and-roll music. Whatever barbs Chaplin the filmmaker aims at the congressional committee seem gentle—at one point his character douses the committee members with a fire hose that has become stuck to his hand—compared to the reality of the treatment he himself actually received, and his HUAC subplot becomes just one of a series of awkward and anachronistic slapstick shticks in a movie that lacks both bite and focus.

The Front's story concerns Howard Prince (Woody Allen), an amiable cashier and part-time bookie who can never quite pay off on winning bets. One day a high school friend named Alfred Miller (Michael Murphy), who has become a successful television writer, asks Howard to front for him. Blacklisted for his liberal politics, Alfred can no longer get his scripts past the network watchdogs who report directly to the committee. When Howard agrees to become his front, Phil Sussman (Hershel Bernardi), the producer of a dramatic anthology show called *Grand Central* is so impressed with Howard's work that he soon makes him the head writer. Before long, Howard is fronting for two other blacklisted writers, Delany and Phelps (characters based on Bernstein's friendship with Abraham Polonsky and Arnold Manoff), living in luxury, and dating Florence Barrett (Andrea Marcovicci), a script editor who is in love with his "talent." He is thoroughly enjoying a reputation as television's hottest new writer.

The only hitch is that even Howard can't escape the madness of the Communist hunters. Although he has never had a political impulse of any kind, he falls under suspicion and is forced to decide whether he will cooperate with HUAC or defy the committee and so risk his glamorous new life. Making Howard a HUAC victim establishes the important point that the committee members are not really searching for subversives; they are just hypocritical publicity seekers looking for any scapegoats they can find in order to prolong their time in the spotlight.

The film opens with a newsreel montage of the fifties, showing the marriage of Joseph McCarthy amid shots of Joe Dimaggio, Eisenhower, Truman, Marilyn Monroe, American warplanes over Korea, bomb shelters, soldiers coming home from Korea, and the Rosenbergs. All of the bland visual imagery is ironically charged by Frank Sinatra singing "Young at Heart," and this distancing device, which is unique in Ritt's work, immediately defines the film as a meditation on history, not a re-creation. During the American Film Institute seminar he conducted in 1974, Ritt spoke of the problems of making a period film in New York City and referred to the project as a "talk film," which goes to the heart of its style.

In part because of the lack of exterior locations, *The Front* is very much an indoor film. Most scenes are shot in apartments, studios, offices, and restaurants, attempting little representation of fifties New York. Directing briskly and skillfully, Ritt manipulates space to disguise the essentially theatrical nature of his narrative, except when he wants to draw attention to the HUAC enterprise as theater. For the most part the historical era is evoked indirectly, through the portrayal of supporting characters like Hecky Brown (Zero Mostel), whose Catskill act reflects the period but also eerily parallels Mostel's own experience. Ritt also embodies the period in the television studio sets and in the office of Hennessy, head of a watchdog organization, whose wall is decorated with pictures of Eisenhower, McArthur, and other contemporaneous authority figures.

After the opening montage of pictures and song, setting the time and tone,

Ritt cuts to Howard Prince at his cash register reading the racing form. Bernstein's original script opened the film with a dramatic sequence in which Alfred Miller is told by a producer that he can't use his scripts and is then shown unsuccessfully trying to find a front, concluding with him in a theater watching a John Garfield movie. Ritt's beginning with Howard is a more effective narrative strategy, however, because introducing Woody Allen in close-up immediately confirms both the film's tone and its visual strategy. As Alfred walks into the bar, Ritt widens the shot to emphasize the narrowness of the barroom, and this gradually becomes a visual signature, as even in long shots, Ritt repeatedly demonstrates how space confines the characters rather than liberating them. The tight visual style plays off the comedy to create an uncomfortable edge.

The scene then shifts first to a chess parlor where, in alternating close-ups, Alfred tells Howard that he has been blacklisted for being a Communist sympathizer. The filmmaker's strategy is not to make the writers innocent of the charges, for they all admit to being Communists. This ready admission eliminates any element of suspense about whether the characters are rightly or wrongly accused, focusing the film's attention instead on how events affect the individuals involved and on the committee's ability to interfere in people's lives. It also allows Ritt and Bernstein to suggest a parallel between the writers' opposition to the Korean War and the current generation's resistance to the war in Vietnam.

The close-up strategy continues as the scene subtly shifts to a candy store, where Alfred asks Howard to be his front. When he explains that the front's job entails not only putting his name on another man's work but meeting with producers as well, the film's thematic focus on shifting identities is established. Unlike a film such as *The Spy Who Came in from the Cold* or *The Molly Maguires*, in which assuming a false identity becomes part of a Machiavellian government scheme with tragic consequences, here the device activates a Pirandellian masquerade whose comic possibilities are perfectly matched to the satiric wit of Woody Allen.

The Front marks an interesting transition from the early Woody Allen persona to the darker, more complex characters he would create in later films. It was his first film appearance solely as an actor in another director's project—a service he would not repeat until 1991, when he starred in Paul Mazursky's *Scenes from a Mall*. The character of Howard Prince is the culmination of such earlier Woody Allen film incarnations as Fielding Mellish (*Bananas*), Miles Monroe (*Sleeper*), and Boris (*Love and Death*), each of whom must confront social disorder, physical chaos, and the detritus of the modern world armed only with the sweet sincerity of the schlemiel/victim. This archetypal character is repeatedly challenged to negotiate his way through closed systems of cultural or political reference while remaining merely anxious and confused. Throughout his comic trials he struggles to maintain an alternative point of view as a way out of the absurd situations he finds himself in.

Bernstein's screenplay exploits these thematic oppositions within the delicately balanced dynamics of Allen's comic persona. Unlike his fellow stand-up comedians of the sixties, such as Mort Sahl and Lenny Bruce, Allen had avoided political humor; the events of the decade were rarely reflected in his material. His concerns were too personal, his world too self-centered to admit wider social issues. This determined inward focus is also a salient aspect of the character of Howard Prince, who initially refuses to be involved in the blacklist and who does not even know what the Fifth Amendment is. Howard's exclusive concerns in the midst of the McCarthy era are his developing relationship with Florence, his luxurious new apartment, and the gratifications of wealth and celebrity.

Like other successful comics, Woody Allen developed his distinctive comedic persona by becoming his own material. Allen's schlemiel character originates in his own personality, but when he exploits it as a stage persona, the relationship between life and theater becomes blurred. The comedian learns to feed off of his "real" self, which is the source and substance of his jokes. This concept is brilliantly exploited by Bernstein in shaping the front figure as a thematic device. Howard Prince's real self plays host to Howard Prince the successful front. The comic twist becomes, at least for a while, that instead of maintaining a split personality, the real Howard collapses into his persona. Like Walter Bernstein's presumptuous front, he even starts rejecting scripts for not being up to his standards as a "writer," and he lectures Phelps (David Margulies), another writer he is fronting for: "[Y]ou don't expect me to hand in just anything. I've got a reputation. My name's going on that script." He then pushes the gag over the top with the comment that he would like something along the lines of Eugene O'Neill.

As in his best films, Ritt's direction and mis-en-scène emphasize thematic parallels of character and space. Howard Prince's life as a cashier and bookie is presented visually as a closed, restricted environment. His one-room apartment is cramped and cluttered; Ritt provides shots of him crowded in by his desk as he deals with his clients by phone. Hemmed in also by constant debt, he must beg his successful brother, Meyer, a furrier, for money. In the scenes in Meyer's offices, Ritt emphasizes the narrow hallways through which Howard pursues his brother, asking for yet another loan while promising that his life will improve.

In addition to the story of Howard Prince, the film focuses on that of Hecky Brown (Zero Mostel), an actor on the program *Grand Central* (for which Howard provides Alfred Miller's scripts), an actor who is having trouble with HUAC. In his first extended scene, Hecky is questioned about his Communist past by Hennessy (Remak Ramsay), head of the Freedom Information Service. Ritt sets up this interrogation with a satiric thrust, cutting from a scene in the television studio where Howard has introduced himself to the producer Phil Sussman and to Florence Barrett and has briefly met Hecky. When the others leave, Florence compliments Howard on the "substance" in his scripts, remarking that they are "about people." Howard replies, "Well, if you're going to write about human beings, you might as well make them people." Ritt's swift cut to Hennessy's office thereby ironically implies that Hennessy is the very opposite of "people." Whereas Bernstein's script continued the scene in the television studio, showing Howard trying to arrange a date with Florence, the director's cut away on that profoundly absurd line of dialogue is both more dramatic and more thematically meaningful.

In Hennessy's office Hecky is desperately trying to clear himself, but his show-business bravado has no effect on the stolid and humorless Hennessy. Hecky admits marching in a May Day parade and subscribing to the *Daily Worker*, although he denies reading it—"From the mailbox right to the garbage can." He insists all of his suspect actions were undertaken only to impress a Communist girlfriend. Questioned further about a contribution to Russian War Relief, Hecky responds, "We were on the same side. Weren't we?" but Hennessy insists that Hecky write a sincere apology, "from the heart." Despite its humor, this scene effectively conveys the degradation visited upon the accused in the process and makes clear that the interrogators already had all the information about the people they were investigating; they just delighted in humiliating them. Hecky, a successful entertainer, here must give a command performance in Hennessy's political theater, enacting a desperate struggle to bridge the gap between what is real and what is not.

Ritt structures this ominous scene by reversing the symbolic positioning devised for the sequence between Control and Leamas at the beginning of *The Spy Who Came in from the Cold*. There Control walks about the room as the camera follows him, emphasizing his dominance and the entrapment of the seated Leamas. Here Ritt instead keeps Hennessy physically stationary behind his desk, implying that all he needs to control Hecky are his powerful accusations. Hecky is the one constantly in motion, restlessly utilizing the office as a stage but making no impression on his audience. Ritt's camera also draws attention to the pictures on Hennessy's wall, authority figures who function as a mute audience to the victim's squirming self-defense: Eisenhower, McArthur, Chiang Kai-Shek, and J. Edgar Hoover. At one point Hecky takes a seat by the window, hinting at his suicide later in the film.

The scene derives additional poignance from its real-life provenance; it was based in part on Mostel's own experience and on that of Philip Loeb, the actor who played Gertrude Berg's husband in the television series *The Goldbergs* (1949–1951). Loeb, like Hecky, swore under oath that he had never been a member of the Communist Party, but that denial did not permit him to work. Like Hecky, who tells Hennessy of the family he has to support, Loeb was the sole support of a seriously disturbed son whom he kept in a private mental home. Threatened by the blacklist, he feared that he would be unable to keep up the payments and would be forced to put his son in a state hospital. When Loeb lost his apartment, he lived for a time with Mostel and his wife (Bernstein, *Inside Out* 185). Five years after he was blacklisted, Loeb committed suicide in a hotel room by taking an overdose of sleeping pills.

In a subsequent scene, Hennessy asks Hecky to spy on Howard, whom he has befriended, to find out if there is anything suspicious in his new friend's past. (Hennessy's organization, naturally enough, can find no past history on the writer Howard Prince.) Ritt makes it clear that Hecky's guilt over his compliance with this scheme partly motivates his eventual suicide. The capitulation scene in Hennessy's office is again deftly composed. Once more Hennessy humiliates Hecky, forcing him literally to beg for his livelihood. As in the earlier scene, Ritt shoots the action with Hennessy seated and Hecky moving, but this time the pretense of a performance is gone; the accused man is pacing like a caged animal. At the conclusion of the scene, when Hennessy suggests spying on Howard, Hecky finally sits down, and Ritt shows him literally cornered in the left part of the frame, his face drawn and anguished. Positioned like Leamas, his freedom and dignity lost, Hecky, too, is being forced to assume the role of spy and informer.

Hecky begins questioning Howard as they drive up to a Catskills hotel where he has agreed to perform for a fraction of his usual fee. No longer working on *Grand Central,* he must pick up work where he can get it. Again the lines between actor and character are blurred, as this incident is based on Bernstein's experience of watching the blacklisted Mostel perform at the Concord Hotel in the fifties. As Bernstein recalled, "His performance was filled with rage—he'd keep breaking off to curse his audience, and the more he cursed, the more they kept applauding and laughing. He was brilliant and frightening" (Interview). Bernstein even incorporated that scene into the script, but Mostel refused to do it— the memories were too painful and he couldn't bring himself to relive them. Instead he performs a song-and-dance routine, "Anything for a Laugh."

In the office of the hotel owner (Joshua Shelly) before the performance, Hecky is told that his $500 salary has been cut to $250. The long, narrow, white office setting recalls a scene in which an actor named Harry Stone chases Hennessy down a long, narrow, white corridor, crying that he can't get work because he has the same name as that of a blacklisted director. Hennessy replies that he can only help those "who are willing to make a clean breast of they've done."

> Actor: But I haven't done anything!
> Hennessy: That's why I can't help you.

This absurd conundrum, so representative of the film's corrosive humor, is reinforced by the surreal visual setting of the narrow, white corridor.

This eerily elongated composition is repeated in the hotel office. Unlike the scenes in Hennessy's office in which medium shots and close-ups compacted the action in horizontal constructions, here Ritt projects a depth that is equally confining. Sam, the hotel owner, also has pictures on his wall, although they are to the right of Hecky, not behind him, but here it is Sam who nervously paces while Hecky remains seated. When Sam lowers his offer to $250, however, Hecky rises and yells, "I'm still Hecky Brown. Don't you forget that. You don't pay two-fifty for Hecky Brown!" But the man's assertion of identity and of the sanctity of his name—an important motif in the film—is as meaningless to Sam as Harry Stoner's declaration was to Hennessy. Sam's heartless "business is business" attitude is clearly interchangeable with Hennessy's corrupted notion of patriotism.

Meanwhile, in this same scene, Ritt marks another thematic development in the manipulation of dramatic images. As Hecky makes his declaration of personal and professional integrity, he is standing and then, in profile, faces screen left. Howard, who stood behind him throughout the scene reading a newspaper, then faces screen right. The two figures coalesce in a Janus-like effect, visually linking their characters. And indeed, Howard's process of change, in effect, begins here, when he merges with Hecky Brown.

In a scene prior to this incident, Florence arrives at Howard's new apartment and, after a passionate kiss, announces that she has quit her job. She can no longer tolerate blacklisting and has decided to put out a newspaper exposing the practice. But Howard refuses to go along, preferring his apartment to "living in the world." When Florence declares her belief "in personal responsibility," Howard refuses to budge, and she walks out on him. The scene with Hecky that follows then shakes him further and moves him closer to his eventual change of heart.

After the show, Sam gives Hecky an envelope filled with money, but when he finds only $250 inside, Hecky flies into a drunken rage and attacks Sam. As he is dragged out, screaming "I'm Hecky Brown!" Sam calls him "a Commie son of a bitch." This is the first time in the film that anyone has been called a Communist to his face, and it is at this moment that the comic tone all but disappears.

This incident, although reworked for dramatic and thematic purposes, was also based on reality. Bernstein had driven Mostel to the Concord, where he was to appear for $500 for one night. Before the blacklist, Mostel had commanded $3,000 per appearance, but now when he arrived at the hotel, the manager told him that his fee had been reduced to $300. Bernstein recalled that Mostel did not put up a fight; he merely shrugged and walked away. After the show, having consumed the better part of a bottle of scotch, Mostel demanded to see the manager, but Bernstein managed to get him to his room. The next morning, Bernstein collected Mostel's fee and drove him back to New York City (Bernstein, *Inside Out*, 190–93).

In Howard's apartment, the distraught Hecky proclaims, "It's all Brownstein's fault. I wouldn't be in trouble if it wasn't for Brownstein." Hecky is blaming his real self (using his true surname) for his inability to compromise and act as an informer. Later, Bernstein recalled that he had based this poignant insight on the experience of John Garfield, who was originally Julie Garfinkel and who died of a heart attack while trying to cope with the pressure from HUAC (Bernstein, *Inside Out* 197–98, and Interview). Howard at first doesn't understand, protesting, "People change their name, it's no big deal." But his own facility in subsuming other people's identities into his own will soon make him a HUAC victim as well. As with the comic persona, the theatrical self co-opts the true self, and in *The Front*, the real-life result is not an occasion for laughter. Bernstein had made this concept more emphatic in an earlier version of the script, wherein Howard buys himself a typewriter and tries to become a writer. He cannot even begin, however, and when he gets a call about booking a baseball game, he reverts to his true calling. These scenes were eventually dropped.

Hecky's anguished visit to Howard's apartment is followed by a series of scenes in which Howard becomes increasingly conscious of the effects of the blacklist. At a party, he is outraged to learn that a sponsor can dictate to the network whom to hire. He later tells Sussman, the producer, that he should take a stand against the committee. Howard's good intentions get sidetracked, however, when he is subpoenaed; and, visiting Alfred in a hospital room, he rationalizes cooperating so that everyone can continue working. Alfred disagrees and tries to raise Howard's consciousness, telling him, "They don't care about names. They care about getting people to *give* names." Later he drives home the point: "You always think there's a middle you can dance around in. I'm telling you there's no middle here."

This dire warning is soon confirmed, as in a sequence with ominously surreal overtones Hecky Brown kills himself. He walks to a hotel room and with a flourish tips the bellhop. The light goes on, illuminating a room that is bright white (like the corridor in the Harry Stone scene and the hotel owner's office). The action is played without words, as Hecky enters the room and tries the bed. A knock at the door is heard and a waiter enters with a bottle of champagne in a silver bucket. Again Hecky theatrically presents him a tip. After pouring himself a glass of champagne and downing it, he takes the bottle out of the bucket, cradling it like a baby, and looks at himself in the mirror. Only his reflection is shown, as Ritt repeats to high dramatic effect the frame-within-the-frame device employed so effectively in *Spy*. Hecky toasts himself and then takes a drink directly from the bottle. His image disappears from the mirror, but the camera remains on the empty reflection, until the sound of wind blowing in the room is heard and a part of the fluttering curtain is seen in the mirror. The camera's slow pan to the open window is made in one unbroken take; this remains one of Ritt's most cinematically powerful sequences.

Walter Bernstein remembered that Ritt and the cameraman, Michael Chapman, devised the visual strategy for the suicide scene on the day it was shot at the Plaza Hotel. Bernstein's script had originally called for Hecky to take sleeping pills, but Ritt's decision to change to a minimal representation of a leap from the window radically simplified the image of death, eloquently merging the motifs of theatrical gesture and assumed identity with the horror that was enveloping a country and effectively destroying both its human life and its soul.

The wrenching suicide scene is followed up and resolved in the image of Howard watching Hecky's funeral from across the street, while an FBI agent takes pictures of the people attending the funeral. Immediately thereafter, Howard goes to Florence's apartment, where he finally confesses that he is a front and reveals his true identity. In recovering his name, like Hecky, he rediscovers himself, and Ritt reinforces the parallel by framing his confession, as he framed Hecky's reaction when asked to spy on Howard, again focusing on the protagonist's head in medium close-up, as if trapped in the left corner of the frame.

The identification between the two victimized characters is sealed in the scene in which Howard appears before the committee. Initially he plays games with the committee's questions, as the old Howard would have done. When he is asked about Hecky, however, his demeanor changes and he expresses shock that the committee would question him about a dead person. When his lawyer asks him to give Hecky's name and the committee's spokesperson then asks for it, Ritt frames Howard in a tight close-up as he gets up, walks over to the committee table, then behind it, and announces that he does not recognize the right of the committee to exist. The film then concludes with Howard kissing Florence and bidding Alfred and others good-bye as he is led off handcuffed to board a train for jail; Ritt rounds out the action by once more playing "Young at Heart" in the background.

While *The Front* garnered its share of good reviews, it received some negative criticism, most of which assessed the film as slight and although basically good-natured, neither worthy of its subject nor equal to its noble intentions. After praising *Sounder and Conrack*, Pauline Kael called *The Front* a throwback to the forties' wartime movies about the need for the common man to become morally involved in the events of the era. She felt that it too closely echoed the kind of film written by those who were later blacklisted (*New Yorker*, October 4, 1976). Some negative comments were also aimed at Allen's performance, claiming that he was not up to the dramatic demands of moving beyond his comic persona.

Much of the critical frustration stemmed from disappointment that the first film about the blacklist was not angrier and darker. Yet, despite its comic veneer, Ritt's film is sharply satiric and damning of the witch hunters. Like a Pinter play, Bernstein's script offers comedy with an edge, comedy whose element of whimsical fun abruptly gives way to a mood of foreboding and death. It effectively embodies a chaotic, upside-down cosmos wherein people's lives are ruined by the mere mention of their names and it is not necessary for charges to be substantiated. Lives are controlled by self-appointed protectors who manipulate truth for their own profit, at the behest of others who deny that a blacklist exists. The absurdist possibilities of this perverted universe are fully explored in the film's comic mode, which here accentuates eruptions of the pathetic and the tragic. Howard Prince's story is juxtaposed effectively with that of Hecky Brown, whose fate is quite devoid of humor. The film makes no attempt to present an inclusive historical drama; its focus remains on how the blacklist functioned. *The Front* is, in Vincent Canby's words, "about plights," not "the ideological debris of those years" (Oct. 1, 1976).

Ideology, however, is neither skirted nor evaded. Alfred Miller and his colleagues admit to being Communists, although Ritt and Bernstein are not concerned with the political issue. Instead, it is the relationship between theater and life, not only in the victims' experience, but also in the actions of the committee, that draws their satiric fire. The film makes it clear that the "investigators" already had the names; what they wanted was spectacle. This ironic perception is *The Front*'s controlling metaphor, deployed effectively in its tragicomic plot and absurdist dialogue.

Woody Allen's Howard Prince, however, does present some problems. Although Allen projects his comic persona skillfully in the first half of the film, the role later seems to get away from him during the darkening turn from light comedy to pathos and death. Howard's gradual transition toward grappling seriously with the issues of the blacklist and with his troubled relationship with Florence is not convincingly portrayed. Part of the problem is that Bernstein has tailored his script too closely to the strong suit of his star, while Ritt, normally a sure-handed actor's director, allows Allen too much leeway, letting him take over the character instead of forcing him to understand and inhabit it.

Nevertheless, *The Front* offers a creative reshaping of the major thematic terrain of Ritt's world. Having explored the problems of informing implicitly in *Spy*, *The Brotherhood*, and *The Molly Maguires*, here, because of the historical nature of the subject, Ritt's judgment is made explicit. Howard Prince, like James McParlan, becomes enmeshed in a world that he knows nothing about, and, like McParlan, he develops relationships and falls in love. But unlike McParlan, Howard ultimately chooses to sacrifice his new success for love, friendship, and honor. Ritt and Bernstein suggest in both *The Molly Maguires* and *The Front* that personal betrayal and perfidy may be part of the price of upward mobility. But if McParlan is willing to buy into that ethic, Howard Prince finally refuses it. Although he is led off to jail at the end, he has found love and rediscovered his essential self. Like David Morgan in Sounder, this protagonist is left in mid journey at the film's end. Upon his release, he will face an uncertain future, but, like David, he has taken an important first step.

Ritt wanted to follow up *The Front* with a film focused on the stories of Enrico Fermi, Robert Oppenheimer, and Klaus Fuchs and their struggles to develop the atomic bomb. He intended to make the film with his friend, the producer Ray Stark, and the two explored various angles and treatments for "The Atom Bomb Story" before eventually abandoning it for *The Electric Horseman*, which Stark wanted Ritt to direct. On Ritt's advice, Stark hired Walter Bernstein to rewrite an earlier script that had been rejected; and Bernstein wrote the character of Sonny, a former rodeo champion and now a pitchman for a breakfast cereal, with Steve McQueen in mind. Robert Redford then got interested and Ritt and Bernstein found themselves out of the project, which was eventually directed by Sydney Pollack, with a screenplay credited to Robert Garland.

The Electric Horseman tells the story of Sonny's reclamation from drunken pitchman to hero, as he saves from a diet of steroids the champion racehorse he has been riding onto a Las Vegas stage, kidnapping and then setting the horse free in a canyon. Stark and Ritt eventually settled on another story about a racehorse, and it became Ritt's next project, *Casey's Shadow*. Ritt had always been enamored of racehorses—he was an expert handicapper and owned a number of thoroughbreds himself. He spent many of his summers at Del Mar, California, where he owned a condominium, racing his horses and watching the races. So, filming a story about horse racing was a natural for him, and he took it on with relish.

Casey's Shadow, which at different times during its evolution was called "A Horse of a Different Color," "The Cajun Colt," and "The Coon-Ass Colt," was loosely based on a lengthy piece of reportage, "Riudoso," by John McPhee. Published in the *New Yorker* (April 29, 1974), it chronicled the fortunes of various people who entered horses in "The All-American Futurity," the world's richest horse race, held annually at Riudoso Downs in New Mexico.

Borrowing atmospheric details and financial facts about the race, the kinds of people who enter horses, and medical information about unscrupulous owners forcing colts to race too young, Carol Sobieski's screenplay blends them into a story about a father and his three sons. McPhee's piece is reportage, not a story, as it is mistakenly labeled in the film's closing credits. Sobieski's story is her own, and like many of the scripts Ritt filmed, it uses source material as a springboard for what is essentially an original work.

The plot revolves around the Louisiana family of Lloyd Bourdelle (Walter Matthau), whose wife has left him to raise his three sons on a run-down horse farm where he trains quarter horses. His home is dilapidated and his truck barely runs, but he is good-natured and content with his life. As he tells one of his sons, "It bothered your mama that we were poor. That our horses didn't win much. It didn't bother me. I had my beer, the farm, you kids. It seemed like enough to me. More'n enough."

Through a stroke of good fortune, Lloyd ends up boarding and training a colt sired by a champion. The horse is raised by his son Casey, hence the name. Unfortunately, the boy can't resist racing Shadow on a bet well before he is fit to race. Having almost "blown out" Shadow's leg, Casey then takes good care of him and the horse heals. Then, before the All-American Futurity in Riudoso, in which Lloyd has entered the horse, Casey is tempted to race Shadow again in a five-dollar race and the colt sprains its leg.

Lloyd is torn between his dream of winning the big race—getting his name in the history books—and choosing not to race Shadow because of the risk of destroying the colt. Lloyd has raised his sons to live ethically, and the film implies that his scrupulous nature is in part responsible for his financial failure. Drawing on the information in McPhee's journalistic essay, Sobieski incorporates into the dialogue the danger and immorality of racing two-year-olds before their legs are ready. The "villains" of the piece are the trainers who will do anything to win, and they are contrasted with those who, like Lloyd, are more concerned with doing the right thing by their animals.

Lloyd is tempted also by the prospect of winning the money. His farm and house are in need of repair, he desperately needs a new truck, and he dreams of a vacation in Tahiti, "where women walk around without any tops on." But he is more interested in fame and the chance at immortality. He refuses a number of opportunities to sell Shadow to Sarah Blue (Alexis Smith) for more money than he could ever hope to win, and he also turns down the offer of an unscrupulous breeder, Mike Marsh (Robert Webber). His son Buddy, more of a pragmatist than his father, reminds him, "Mike Marsh is talking money, dad, not dreams." Lloyd, however, remains caught up in his dream—"To be in the record books. Lloyd Bourdelle. Right up there with Sarah Blue and God."

Like Jack Jefferson in *The Great White Hope* and James McParlan in *The Molly Maguires*, Lloyd loses sight of what he has while chasing a dream that will compromise who he is. Sarah Blue, the embodiment of Lloyd's ambition, reminds him of the blessings he has when she talks about her own failure as a parent, "I got three girls living in Houston. I don't know how many times they've been married and divorced, I can't keep track. And I got one at home, does nothing but drive her old Cadillac up and down the streets of Claude. Cussing on her CB radio." (Sarah's youngest is rather reminiscent of Hud.) Lloyd, unfortunately, is unable to listen to reason.

Lloyd is even more closely related to the Ritt protagonist who immediately precedes him, Howard Prince in *The Front*. Both are good-natured losers who jump at a chance for fame and riches, and both are redeemed only when they realize that they have lost sight of their deepest values and temporarily turned their backs on what is most important to them. In one case it is love of family; in the other, the love of a woman. Both films revolve around a theme very dear to the Group Theatre, "What good is it if a man gains the world but loses his soul?" Both comic in tone, *The Front* and *Casey's Shadow* allow their heroes the chance at redemption that is denied to Jefferson and McParlan, who are both destroyed by their choices. *Casey's Shadow*, like *The Front*, reflects the gentler vision that dominates much of Ritt's later work.

Lloyd finally does run Shadow in the All-American, against the wishes of his sons. Buddy confronts him, asking, "And when it breaks Shadow's legs. How're you going to face Casey? How are you going to raise him up the rest of the way? How're you gonna ask him to trust you?" But Shadow wins the race, and Lloyd is granted his moment of glory in the winner's circle.

In an uncharacteristic move, Ritt filmed the entire race in slow motion. In the margin of his script at scene 178, he penciled in "entire race—5 cameras." Interrupting the narrative flow of a film to draw attention to technique is unusual for Ritt, but he opts to do so here in order to underscore the race's thematic significance. The slow-motion finish had become in the sixties and seventies a standard Hollywood device for heightening audience involvement in a drama. With the protagonist's victory, the audience experienced a prolonged release that intensified the happy ending and confirmed the enduring viability of the American dream of success.

By filming the entire race, not just the finish, in slow motion, Ritt further intensifies the joyful experience, seeming to suggest that Lloyd's dreams of wealth and glory can coexist with his domestic success. This promise is abruptly undone moments later, however, with the news that Shadow has suffered a three-way fracture of his shinbone, and the veterinarian recommends putting the colt to sleep. Lloyd refuses to give up, however, talking the vet into operating and promising that he will keep the colt immobile long enough to allow the leg to mend. The operation is a success, Lloyd apologizes to his sons, the family is reunited, and all return home, where they plan to put Shadow to stud. Ritt thus allows Lloyd and the audience to retain at least some measure of idealism.

A number of significant changes were made to the final script. Sobieski opens her version the film outside Broussard's Bar, where Casey is trying to hustle a local kid to bet a nickel on a race. While this scene is used later, Ritt opens instead with a shot of the Bourdelle home and farm, as Casey wakes up and runs to the barn, the camera panning alongside him, to feed his horse. Ritt then cuts to Lloyd and his son Randy waking up and getting ready to go to Evangeline for the races. Ritt introduces the themes of family and home early on, as he did in *Sounder.*

The opening scenes also establish Lloyd's character. He forbids his son to race a lame horse at Evangeline Downs even though Randy insists the horse will win. (Lloyd, of course, will break this principle himself later in the film.) He also lectures Mike Marsh about raising his daughter on the road instead of giving her a more stable home life. Lloyd's devotion to his sons, despite the family's strained circumstances, and his steadfast good humor make him the prototype for Ritt's later protagonists: Norma Rae, Emma Moriarity, and Iris King, all single mothers who are raising children under very difficult circumstances.

Another, less telling change occurs later in the film when Tom Patterson (Murray Hamilton), an unscrupulous breeder and owner, fearing that Shadow will win the All-American, sends Mike Marsh to poison the horse. Marsh poisons Casey's other colt by mistake, and when Lloyd finds out, he pursues Marsh and beats him up. Sobieski's script had provided a more comic moment, having Lloyd trip up Marsh into a pile of horse dung, but Ritt's scene places greater emotional and dramatic emphasis on Lloyd's feeling for his son.

Ritt shot the film in fifty-one days, beginning at the end of August 1976 and finishing on October 25, mostly on location near Riudoso, New Mexico, although the earlier scenes were shot within a five-mile radius of Lafayette, Louisiana. Precautions were taken during shooting for Walter Matthau, who was recovering from a heart attack. Matthau claimed not to have prepared much for the part except by listening to some Cajun records to help him with the accent. "We didn't have the luxury of rehearsal . . . Martin Ritt will discuss a picture in general, what its social conscience should be" (*New York Times*, March 26, 1978). The film was made for about $3.5 million.

Ritt had several run-ins with Ray Stark after the film was finished. In January 1978 he wrote Stark to express anger at the "low level of technical excellence" of a trailer for the film. When Stark complained that some of the scenes in the film were "hokum," Ritt responded, "I am very committed to what I consider genuinely emotional material as witness a film I made called *Sounder*. I believe I gave every scene in *Casey's Shadow* what I felt it deserved emotionally. If it is hokum you want there are plenty of directors you could go to in this town. What I have to sell is a much rarer commodity" (RC 3-28-78). The film did not attract wide press coverage when it opened, but it drew respectable reviews; Judith Crist even selected it for Dallas's eighth annual film festival.

CHAPTER 14

Unions and Road Movies: *Norma Rae* and *Backroads*

In the seventies Ritt generally followed up a significant and ambitious film with one or more that seem slight in comparison. Thus *The Molly Maguires* was succeeded by *The Great White Hope*, *Sounder* by *Conrack* and *Pete 'n' Tillie*, and *The Front* by the modest but entertaining *Casey's Shadow*. Then Ritt seemed ready again to tackle a weightier subject, and he found it in the story of Crystal Lee Jordan, who was instrumental in helping to unionize the textile industry, particularly the J. P. Stevens Company in Roanoke Rapids, North Carolina.

Ritt became interested in the story when he read Henry Leifermann's article in the *New York Times* on the difficulties—physical threats, ostracism by fellow workers, and community hostility—faced by union organizers. In a 1978 letter, Ritt described his initial reaction: "When I first heard about the situation in this industry, I could not believe that I was not reading a period piece, and was further excited to find how many women were in the forefront of the struggle for civil and economic rights" (RC 1-10-78). When Leiferman eventually turned his article into a book, *Crystal Lee: A Woman of Inheritance*, Ritt bought the rights and determined to make it into a film.

Not surprisingly, he had trouble selling the film to the studios. Most executives found the subject matter too depressing, as did Alan Ladd Jr., the president of Twentieth Century Fox. Ritt countered by demanding to know what was so depressing about a story of a girl who becomes a woman, "who is as close to a complete woman of superior dimensions as any in film history" (*New York*

170

Times, February 25, 1979). Convinced by Ritt's argument, Ladd decided to back the film.

Irving Ravetch and Harriet Frank Jr. were asked to prepare a script for *Norma Rae*, which during its early stages was called "Crystal Lee." Ritt sent their first draft to Paul Newman, although it is not clear whether he wanted Newman to star in the film; some months later he sent a copy to Dustin Hoffman. He also wrote to Patricia Neal, offering her the part of Norma Rae's mother, "[N]ot the best part in the world, but it is a good part . . . would love to work with you again" (RC 2-22-78). The part of Norma Rae herself was offered to two prominent actresses who turned it down before Ritt turned to Sally Field.

While preparing the film, Ritt had some problems with Crystal Lee Jordan, who made it clear through her attorney that she wanted certain scenes omitted from the film; Ritt refused. She also insisted on script control, but Ritt declined to give it to her. He even made a trip to Durham, North Carolina, to meet with her personally, but as Ritt wrote to his own lawyer, "[S]he was not present at meetings, nor had she any intention of showing up" (RC 2-27-78).

Ritt also had some difficulty finding a factory to serve as a location for shooting the film. He originally intended to film in Georgia, which had been so hospitable when he made *Conrack*, but the Georgia Textile Commission, learning that Ritt was coming to scout locations, allegedly sent letters to mill owners advising them to prohibit him from entering their mills. Ritt eventually decided to film in Alabama at the invitation of then-governor George Wallace, who was promoting his state as an accommodating location for filmmakers. *Norma Rae* was filmed in Opelika, Alabama.

More trouble awaited him, however, in the search for a textile mill in which to shoot. Two mill owners, while not happy with the subject matter of the film, were even more outraged at the strong- arm tactics of the Textile Commission and offered their mills to Ritt. One eventually backed out, and when the other started getting cold feet, Ritt raised his offer for using the mill from twenty-five thousand dollars to one hundred thousand dollars, and the mill owner decided a film about unionism wasn't so bad after all.

Ritt maintained that *Norma Rae* was more about the maturation of a woman than about unionism. In an interview he gave in 1985, he discussed what had attracted him to the subject matter: "I read an article in *The New York Times* about this woman who sat down with her children to explain to them why she was going to be ostracized in town. I've known a lot of women in my life, most of them much more educated and sophisticated, who would not have had the balls that she had. *Norma Rae* is the story of a woman growing up and that's the kind of film I wanted to make" (Goldfarb and Ilyashov 20).

The human focus in Ritt's major films invariably dominates any more programmatic topical subject matter. The establishment of a union, therefore, while it is important to the plot, is not central to this film's theme. Ritt, of course, had explored the motif of labor solidarity in *The Molly Maguires;* but there, too, the relationship of Kehoe and McParlan and McParlan's sellout as an informer were more important to Ritt than the background issue.

The two films are linked more deeply by Ritt's continuing concentration on the effects of industrialism on human society. In the sixties he regarded the incursions of modernism and industrialism with a jaundiced eye, idealizing Old World characters like Homer Bannon, Frank Ginetta, and John Russell, who are destroyed by the corrupted values modern America, while vilifying others, such as Hud, Vince Ginetta, and McParlan, who have sacrificed their humanity for success and upward mobility, the by-products of industrialized society. *Norma Rae* is more in keeping with Ritt's major work of the seventies and eighties, in that it exposes the deleterious effects of a modern, industrialized world yet allows the protagonists to triumph over conditions that militate against growth and achievement.

Norma Rae opens with a series of shots of factory machines processing cotton into cloth, followed by a series of scrapbook photographs of Norma Rae. In the first of these Ritt focuses in on a baby picture until it fills the frame, enforcing an effective contrast of innocence with the realities of factory life that preceded the image. Throughout the credit sequence, he intercuts shots of factory scenes with still pictures of Norma Rae that show her growing older. Finally, a photograph dissolves into a close-up of Norma at a machine and then opens up into a long shot and then to a more extreme long shot of Norma surrounded and then dwarfed by the countless machines and the din they create.

Ritt's opening sequence is a minor but effective modification of Ravetch and Frank's original conception, which is retained in the published version of the screenplay. It offers only the series of personal photographs, with the sound of a camera clicking to advance them, followed by Norma Rae in the factory. Ritt's prefatory scene-setting provides a strong thematic statement of a life seemingly constricted and determined by the mill. Norma grows up and begins working in the mill as her parents have done, and Ritt's establishing shots of the factory environment that shapes her life emphasizes the restrictive nature of this modern workhouse, which Norma Rae will have to struggle to overcome.

The sense of confinement to mechanical process is most powerfully evoked in the long shot of Norma Rae surrounded by machines. This remains one of

Ritt's most powerful anti-pastoral images, a reminder that contemporary America has not progressed very far from the subhuman conditions of the coal miners in *The Molly Maguires*. Ritt hits this visual motif even harder in the film's first dialogue sequence, during which Norma Rae and her friend Leona are seen taking their lunch break along with Norma Rae's mother; Ritt, as elsewhere, confirms the claustrophobic dimension of their world by filming the characters framed by a window. The feeling of confinement evoked in all these sequences extends, as the story is to reveal, to the physical and emotional contours of Norma Rae's life. The separation from nature and the enclosed space of the modern world, which form the central visual motifs of the film's opening images, also provide one of its important thematic threads.

During the lunchtime talk, Norma Rae discovers that her mother has gone temporarily deaf from the factory noise, apparently a common occurrence. After taking her to the doctor, who angers Norma Rae by his lack of concern, they go home. Norma Rae lives with her two children in her parents' overcrowded and dilapidated home. As usual in Ritt's working-class films, the re-created environment looks and feels perfect. As he cuts from Norma Rae leaving the doctor's office to a shot of her mother outside the house working on her potted flowers, the expression on the older woman's face is almost beatific. This brief pastoral moment is quickly undercut, however, when in a reverse shot from Norma Rae's point of view, her mother is again framed, here by the kitchen window.

The scene in Norma Rae's home also introduces Reuben Warshovsky (Ron Leibman), the labor organizer who has come to try to establish a union among the mill workers. He, too, is first presented visually through a door frame as he talks with Vernon Webster (Pat Hingle), who insists that he wants no part of the union: "[Y]ou're all Communists or agitators or crooks or Jews." During this exchange Reuben and Norma Rae meet for the first time.

They encounter one another again in the next sequence, when Norma Rae comes into town to meet a married man for sex in a motel room in exchange for dinner and other favors. The scene at the motel, where Reuben has also just rented a room, is again filmed mostly in medium close-up shots that portray the characters trapped in restricted space. Norma Rae's life, it is suggested, is a series of dead ends—working in the factory, returning to an overcrowded home, and then going out to have affairs with married men in dingy motels. When Norma Rae decides to end the current affair, her rejected lover knocks her against the wall. Walking away with a nose bleed, she meets Reuben, who takes her in and provides ice for her wound.

The scene in Reuben's room is filmed predominantly in medium and medium-long shots, suggesting that this relationship will open up Norma Rae's world and expand her horizons. Noticing Reuben's books, she asks about them and then confesses that she has never met a Jew before. When she asks him what makes Jews different and he answers, "History," Ritt films Reuben from a low angle, from Norma Rae's point of view, thus indicating his significance, for he is the agent who will facilitate her growth.

Reuben is the only character in Ritt's work who must confront his Jewishness and talk about it. He is a classic outsider, a stranger in a strange land but also a kind of messianic figure, who will bring union solidarity to the mill and thus transform the lives of the people of Henleyville. In that respect he is like Conrack, a liberal reformer who introduces larger ideals and values to a closed community.

Ritt did not often confront his ethnic identity in his films. His first important Jewish character was Fiedler in *Spy*, a man who successfully exposes an anti-Semitic double agent only to be destroyed in a game of government duplicity. He is among the victims, like Nan Perry (who is Jewish in the novel but not in the film), who must be sacrificed for the sake of cold war politics. In *The Front*, Howard Prince and Hecky Brown are both Jewish, though their ethnicity is not so noticeable in the urban and ethnic world of the film. But Hecky, too, is destroyed by political forces, and Howard is eventually imprisoned when he discovers his political principles.

Ritt's Jews thus are not significantly different from his other outsider characters; though out of step with the status quo, they are shown to be morally and politically correct. In Reuben, however, Ritt confronts the aspect of Jewish character that he considers precious, presenting an individual shaped by history who is of necessity moral and ethical, who acts as a spokesman for the communal ethic. Reuben recalls the Jewish mentors of Ritt's youth, particularly Harold Clurman and Clifford Odets, passionate polemicists on behalf of the ideal of human solidarity, the bedrock of the Group Theatre experience.

Reuben's symbolic status and his mission are made plain in his dialogue with Norma Rae. He talks about the rare experience in his travels of being invited to stay with a family rather than rooming in a hotel: "But every once in a while, somebody'll open a door and put me in the best bedroom and treat me like I was a cousin." This is the communal vision promoted by the film, the closest thing to the pastoral ideal available in the modern world. Ritt films that speech in medium close-up in a two-shot with Norma Rae, the first such shot in the film. As Reuben speaks, he is looking not at Norma Rae but at a point in space, as if describing a faraway place that exists in the imagination. His meeting with Norma Rae will make that vision a reality, but at this point in the film, Reuben still has his work ahead of him.

Norma Rae is the first of a series of late films wherein Ritt articulates a version of the pastoral ideal that his characters are allowed not only to glimpse but to realize. He was to repeat the portrait of transcendence with an artist protagonist in *Cross Creek* four years later, when Marjorie Kinnan Rawlings would be allowed to enter a pastoral landscape but would have to learn to internalize its natural values in order to become a true artist. There Ritt would construct an isolated, lyrical world where he could meditate on art for the only time in his career. Norma Rae, however, remains rooted in real-world experience.

Reuben's evocation of the communal ideal is followed by Norma Rae's question about his being a Jew, thus making explicit the link between Reuben's Jewishness and his world view. Ritt's remark that "being a Jew has been an important part of my life and an important part of my talent" alludes to the same equation of Jewish ethnicity with moralistic vocation. In another context, in a letter answering a query about the Jewish condition in films, Ritt wrote, "I think the fact that I grew up as a Jew in itself has influenced the content of my films" (RC 2-10-69).

The thematic importance of community is enforced again when Reuben gives his recruitment speech at a black church. He describes the funeral of his grandfather, which was attended by "862 members of the Amalgamated Clothing Workers and The Cloth, Hat and Cap Makers Union. Also members of his family . . . They were black, they were white, they were Irish, they were Polish, they were Catholic, they were Jews, they were one. That's what a union is: one." During the speech, which begins with a medium shot of Reuben, Ritt cuts to a long shot of the room, including in the frame all those in attendance. Then, when he cuts back to Reuben, a painting of Martin Luther King Jr. is seen in the left corner of the frame, completing the iconography of humanitarian reform.

This scene is preceded by a sequence detailing Norma's maturation. She is courted by Sonny Webster (Beau Bridges), a mill worker, who makes his proposal beside a lake where they are picnicking with the children. (In earlier drafts, this scene begins at a burger joint and then moves to a field; in view of Ritt's penchant for water imagery, the change of setting is significant.) A brief vignette of their wedding and then various short scenes of Norma, who has recently been promoted to spot-checker, being shunned by her coworkers. Ritt himself even appears in a cameo, calling Norma a "fink." Norma resigns her new position and rejoins the workers. Hearing Reuben speak then seals her commitment to the union.

Once Norma Rae becomes a union member, the drama sags a bit. The scenes depicting union organizing are sporadic, and most of the workers seem so apathetic that by the end of the film when they vote in favor of a union, it is not clear how Reuben and Norma Rae have generated so much support. Also, Ritt makes little notice of Norma Rae's home life, alluding to it mainly in scenes in which Sonny complains that she is spending too much time on the union and so neglecting the family. Earlier script versions do provide more scenes of the family, including one in which a social worker visits Sonny and questions him about adopting Norma Rae's children, but Ritt apparently decided to streamline the story to focus more closely on the relationship between Norma Rae and Reuben.

After this the two go to a lake where Reuben swims while Norma Rae washes his clothes and then joins him in the water. It is the most idyllic moment in the film, with erotic overtones, as they swim naked together. Both reminisce, delighting in each other's company in their one shared moment outside the factory and the town. The earliest version of the script presents Reuben reading to Norma Rae from Dylan Thomas's "Fern Hill"; this scene was cut from later versions, though Norma Rae still does read Thomas. This scene at the lake achieves the spirit of the Thomas poem with its evocation of the beauty of nature and of youthful possibility.

Norma Rae's story reaches its climax in the triumph of the union. Her marriage to Sonny remains strong despite some setbacks and her extraordinary personal growth. Just before the end, Ritt offers an emotional set piece that has become one of the most often shown clips from his work. Norma Rae has just been fired for copying a notice from management designed to incite whites against blacks. As she is being escorted from the mill, she gets up on a table, writes UNION on a piece of cardboard, and holds it up for all the workers to see. In a series of quick cuts, Ritt shoots her first from a low angle, then in a medium close-up, then a long shot that takes in most of the room. Next, a series of cuts show various workers, followed by another shot of Norma Rae. Slowly, one by one, the workers shut off their machines in a show of support, as Ritt's camera slowly circles around her.

Like the final moments in *Conrack*, moments which were devised for the film, this is a real movie moment that has only a peripheral relationship to the actual story. In reality, Crystal Lee Jordan did hold up such a sign, for which she was arrested and fired, but no union solidarity was expressed by the workers, nor was there any vote for the union like the one that concludes the film shortly thereafter. By the time the film was made, Jordan was divorced, out of a job, and blacklisted by the southern textile industry. As in *Conrack*, Ritt, Ravetch, and Frank isolate the protagonist's moment of defiance and turn it into a moving and effective gesture of heroism.

The film concludes with Norma Rae and Reuben saying good-bye after the successful vote for the union, displaying the same remarkable restraint that has characterized their dealings throughout the film. Despite occasional hints at sexual attraction, the two never compromise their professional relationship; this makes it all but unique in a Hollywood film. They part without so much as a kiss, but with a strong bond that has been cemented through hard work and shared commitment. Ritt commented, "I didn't allow the organizer to have an affair with her . . . because he had to go on to another town, and, if the audience felt he was going from one town to another screwing every dame he made connection with, the whole moral fibre of the film was in jeopardy" (Goldfarb and Ilyashov 20).

Ritt also recognized the need to idealize his characters in order to get the film made and to ensure that it would appeal to a national audience. He received a letter from his friend Albert Maltz, a screenwriter and one of the Hollywood Ten, who both complimented the film as "a marvelous first that will always . . . be a reference point in the history of American film" and then complained about what he considered an inadequate dramatization of what a union would actually do for workers (RC 2-18-79). Ritt, although he understood Maltz's ambivalence, responded, "[If] I had gone the way you suggested, the film would have become too polemical to reach the kind of audience I want" (RC 3-13-79).

Ritt always remained conscious of the demands of his commercial medium, striving to balance his personal vision with the requirement of appealing to a mass audience. He never really got over the disappointing reception of *The Molly Maguires*; more than fifteen years later, he was still analyzing its failure to connect with audiences: "The picture was much too sophisticated in the sense that the audience in this country—a totally unsophisticated audience—really didn't know who the hero was. They weren't sure it wasn't Richard Harris, the informer. I should have made it simpler for them" (Goldfarb and Ilyashov 21). Norma Rae can be seen as a corrective to the commercial disappointment of the earlier film, but on a deeper level, it simply reflects the older Ritt's more optimistic reading of American history and his willingness to accept and even embrace the human spirit rather than turning away in disgust.

Norma Rae received almost uniformly positive and enthusiastic reviews, which far outstripped the film's box office. It was a great success at the Cannes Film Festival where, as Ritt noted, "they were delirious about Sally Field" (RC 6-14-79). It also received three Academy Award nominations, including "Best screenplay based on material from another medium," "Best Actress," and "Best Song." Sally Field won the Oscar, as did David Shire and Norman Gimbel for their song, "It Goes Like It Goes." But Norma Rae was only a modest commercial success, and Ritt blamed this on the mood of the country. In a letter, he claimed, "I think I have had enough of labor films right at this moment . . . I feel I should strike in other areas to speak my piece" (RC 6-26-79). At that moment he was thinking of shooting a film about American migrant workers in Florida, but that project never got beyond the talking stage. Instead, he would soon be going down South with Sally Field again.

In early 1980 Ritt was busy planning a film about the life of Joseph Warren Stillwell, who commanded all the U.S. forces in the China-Burma-India theater of World War II and later served as chief of staff to Chiang Kai-Shek. After some preliminary planning, however, the Stillwell project was shelved, and Ritt turned his attention instead to a project that would develop into *Backroads*. He had received a synopsis of the screenplay, then called "Lovers," in 1978. It was an original screenplay by Gary Devore, a young writer who was then developing several projects at Fox.

Backroads was eventually released by CBS Films as its first venture in making films for both theatrical release and television. As the couple who hitchhike to California, where they will change their lives, Ritt chose to cast Sally Field in the lead role of Amy, a prostitute in Mobile, and Tommy Lee Jones, whom he had liked in *Coal Miner's Daughter*, as Elmore, a down-and-out boxer and drifter.

The final script differed from the original treatment primarily in cutting back the role of Mason, a sailor on his way to San Diego and a pinball wizard, who picks up the couple and stays with them on their journey. In the final version, Mason picks them up, becomes infatuated with Amy, and convinces Elmore to bet all his money in a pinball contest, which he loses. When Mason discovers that Amy is a prostitute, however, he leaves them. Ritt cast David Keith in the role.

Ritt gathered his support staff of John Alonzo as the camera man, Sidney Levin as editor, and Walter Scott Herndon as production designer. He also chose Henry Mancini, who had scored *The Molly Maguires*, to write the music for the film, which also includes a song, "Tell Me No Lies," with lyrics by Marilyn and Alan Bergman. The film was shot over a period of two months, primarily in Mobile, Alabama, with some location work in Brownsville, Texas. It cost about $7.3 million, almost $3 million more than *Norma Rae.*

The film tells the story of Amy, a prostitute who works out of a hotel in Mobile. Earlier, it is established, she was forced to give up a child for adoption; now she occasionally watches him from afar as he goes to school. One night she is propositioned by Elmore, who, after sex, confesses that he has no money. Outraged, she throws him out, but Elmore follows her back to the street and promises to pay. While he is apologizing, Amy is propositioned again. This time, however, her customer turns out to be an undercover policeman. Elmore punches him, forcing them both to pack up hastily and leave town. Amy has an additional reason to go, for she has been warned by her son's adoptive mother that if she is seen near the boy again, her husband will call the police.

Elmore, who is charmed by and attracted to Amy, joins her on an odyssey to California, where Amy plans to give up prostitution to become a manicurist and Elmore promises to get a regular job. The rest of the film depicts their various adventures on the road to California. It concludes with the couple still on the road, waiting for another ride, but obviously now in love and committed to each other.

Amy is another of the series of strong, independent, and self-reliant women whom Ritt put at the center of his films, from *Norma Rae* to *Stanley and Iris*. *Backroads* also features the positive, upbeat ending, promising that the protagonists will go on to live productive and committed lives, that became characteristic of Ritt's films after *Norma Rae*.

This film, however, is not a successful work; coming after *Norma Rae*, it was a disappointment, partly because of Ritt's obvious lack of affinity for the material. *Backroads* is essentially a romantic comedy, conceived along the lines of *It Happened One Night*, but as he demonstrated in the humorous moments of *Pete 'n' Tillie*, Ritt was not a comedy director. This film in particular needed a much lighter touch than he was able to give it.

In Frank Capra's *It Happened One Night*, for example, the mixture of realism and farce creates a comic energy that builds from a succession of well-timed and intricately patterned scenes. *Backroads*, however, lacks any such dynamic coherence. Ritt seems to have wanted to give the film a more realistic mixture of comedy and drama, but the switching of moods creates confusion rather than complexity. The mishandling of material becomes apparent in a scene in which Amy and Elmore try to jump on a moving train. Elmore, carrying Amy's suitcases, finally succeeds in scrambling aboard, but when he catches Amy in his arms as the train moves by her, he is unable to hold onto her, and they both fall into a pool of muddy water.

This moment, clearly intended to be a lighthearted homage to 1930s comedy, does not come off, in part because Ritt does not pace the scene with any zest or energy, and in part because it is directly preceded by the scene in which Mason angrily rejects Amy after discovering that she's not the all-American girl he thinks she is. Elmore physically stops him from yelling and demands that he leave. Such juxtaposition of opposing moods and clumsy pacing undermine the film all too often, and the problem is exacerbated throughout by the undifferentiated handling of the comic and the darker moments.

Ritt also miscalculated by deciding to shoot too much of the film at night.

While the earlier scenes showing the street life of Mobile may have benefited from this touch of realism, the persistent gloom does not effectively convey the mood of a romantic comedy. Even a romantic scene, in which the characters discuss their pasts near a lake and move closer to each other emotionally, is so dark that Ritt's signature water setting is lost in a mis-en-scène that remains visually confusing and contradictory.

This muddling of moods is even more striking at the end of the film. After a fight on the bus, Amy and Elmore go their separate ways at a border town. Amy tries to earn some money as a prostitute but is stopped and threatened by the local madam, while Elmore tries to hustle his way into a prize fight. Tipped off by his trainer that his opponent is always late coming out of his corner, Elmore runs up to him at the bell and wallops him before he gets his bearings. His one hundred dollar winnings prove to Elmore that he is not a loser.

He gets back to the hotel room, however, to find Amy being roughed up by the madam and her henchmen, who burn a letter to her son and then knock out Elmore and take his prize money. Ritt films this abrupt reversal of fortunes as if it were a sinister sequence from a film noir, more in keeping with his dark opening than with Elmore's comic triumph in the boxing match.

Devore's original treatment also features a fight scene, but there Amy decides to demonstrate her confidence in Elmore by betting on him the money she has been saving to send to her son. Here Elmore's victory and their boarding the bus together for Los Angeles is more in keeping with the romantic/comic spirit of the story than the final mixed-mood sequences that conclude the film and finally overwhelm its structure.

Whatever comic or romantic possibilities the film may have had are further undermined by the writer's (and the director's) attitude toward all the film's supporting characters. Nearly every personage encountered during the course of Amy and Elmore's odyssey is either malicious or simply stupid. A happy ending hardly seems in order even for such nice people as the protagonists in so utterly corrupt a world. Of all Ritt's films after *The Front*, *Backroads* is the most ill-conceived and poorly executed work. It feels like the effort of an exhausted craftsman who is merely going through the motions.

In 1981 Ritt began working on what was to be his next film, *No Small Affair*, which was to be produced by William Sackheim and to star Matthew Broderick and Sally Field. He soon fell ill, however, and asked to be released from his contract. (The film was later produced by Columbia and released in 1984.) Because of his poor health, Ritt took some time off, but he decided to return to directing when Robert Radnitz interested him in *Cross Creek*, a property that stirred his imagination and fully engaged his creative energies.

CHAPTER 15

A Portrait of the Artist: *Cross Creek*

In an interview with the *Los Angeles Times* (Oct. 6, 1983) to promote *Cross Creek*, Ritt said, "Most of the studios try to make last year's hit and repeat what's worked before. That's not why I start a film. I wait for some impulse I have for the material. There are no other considerations." Of the director's contribution, he commented, "His movies must reflect himself. Skill is a marvelous weapon, but it doesn't expose you. It's the ability to expose yourself that distinguishes a director."

Ritt's work was always a reflection of his concern for the underdog, the outsider. With the exception of *The Spy Who Came in from the Cold*, all of his major films looked unsparingly at the evolution of American society and the individual's precarious place in a system that kept pushing him or her out. As the years went on, an increasing number of those films dealt with real people whose stories required only a little shaping for the purposes of drama: *The Molly Maguires*, *The Great White Hope*, *Conrack*, *The Front*, and *Norma Rae* were based on real-life individuals caught up in important historical moments. *Cross Creek*, based on the life of novelist Marjorie Kinnan Rawlings, continued this pattern. Excepting *The Front*, it is Ritt's most overtly personal film, selectively highlighting aspects of Rawlings's life and art to illuminate his own.

In 1928 Rawlings had left a relatively comfortable lifestyle in New York to buy an orange grove in Cross Creek, Florida, where she hoped to learn to express herself as an artist. Her life as a newspaper reporter and several unsuccessful attempts at writing formula novels had depleted her energy and her spirit. But in Florida she found that the land and its inhabitants enchanted and inspired her as a writer. There she was able to forge her own idiom in such novels as *The Yearling*, which won her the Pulitzer Prize (and became a much acclaimed film in 1946), *South Moon Under*, and *Golden Apples*.

Cross Creek, published in 1942, is a memoir of Rawlings's experiences at Cross Creek and her ruminations on nature and the country life. At its best it eloquently evokes the atmosphere of the North Florida backwoods, whose lakes and rivers echo the writer's surrender to a meandering rhythm of life. Her growing sense of connection with her natural surroundings and the discovery that what Cross Creek lacked in human pageantry was overcompensated for by the rich variety of experience she discovered in the land and in natural cycles comforted her and renewed her strength.

Ritt, like Rawlings, was an easterner who found his deepest inspiration in the rural South. Of Ritt's twenty-six films, nine are located in the South and four others are in rural locations. He once remarked in an interview, "I like the South. The essence of drama is change, and the section of the country that is most in flux appears to me to be the South; therefore I go there to make films" (Chase 45). This rather simplistic explanation of his attraction to his recurrent setting obscures the fact that much of Ritt's work falls within the pastoral tradition that forms a significant strain in American culture. Focusing on characters of low socioeconomic class living simply and harmoniously in a rural area, the pastoral typically locates its dramatic conflict between the sophisticated world in which the protagonist feels trapped and a wistful longing for a simpler life in closer harmony with nature.

Ritt's first major films to invoke aspects of the pastoral, *Hud* and *Hombre*, present its central conflict in bold, dramatic terms. This is especially true in *Hombre*, where Russell's outdoor life is threatened both by the death of his father and by the coming of the railroad. This basic confrontation also provides a framework for *The Brotherhood*, which contrasts city life with the more bucolic Sicilian countryside, and it is prominent in *Conrack*, wherein the island is contrasted to the town of Beaufort. One of the primary weaknesses of this latter film, in fact, was Ritt's failure to exploit fully that thematic vein, but he would return to it effectively in *Norma Rae* and again in *Murphy's Romance* (which followed *Cross Creek*). In these films a nostalgia for traditional beliefs, rooted in an agrarian past, plays against the alienation endemic to the modern urban world. Ritt managed to dramatize this conflict most effectively in *Cross Creek*, by identifying with the affinity Rawlings developed for the land and its hypnotic rhythms. He called *Cross Creek* "the most lyric film I've ever made" (Weinstein 12); and, indeed, it contains some of his most poetic images and richest pictorial compositions.

Robert Radnitz purchased the film rights to *Cross Creek* in 1976 and soon thereafter began developing what was to be his first film featuring an adult protagonist. It was his vivid childhood memories of *The Yearling* and the powerful film version of that novel that attracted him, as well as his admiration for Rawlings herself: "Marjorie was a courageous woman. In the late 1920's, she decided to strike out on her own, divorced her husband, and bought land in the wilderness of Florida—all because she had a burning desire to stand on her own two feet and thought she could become a writer."[1]

Her memoir, however, was not readily adaptable as a film vehicle, for it mostly consisted of Rawlings's meditations on a variety of subjects and yielded only a loose assortment of incidents that had to be fleshed out and knit together into a coherent story. Realizing that he needed additional material to anchor the screenplay, Radnitz sought out Rawlings's husband, Norton Baskin, who had courted and married her after her move to Florida, and who now agreed to serve as a consultant. The additional layer of detail that he supplied solidified the project, and Radnitz was later to take great pleasure and pride in the fact that Baskin admired the script: "One of the happiest moments for me was when he read the screenplay and called me on the phone to say that he was just overjoyed with it. He kept saying, 'I don't know how you could have captured so much of Marjorie. This really is Marjorie!'" (Interview). (Baskin even appeared in the film, in a cameo role as the Island Grove resident who directs Rawlings to the hotel proprietor, Norton Baskin.)

Radnitz received a completed script from Dalene Young, the writer of several memorable television biographies and dramas.[2] He then began looking for financing and promptly encountered the same problems he had with *Sounder*: the major studios admired it but found it too risky. While Sounder would eventually be released by Fox, Cross Creek was turned down by all the major studios. "Everybody said, My God, it is absolutely beautiful! A touching, moving story, but . . . it's not this . . . it's not that." One studio was willing to finance it only if Radnitz could get Jane Fonda or Meryl Streep. When another suggested Barbra Streisand, Radnitz struggled to envision it: "Well, I admit it's off-casting, but it could be interesting" (Farber 23). Finally the project found a home when Barry Spikings and John Kohn at EMI (an English company that had backed *The Deerhunter* and *Tender Mercies*) agreed to finance it. Radnitz later recollected that "they were prepared to take the project on the project's sake alone" (Interview).

From the beginning Radnitz had wanted Ritt to direct the film. Ritt shared his friend's an admiration for Rawlings and his ability to see in her life and work elements with which he could identify:

> I chose to film Marjorie's life because of her fierce need to express herself and the fact that she did it. I've been involved in the arts for forty-five years, and I have met a lot of people who wanted to paint or write but ended up falling by the wayside. They weren't able to fight. Talent is, after all, like the color of one's skin, a genetic accident. What you do with it is the mark of a person, and Marjorie made the most of hers. What intrigued me was how she became a good writer, and I believe that had she not gone to Florida, she couldn't have done it. I relate strongly to her strength and her need for self-expression. This has always been my need, too, and for a long time my kind of expression wasn't popular. (Yakir 46)

Having completed *The Front,* in which he was able to exorcise the demons of the blacklist, Ritt turned to *Cross Creek* to investigate his own need for self-expression as an artist. It is perhaps significant that these most personal films were made in collaboration with two of his closest associates, Radnitz and Walter Bernstein.

Ritt and Radnitz also shared a passion for location filming. In Rawlings's story especially, the setting is practically a character in itself, and so achieving a sense of place became integral to the conception of the film. Rawlings's own home had been restored as a state landmark to reflect its condition at the time of her death, and it had become a popular tourist attraction. But a paved, well-traveled highway now ran in front of the house; this would have seriously hampered the film's verisimilitude. Radnitz scouted locations in Florida intermittently for nearly three years before finding what he was looking for only a few miles from the Rawlings home: "It was exactly what I wanted, a huge arbor of trees, with orange groves in the back and water in the front where we put the set house."[3] Production designer Walter Scott Herndon designed and created entire period sets, including replicas of Rawlings's dwelling, Marsh Turner's home, and the settlement of Island Grove.

Cross Creek opens with a shot of a sunset over a body of still water. As the camera pulls back, it slowly moves to the left to reveal a narrow road that runs beside the water. From a distance a car approaches, its headlights moving toward the camera. In Ritt's films water is always a symbol (at times employed ironically) of cleansing and rebirth, as well as a pastoral image of peace and harmony. The intrusion of an automobile into this tranquil picture transforms it, evoking the classic sense of dislocation best described by Leo Marx's phrase "the machine in the garden." This archetypal juxtaposition, employed effectively by countless American writers and artists, also provides unifying thematic motif in both *Hud,* which opens upon a peaceful landscape horizon that is suddenly disturbed by the noisy appearance of a truck, and *Hombre,* which begins with a roundup of wild horses and then moves to a town decimated by the arrival of the railroad.

In these modern Westerns and such other films as *The Molly Maguires, The Brotherhood, Norma Rae,* and even *The Great White Hope,* however, Ritt was examining the effects of industrialism (the machine) on an agrarian landscape. The complex interrelationship of opposed forces formed a thematic thread that highlighted the schism this industrial assault created in American culture. *Cross Creek,* however, is not a study of society or history, but, like its literary source, a meditation on the restorative powers of natural beauty. It is not an overtly dramatic film even though it deals, in part, with the same nature-machine dichotomy as its predecessors. It offers, instead, a lyrical reflection on the life of the artist, the nature of art, and the pastoral ideal. Its focus is established when Marjorie Rawlings (Mary Steenburgen) opens the film in a voice-over: "My journey to maturity began in New York." Her journey, like Ritt's (which also began in New York), is a spiritual and intellectual one, and it supplies both the film's subject and its minimal plot.

These words, which Ritt chose to introduce his film, stand in significant contrast to the screenwriter's intended opening. Early drafts, including one labeled "final shooting script," start in a movie theater that is showing the film version of *The Yearling.*[4] The voice-over begins, "I never dreamed my novel *The Yearling* would be filmed," and moves toward the line that begins the released film. Both Ritt and Radnitz felt that the screenplay's opening reference to *The Yearling* made too explicit its connection to a similar story that was to be retold in the film. The more elegant, personal image Ritt chose instead made clear that his film's focus was to be less on the artistic process (which a number of critics still mistakenly seized on as its subject) than on the pastoral retreat from the modern world.

This thematic focus is further defined by Ritt's choice of the extended episode in Rawlings's life that he wishes to examine. His is not a standard biography, for he ignores Rawlings's varied experiences in Washington, D.C., Wisconsin, and New York City, and even the death of her father, all of which shaped her personality in important ways and preceded her move to Cross Creek. Instead, the film concentrates on a series of moments at Cross Creek, moments that solidified her sense of personal connection to the land and the community. Ritt reveals little of what came before, and nothing about what came after. The minimal plot is presented less for its inherent dramatic value than for its poetic resonance.

Ritt's camera also revises the scenes that embody Rawlings's spiritual journey in significant ways. Dalene Young's script devotes four sequences to the breakup of Marjorie's marriage to Charles Rawlings, including a scene in their New York apartment. Ritt telescopes those sequences into a single confrontation at an elegant Long Island party where Marjorie announces that she has purchased the Cross Creek property, and Charles decides not to accompany her. The action is further compacted as Ritt presents this scene as merely Marjorie's recollection as she drives toward Cross Creek. Intercutting the flashback with shots of the car on the road, Ritt links the disintegration of Marjorie's marriage and her stalled writing career with the artificiality of the world she is leaving behind; her confinement within the car represents her last separation from the landscape she is fleeing toward.

Her introduction to Island Grove, Florida, and Norton Baskin, the proprietor of its hotel, is heralded by a close-up of the car's grid, from which steam is escaping, signaling its breakdown. Marjorie must ask for a ride and so begins her life at Cross Creek by abandoning her machine. Ritt and Young have drastically altered the literal details of Rawlings's arrival at Cross Creek: in reality, Marjorie moved to Cross Creek with her husband and they lived there together for five years before the divorce. The film's concentration on Marjorie alone fixes its focus tightly on the artist's journey into the pastoral landscape.

The narrative of *Cross Creek* follows a number of story lines, which are only loosely tied together. One plot thread portrays Marjorie's acclimation to her new life as she refurbishes a dilapidated shack and makes it habitable, then, with the help of some neighbors, sets out to revive the orange grove that is to support her, and finally harvests the first crop. The film also chronicles her relationship with Norton Baskin (Peter Coyote) and her decision to marry him, as well as her affection and friendship for her maid, Geechee (Alfre Woodard). The most important plot line, however, is Marjorie's growing involvement in the lives of Marsh Turner (Rip Torn), his daughter Ellie (Dana Hill), and her pet fawn, Flag, all of whom will figure in her most famous novel, *The Yearling*.

The film was lambasted by a number of critics, particularly at the Cannes Film Festival, for seeking to dramatize an inherently nondramatic subject: a writer learning to write. Nancy Kinney complained that the multiple stories had the effect of isolating Marjorie and overshadowing her: "The vignettes, while interesting in themselves, overpower the structure that is intended to contain them." She adds, "The interpretation of Rawlings's role as primarily that of an observer muffles the abilities of Mary Steenburgen, destroys the film's cohesion, and prevents it from fulfilling its rich potential" (Kinney 116–20).

Steenburgen herself was aware of these potential dangers in the role: "Writing is essentially an internal process. To try to make that external has always been a trap for actors. You tend to get self-indulgent and overly dramatic. I don't know if I licked the problem but I don't think I make people cringe" (Farber 23). But her Marjorie Rawlings does not come across as a compelling character in Steenburgen's essentially emotionless performance. The lively comedienne, who was so engaging in her award-winning performance in *Melvin and Howard*, emerges in only one scene here, and her otherwise unsympathetic presence merits David Denby's comment, "She appears to have swallowed a pound of starch" (88).

The film's central subject remains, as the title suggests, Cross Creek itself, and Ritt stressed this point in an interview: "I had read several of [Rawlings's] books, and I was not set on fire by her at all. But I cared for those people [the characters Rawlings depicted]. I began to realize that *Cross Creek* is as much about the land and the community as about her career" (Pollock 9). Ritt might have gone further, to say that the land, the community, and the pastoral tradition are the film's real subjects, with Marjorie Rawlings functioning mainly as a filter for the director's vision.

Although it continues the exploration of the pastoral motif begun in earnest in *Hud* and *Hombre*, *Cross Creek* is not, as a number of critics inaccurately suggested, Ritt's homage to an ideal of American rural purity. Nor were the scenes showcasing natural beauty simply thrown in to cover up weaknesses in the acting or the plot; in an important sense those idyllic images are the plot. Early in the film, as Marjorie begins the process of cleaning her new house, she selects a record to play, and Ritt cuts to a stunning shot of the lake with a lone tree in the background. Marjorie then carries her typewriter out to her porch, overlooking the lake. Ritt composes the shot so that the lake is foregrounded and framed in almost circular fashion by the trees; when Marjorie sits down to type, it is as if she is entering that space. Ritt then cuts to an extreme long shot of her house, dwarfed by the lake, which takes up the entire frame, and this expansion of focus is followed by a series of shots of the land.

John Alonzo's lush photographic style establishes the power of the natural setting, as the editing and composition accentuate the thematic point that Rawlings is to be contained and embraced by the world around her. In these shots Ritt's camera remains divorced from his protagonist. What Ritt and Alonzo show us is not what Marjorie sees or even what she is writing about. (She is still working on her gothic romance at this point.) These visual references to the natural world are not called for in the script; Ritt deliberately plays upon this motif in order to shape the narrative to his own vision. Marjorie herself will have to enter Marsh Turner's world before she fully apprehends the pastoral landscape in which Ritt has framed her and before she begins to understand and internalize it.

The Marsh Turner–Ellie story is the film's central narrative, in which Marjorie functions primarily as an observer. In her memoir, Rawlings devotes only three pages to Turner, who lives with his mother in a decaying house, surrounded by a considerable number of hogs and cattle, which roam freely in the woods. After a number of incidents in which Turner's cattle have vandalized Rawlings's property, she sends word to him that either he must do something to control his animals or she will do so. The next day he appears, drunk, and proclaims, "The next time them cattle and them hogs comes over here a-botherin' of you—them's your cattle. Them's your hogs."

Rawlings finds him to be a contradiction: often a troublemaker and a drunken hell-raiser, he is also, at times, a chivalrous gentleman, as well as a music lover and an accomplished fiddler. She recounts the tale of his death at the hands of the sheriff, who has come to arrest him for damaging a stranger's house; Turner holds out his gun to surrender it, but mistaking this motion as a threat, the sheriff shoots him. Convinced that Marsh intended no harm, Rawlings describes his death as "the end of glamour at Cross Creek."

In the film, Marsh retains his chivalrous nature, his prowess as a fiddler, and his predilection for alcohol. His personality, however, emerges as an amalgam of several other characters from the book. One of these figures is Moe, who gives Marjorie a bed, and whose daughter she helps to save. In the film, Moe's relationship to his daughter has been transferred to Marsh and Ellie, and now it is Marsh who gives Marjorie the bed. Another significant incident in the book is that of Marjorie shooting Mr. Martin's pig. That entire sequence, including the dialogue, is incorporated into the Marsh Turner story in the film.

The film's most dramatic departure from Rawlings's book is in giving Marsh Turner a family: instead of living with his mother, he now has a wife and four children. The Turner family is clearly based on the book's Townsend family, and the "pound party" given by the book's Mrs. Townsend is hosted by Turner's wife in the film. The film's Turner home, unlike the original, is well kept, although Mrs. Turner, who seems somehow to have been destroyed by life at Cross Creek, has retreated to memories of the more elegant social world of her childhood. Marsh explains to Marjorie, "The Creek's hard on folks . . . particularly women." For his wife, the isolated natural world clearly has not been a haven.

Marsh's more compelling relationship is with his daughter Ellie, whom he adores. Against his better judgment, he has allowed her to keep a pet fawn, which, as it grows into a deer, is becoming increasingly difficult to control, breaking out of its pen and eating the family's vegetable garden. Marsh feels that it is wrong to keep the deer, and after an especially destructive incident, he orders Ellie to shoot it. When she refuses, he kills the animal himself, which causes a violent rift in their relationship. This leads to a drunken spree, during which he throws his liquor bottle through the window of a pool hall. When the sheriff comes to arrest him, Marsh is shot offering the sheriff his gun.

This story is obviously a variation on the plot of *The Yearling,* and the film implies that Marjorie will eventually use the material to fashion her most famous novel. In that novel and in the early drafts of the film script, the Ellie character is represented by Marsh Turner's son Paul, reflecting the actual fictional relationship between Penny and Jody Baxter. The transformation of Paul into a girl resulted in large part from Ritt's desire to cast Dana Hill, whose work he had much admired in the film *Shoot the Moon,* but it also served, in addition, to echo and enrich the story of Marjorie's development as an independent woman; for Ellie, by becoming head of her household upon the death of her father, must also learn to face the world alone.

Ellie's developing attachment to the newcomer is indicated in her inviting Marjorie to the "pound party." Marjorie accepts and promises to bring a cake, an indication of her growing participation in the life of the community she has discovered in Cross Creek. Soon afterward, Norton Baskin comes to deliver Marjorie's car, which he has fixed and repainted. At first she refuses the car and rebuffs his invitation to a picnic, but then, regretting her rudeness, she invites him to stay for coffee. The scene concludes as they sit, backs to the camera, with the car in the center of the frame and the lake in the background—Baskin has brought the machine back into Marjorie's idyllic world. The shot is thematically significant, for Ritt's composition suggests that their union will require an intelligent integration of the elements contained within the frame.

The "pound party" introduces Marjorie to the Turner family. Formally dressed and bearing a chocolate cake, she is greeted by Mrs. Turner with exaggerated social etiquette. It quickly becomes apparent that Mrs. Turner is "slipping away," for she insists to Marjorie that the weather is keeping other guests away, although it is clear that no other guests are expected. Ritt films the scene in a naturalistic mode, with little dialogue and no music. The only background sounds are the chirping of birds and the chatter of animals. The children entertain Marjorie with music and dance and then hungrily eat the cake in disconcerting silence, with Ellie giving a piece to Flag.

Such scenes as this dramatically refute the charge of sentimentality leveled by some critics at Ritt's film. With no bathetic overtones, Ritt confronts directly the psychological and material deprivation of living in isolation and poverty. His camera may revel in the physical beauty of the place, but he is unsparing in his depiction of the emptiness of the rural life. Ritt is operating within the Virgilian conception of the pastoral, as articulated by Leo Marx in his analysis of the first Eclogue: "This ideal pasture has two vulnerable borders: one separates it from

Rome, the other from the encroaching marshland. . . . Hence the pastoral ideal is . . . located in a middle ground somewhere 'between,' yet in a transcendent relation to, the opposing forces of civilization and nature" (22–23).

Marsh Turner acknowledges the difference between his world and Marjorie's when he brings her the ornate bed. In Rawlings's book, the bed is described as a valuable antique (115); in the film its elegance merely suggests a world other than the Turner home. Marsh also comments on Marjorie's newly painted car and house, and then he suggests that he will take Marjorie on a "gator hunt," an attempt to bridge their two worlds. Marsh apparently understands that Marjorie is becoming comfortable in that world "between" his natural one and the mechanistic Yankee world he alluded to earlier.

Ritt's camera reinforces her growing sense of belonging as that scene is followed by another shot of a tree and the water, with a voice-over by Marjorie, and then a medium shot of her typing. The camera has moved in closer than in the first shot of her on the porch, and the linkage of this diminishing range with Marjorie's voice shows that she is no longer so far separated in spirit from the land and water. The point is made even more emphatic moments later when, in another voice-over, she recites a letter to Max Perkins detailing her life at Cross Creek, again accompanied by successive shots of the countryside. Her words are lifted directly from the book: "If there can be such thing as instinctual memory [replaces Rawlings's 'racial memory'] . . . the consciousness of land and water must lie deeper in the core than any knowledge of our fellow beings. . . . We were bred of the earth, before we were born of our mothers."

In the draft dated January 4, 1982, the scene shifts here, but in the final version Ritt continues the voice-over as Marjorie and her helpers, Tim and Paul, are shown completing the irrigation ditch they started earlier. The shots of their labor and then of water running toward the orange groves provide strong images of the redemptive power of men's engagement in nature. Marjorie's voice-over then finishes Rawlings's meditation on the land: "Once born, we can live without mother or father, or any other kin, or any friend, or any human love. We cannot live without the earth or apart from it, and something is shrivelled in man's heart when he turns away from it and concerns himself only with the affairs of men" (3).

This is a clear enunciation of the pastoral ideal, underscored by pictures of people working to bring the land into harmony with their lives. Leonard Rosenman's symphonic score wells up here to enhance the scene's grandeur (for which Ritt is indebted to King Vidor's *Hallelujah* [1929]). The following scene shows Marjorie's first dinner guest, Norton Baskin, who declares his love for her, and the next depicts Marjorie bringing clothes for Tim's newborn baby. Thus Ritt assembles episodes from different parts of the film script to fashion a coherent sequence suggesting life's progress of renewal.

This hopeful movement is abruptly brought to a close when Marjorie's story is rejected by Maxwell Perkins. In a voice-over, Perkins (Malcolm McDowell) suggests that her truest writing is in her letters about Cross Creek and recommends that she write about her experience there.[5] Marjorie's subsequent natural rebirth is a bit overdone, as, in a rainstorm, she rereads the letter while walking about barefoot in her nightgown. Then, drenched and looking nearly naked, she reenters the house, sits at her typewriter, and begins typing. The rebirth imagery is excessive, even rather ludicrous, but this is the first time that she has been seen typing indoors, and the suggestion is thereby conveyed that she has finally become one with her environment, as her subject has become a part of her.

The final movement of the film parallels Marjorie's emergence as a writer with Ellie's coming of age. Having rejected Norton's proposal because she feels that she must remain isolated if she is to become a writer, Marjorie receives a visit from Maxwell Perkins, who, after reading her story "Jacob's Ladder," accepts it and offers her seven hundred dollars. In the next scene, Ellie interrupts Marjorie's writing to beg for her help in finding the runaway Flag. Earlier, at Ellie's birthday party, the deer's escape had created chaos; but at Marjorie's intervention, Marsh then allowed Ellie to keep Flag. Now the deer has escaped again, and Marsh insists that Ellie shoot Flag because "a family can't starve over the love of an animal." When she refuses, Marsh shoots Flag himself.

In the novel, coping with loss and hardship forms the thematic core. As Penny tells his son, "Life knocks a man down and he gits up and it knocks him down again. . . . What's he to do when he gits knocked down? Why, take it for his share and go on" (Rawlings 426). When Jody shoots Flag, he feels he will never love again: "He would be lonely all his life. But a man took it for his share and went on" (427–28).

In the film Marsh is unable to cope with the loss of Ellie's love; not even his liquor helps. The stoic resignation of Penny Baxter is not part of Marsh's makeup. Ellie's rejection leads to his death, but the double loss of her father and Flag forces Ellie to confront her own adulthood, and it cements her relationship with Marjorie. It also helps Marjorie to realize that solitude and isolation are antithetical to human happiness, and she finally accepts Norton. Love and the human need to connect, essential elements in Ritt's universe, triumph here. The affirmation of community is realized when all come together at the end to help Marjorie save her orchard from the frost.

Marjorie's realization is again connected with the water. After Marsh's funeral and her own rejection by Ellie, Marjorie takes out her boat and eventually falls asleep in it. As the boat drifts among lily pads, she wakes up, surrounded by water and greenery. This episode is based on the book's chapter "Hyacinth Drift," which appeared originally as a separate piece in *Scribner's* in 1933. Therein Rawlings recounts a therapeutic journey on which she regained a renewed appreciation of Cross Creek. She concludes, "I shall never be happy on land again. I was afraid once more of all the painful circumstances of living" (357). Ritt's version portrays this journey accompanied only by Rosenman's score. When Marjorie returns to the land, she, like Ellie, will be ready to face her life.

Having reached a transcendent appreciation of the land, the film's Marjorie recites Rawlings's own hymn to nature in a concluding voice-over, as Ritt offers some final images of the primeval world that has now become hers. The sequence of shots repeats the film's first framing sequence, which declared the camera's separateness from Marjorie. Now Ritt begins with a medium shot of Marjorie's house, the lake in the foreground, and drifts farther away as the voice-over moves from "I had become part of Cross Creek. I was more than a writer, I was a wife . . . a friend . . . a part of the earth" to "Who owns Cross Creek? The earth may be borrowed, not bought." Ritt then layers shots of the trees, the lake reflecting clouds, the stunning image of a white bird flying out of the water-filled frame. He concludes as the camera moves through the creek, winding through trees and forests.

Again Ritt has amended Young's script, which called for a picture of Marjorie and Norton embracing. Ritt's sequence of nature shots instead constitute a paean to the land and water, which, if properly appreciated, offer redemption. It is significant, however, that Marjorie's narration follows upon an acknowledgment of the need for community and her accommodation to the challenges of life at Cross Creek and outside it. Like his protagonist, Ritt reflects an awareness of the need to distinguish between the pastoral ideal and the realities of life.

Ritt would make three more films after *Cross Creek*, but this, his last film with Robert Radnitz, remains his most lyrical and his most personal statement, coming as close as he ever could as a filmmaker to embodying his own deepest values. *Murphy's Romance*, his next film, would explore similar themes in a more dramatic, yet prosaic form; in *Cross Creek*, Ritt attempted poetry.

CHAPTER 16

On the Road Again: *Murphy's Romance*

After *Cross Creek*, Ritt was about to take on the direction of *Roadshow*, which was to star Jack Nicholson, Mary Steenburgen, and Timothy Hutton, when he had to pull out because of health problems. Instead, he appeared as an actor in the Neil Simon–scripted and Hal Ashby–directed *The Slugger's Wife* (1985), playing a character loosely modeled on Tommy LaSorda, manager of the Los Angeles Dodgers.

While that film was being cut, Ritt became involved with another project in which he would again collaborate with Ravetch, Frank, and Sally Field. Ravetch and Frank had developed a screenplay from Max Schott's 1980 novel, *Murphy's Romance*. Ravetch and Frank were never strictly faithful to their sources, in many cases fashioning essentially original screenplays from the source material instead; and this was certainly true of *Murphy's Romance*, a rather monotonous tale of unrequited love. Scrapping Schott's work almost entirely, they retained only the name Murphy Jones and the ranch owned by the heroine (whom Schott calls Toni Wilson and Ravetch and Frank call Emma Moriarty). Whereas Schott sets his story in the desert locale of Pearblossom, California, which is still populated by cowboys in the 1960s, Ravetch and Frank retain the desert setting but place their story in Eunice, Arizona, with a contemporary time frame and characters who are simply westerners rather than real cowboys.

Schott's novel is narrated by Murphy Jones, who, after the death of his wife, sells his store in Oregon and moves to Pearblossom, where he marries Toni's aunt, Margaret. He meets Toni after buying a horse, which he boards at her farm.

Eventually he also buys the Auction Yards where horses are bought and sold, and these activities cement their relationship. Murphy falls in love with Toni, but she makes clear to him that romance is impossible. Toni, who lives in an apartment in town, has had numerous affairs and romantic relationships, and by the end of the novel, she marries an old friend of Murphy's and settles in Oregon.

Ravetch and Frank's protagonist is Emma Moriarty (Sally Field), a recently divorced woman who moves to an Arizona horse ranch with her twelve-year-old son (Corey Haim). She gradually falls in love with Murphy Jones (James Garner) an eccentric pharmacist who still drives a 1927 Studebaker, choosing him over her ne'er-do-well ex-husband Bobby Jack (Brian Kerwin), who shows up at her new home, moves in, and tries to win her back.

Like much of Ritt's later work, *Murphy's Romance* is a quiet, understated story which again, he had trouble selling to Columbia. The project's eventual approval owed much to the sponsorship of Sally Field, who was by then a big star and head of her own production company, Fogwood Films. Field herself served as executive producer, with Laura Ziskin as producer.

One of Ritt's main difficulties was over the casting of James Garner, who he felt was perfect for the role of Murphy. Columbia objected that Garner was not enough of a box office draw, despite his popularity on television, suggesting instead George C. Scott, Robert Duvall, Jason Robards, or Walter Matthau. But Ritt fought for Garner and eventually won: "I think he's been underrated for a long, long time. An actor needs a vehicle, the right material, the right script and the right director in order to achieve what he is capable of achieving" (*Chicago Tribune*, Jan. 16, 1986). His confidence was rewarded when Garner was nominated for an Academy Award as Best Actor.

Ritt shot most of the film on location in Florence, Arizona, completing it in fifty-five days, a day ahead of schedule, and at a cost of $11.5 million, a rock-bottom figure in 1985. *Murphy's Romance* initially did quite well at the box office: in April 1986 *Variety* reported that it was among the ten top-grossing films in Los Angeles in its first thirteen weeks.

Hiring William Fraker, with whom he had worked on *Roadshow*, as his cameraman, Ritt described the film to him as "romantic": "It's a love story and it's an optimistic film. It's a comedy in the classic sense and in the actual sense, which means it has a happy ending. I wanted the picture to look good and rich" (Harnisch 30). Fraker achieved this effect by shooting numerous scenes at dusk. Ritt remarked, "There's a lot of magic-hour shooting, with a series of scenes set in the late afternoon in which characters are invited to dinner or go for rides in the country. It's difficult to shoot because there isn't much time, so it must be well-prepared. All of it is very handsome to look at" (Harnisch 30).

Murphy's Romance is a logical follow-up to *Cross Creek*, repeating its basic focus on a recently divorced woman who leaves her home to strike out on her own in a new locale. Both films deal with the maturation of this protagonist, although *Cross Creek* is more concerned with artistic and intellectual growth; *Murphy's Romance*, with emotional change. Emma Moriarty and Marjorie Rawlings both fall in love again, and both films end with the promise of renewal through marriage. Harriet Frank Jr., who co-wrote *Murphy's Romance*, described her view of the film: "It's a triangle involving a woman who's finding her spiritual and emotional center. It's about becoming an adult in one's emotional choices. Climbing out of the playpen and falling in love grown-up. It's about people picking up the tab and having a sense of responsibility for their lives. The ultimate sign of maturity is to pick up the tab, to pay one's way in every way— emotionally, professionally, and humanly" (press kit).

More tightly structured than *Cross Creek*, its dramatic line firmer and leaner, its central characters more full-bodied, *Murphy's Romance* is a less visually and thematically ambitious work that still manages to extend Ritt's exploration of the pastoral ideal within a mechanized and increasingly modernized society. His determination to emphasize these themes is indicated in a studio memo describing the planned location as "dry, tough cattle country . . . Big skies, far-reaching vistas."

The film begins with a shot that recalls the opening of *Cross Creek*. A nearly still picture of the moon over a desert landscape, with a road running through the middle and a mountain in the background, is soon animated by lights in the distance, as a truck appears traveling along the road. It disappears, and then there is a cut to morning, where again the truck is seen moving along the road. Inside a woman (Emma) is driving, her son asleep beside her. The camera shows all their possessions tied to the back of the truck, and then it moves around the back to the driver's side to rest on Emma in a medium-close profile as she drives.

Much like Marjorie, Emma arrives at a run-down house, and again there are scenes of her cleaning up the house, moving in her furniture, repairing fences, and painting. The last thing she does during this sequence is to pull a flowering plant from the ground, pot it, and place it above the fireplace. As she does so, the final credit, "Directed by Martin Ritt," comes on screen. It is a signature moment, the merging of the natural world with the domestic one that Emma will build for herself and her son.

After this homemaking sequence Emma repairs the hot walker, recalling Marjorie's achievement in starting the generator. In each case the machine is part of

the rural world, and in each case a woman's mastering of the machine is drama-
tized as a triumphant moment. In *Murphy* the presence of the modern is made
even more apparent by Ritt's inclusion of telephone lines in a number of early
shots. In Ravetch and Frank's script, the moving into the house and the repair
work to the barn area are interrupted by Emma's going to town, but Ritt keeps
the farm scenes together, making for a unified sequence. Only after doing some
work on the barn does Emma go into Florence.

The transition is accentuated by the cut to town, which offers at first an extreme close-up of a flyer advertising Emma's horse training and boarding business. The camera pulls back to show that there are flyers on the windshields of
several dozen cars in a parking lot. The movement from Emma's isolated farm
to the parking lot is dramatic, emphasizing that this small western town is very
much a part of the modern world. Ritt provides an amusing comic spin on this
perception as Emma, who continues to place her flyers on cars parked in the
business area, tries to put one on the windshield of a 1927 Studebaker that already
features "No Nukes" and "Reforest America" stickers.

This car belongs, of course, to Murphy Jones, owner of the town's pharmacy
and spokesman for the values of the individual and personal responsibility. Murphy objects that Emma's flyer is covering up his causes, but he lets her put her
ad in his store window, explaining, "I'm for free enterprise." As Emma enters
his store, Ritt's camera follows to take in the interior, which is a reflection of
Murphy himself—immaculate and old-fashioned, with a long, marble counter
and burnished oak fittings. The soda fountain instruments are gleaming, suggesting the thirties and forties rather than the eighties. Murphy serves Emma a lemon
coke made with a real lemon grown in his backyard.

Murphy tells Emma that he has lived in the town all of his life; when she asks
him to describe it, he replies, "[W]e've got a Rhodes scholar, we've got a homo-
sexual, we've got marijuana growing in the tomatoes, we've got a man wearing
his wife's nightgown. We're in the mainstream." Emma complains that they
haven't made it quite yet, because "this morning I got called honey, missey, and
little lady," and Murphy responds, "If it's consciousness-raising your looking
for, better head East." His point is to be driven home to Emma later when she
is turned down for a business loan in large part because she is a single woman.

The eccentricity characteristic of both Murphy and the town he lives in is
revealed when he objects to putting coins in the meter for his parked car and he
pays over two hundred dollars in tickets rather than deal with the meter. He
considers his car an inheritance, and he insists on parking it where he can keep
his eye on it. When he offers to plant a tree in the meter's place on the sidewalk,

the town accedes, and soon Murphy's store is shaded by the tree, which links him to Emma and her potted plant, joining them as advocates of a pastoral ideal.

It is apparent from Murphy and Emma's first meeting that they will fall in love. The film's considerable appeal therefore, is created not by suspenseful plotting, but by Ritt's patient handling of the comic courtship formula; he lets the characters reveal themselves gradually to the audience as they do so to each other. *Murphy's Romance* is a richly observed film, focusing on how its mildly eccentric characters behave in a specific time and place. Such close attention to the colorful particulars of personality and place was one of the hallmarks of *Sounder*, and it would be the primary theme of Ritt's work in his final film, *Stanley and Iris*.

In an early scene in which Emma and her son, Jake, go into town one evening, Ritt takes the time to observe the people coming and going, the displays in the store windows, teenagers roughing it up on the back of a truck. At one point the camera follows Emma at a distance as she crosses a street, and then, as she leaves the frame, its focus remains fixed to observe more of the street life. As in *Sounder* and *Cross Creek*, not only does the setting become a character in the film, but its role in shaping the character of the people who live there is made central to Ritt's design. Indeed, Ritt chose to film in Florence, Arizona, in large part because its physical layout accommodated his design: "It has a main street that everything opens on to. If your shooting in the drugstore or cafe or wherever; as you turn to the entrance you're shooting the center of town, so there's always a certain amount of life in each shot" (press kit).

While in town, Emma and Jake are drawn to the sound of music, and following it, they come across a dance, where Murphy is discovered playing the fiddle in the band. Again Ritt's camera shows Emma observing Murphy as he plays while dancers in the foreground fill the frame with action and life. Emma smiles when she sees him; the camera observes this, although Murphy does not.

This visual strategy of establishing connections between characters is repeated in the drugstore when Emma comes in to vent her frustration after being turned down for a loan. As she complains to Murphy, their exchange is filmed in medium long shots as Murphy remains spatially separated from her. When he comes closer and stands behind the counter, Ritt films their exchange in shot–reverse shot sequences without ever bringing them together.

The nearer approach of this distanced couple finally comes about during the horse auction, where Emma helps Murphy buy a horse. Horses, a passion of Ritt's, regularly appear as a symbol of the majesty and beauty of nature in his films, from *Hombre* to *Casey's Shadow*, and they also function, like the water imagery in *Cross Creek*, as a natural force that pulls together the lives of the people around them. It is no accident that in this film, which lacks a water scene, Murphy and Emma come together at the auction. After buying a horse, Murphy tells Emma that he will board it at her farm.

This scene is preceded by one in which Murphy takes Jake out for a drive through the countryside surrounding Florence. Murphy's "inheritance" motors slowly down the road, seemingly very much a part of the quiet farm community that surrounds him. Like Marjorie's car, Murphy's Studebaker is a reminder of the modern world, neatly accommodated amid the unified pastoral images of the film. This sequence, followed by the auction at which Murphy buys a horse, brings the three together and, at the same time, unites Murphy and the town with Emma and her farm.

This linkage becomes stronger in a montage of scenes showing Emma training Murphy's horse while he watches. In the first two sequences, Ritt again keeps the two in separate frames, although the scene of Murphy watching Emma ride his horse is sexually suggestive. Ritt dropped from the earlier scripts a scene in which Murphy tries to ride and is thrown by the horse; such an episode would not be in keeping with the mood of the scenes demonstrating their increasing attraction.

The evolving relationship of Murphy and Emma is suddenly disrupted by the arrival of her ex-husband, Bobby Jack, an immature and irresponsible sweet-talker. Emma describes him succinctly when she challenges him, "How come you were never as good on your feet as you were in bed?" Reluctantly, however, she lets him move in because Jake likes having his father back.

The episodes illustrating Bobby Jack's feckless charm constitute the film's major weakness, for they go on too long and grow increasingly heavy-handed. It is quite apparent early on what kind of man Bobby Jack is without multiplying the examples of his inadequacy. When at last another girlfriend arrives from Tulsa with the twins he fathered, Emma tells him it's time to grow up and assume responsibility: "The party's over, and somebody's just handed you the check. Pick up the tab for once in your life." She asks him to leave, which opens the door for Murphy.

Following a proposal scene that offers the film's first kiss and thus an elegant climax to the love story, the concluding sequences are filmed against a sunset that exudes the romantic glow Fraker wanted to achieve. As Emma drives home in the sunset, Ritt's camera concentrates on her face as it gradually assumes a look of loving recognition. Unlike the opening scene, in which Emma is filmed in profile, the camera now pictures her full-face as she watches Murphy riding his horse down the road. The heroic cowboy image might have seemed clichéd, but Ritt introduces it as such a naturalistic, casual moment that the scene perfectly captures the mood of romantic fulfillment.

Ironically, in presenting a romantic film with no sex and with only a satiric nod to the pervasive violence of the currently popular "splatter films," Ritt encountered trouble with the ratings system, initially receiving an "R" rating because of a four-letter word used twice. Outraged, Ritt appealed the decision, declaring, "In close to thirty years of filmmaking, I have never made an 'R' rated film. I have never made an exploitation film. I am quite sure that *Murphy's Romance* is one of the more moral films you will see this year. To saddle the film with an 'R' rating is, in my opinion, a ridiculous miscarriage of justice" (RC 11-6-85). In the end, however, he agreed to cut six seconds, including one use of the damaging expletive, and the film was released with a "PG-13" rating.

Murphy's Romance is Ritt's most visually eloquent and beautifully written exploration of the theme of human love; its richness is achieved in part because of the strong underpinning of the pastoral motif. It's mature love story is carefully integrated with the romantic charm of the locale, and Ritt managed to elicit appealing performances from his two stars. The working-class love story would be reinterpreted in a different key in his last film, *Stanley and Iris*, Ritt's final testament to the endurance of the human spirit.

CHAPTER 17

Funny Girl: *Nuts*

Nuts (1987) became Ritt's most unpleasant experience as a director. As a novice director he had experienced problems with Orson Welles on the set of *The Long Hot Summer*, and he had faced artistic disagreements as well as personal difficulties with Richard Burton on *The Spy Who Came in from the Cold*. But working with Barbra Streisand, especially while Ritt himself was suffering from health problems, proved to be an emotionally and physically debilitating experience. He even took what was for him an unprecedented step in writing to Michael Franklin, the executive director of the Directors Guild of America, to articulate his problems with Streisand. Franklin replied that since Streisand was also a producer, Ritt had little recourse but to persevere and finish the project (RC 11-3-86). In an interview with *Penthouse*, November 10, 1987, Ritt later labeled *Nuts*, "the most commercial movie" he had made, which was his way of dismissing the whole experience, much as he had done with *Five Branded Women* twenty-seven years earlier.

Ritt's path to this film was a circuitous one. Universal Pictures, which had in part financed the Broadway play by Tom Topor in 1980, announced in 1981 that Mark Rydell, fresh from his successes as director of *The Rose* and *On Golden Pond*, would direct the film version. Rydell originally planned to cast Bette Midler, whom he had guided to an Academy Award nomination as Best Actress in *The Rose*, in the lead, but her breakdown on the set of *Jinxed* had since derailed her career. Instead, Rydell opted for Debra Winger, but she bowed out when Rydell put the project aside to direct *The River*. Finally remembering that Barbra

Streisand had been interested in starring in the film as her follow-up to *Yentl*, Rydell again sent her a script. Streisand again indicated interest, if the script could be revised to highlight the theme of child abuse and the issue of what is considered "normal." Claudia Draper, the protagonist, is a woman who gets in trouble for speaking the truth, and in that character Streisand saw a parallel to her misunderstood self.

Once Streisand had committed to the project as both star and producer, what Universal had planned as a modest film with a small budget ballooned into an expensive project with a budget over $20 million—$5 million going toward Streisand's salary as an actress and an additional $.5 million to be paid to her as producer. In September 1985, Universal placed the picture in turnaround, and it was then picked up for $575,585 by Warner Brothers. Executives at the new studio were less than excited by a collaborative work by Darryl Ponicsan (*Cinderella Liberty*) and Alvin Sargent (*Ordinary People*) and asked for a script revision. Streisand herself had a hand (uncredited) in revising the final draft, which was finally approved by the studio. Warners then decided that it no longer wanted Rydell, who was dismissed after having received his entire salary.

Faced with finding a new director, Warners asked Streisand to direct the film herself, but she didn't want to take on that responsibility so soon after *Yentl*. For years she had wanted to work with Ritt, regarding him as a serious artist who directed prestige projects. She phoned him and sent the script. Although friends tried to talk him out of it, Ritt was reportedly thrilled at the prospect of working with Streisand, whom he regarded as a great singer. Agreeing to meet Streisand, Ritt shocked her by stating, "I don't know if you could play the part," but she found his straightforward approach irresistible and asked him to direct.

The next important step was finding someone to co-star with Streisand in the secondary role of the public defender; Aaron Levinsky, Richard Gere, Marlon Brando, Paul Newman, Jeff Bridges, and Robert Duvall declined the role, and Al Pacino's $5 million salary demand was refused. Ritt and Streisand finally settled on Richard Dreyfuss, whose performance in the Los Angeles production of Larry Kramer's *The Normal Heart* had much impressed the star. While Dreyfuss's deal was being negotiated with Warners, he suddenly backed out to appear in Barry Levinson's *Tin Men*. Ritt then turned to Dustin Hoffman, who was impressed with the cinematic quality that Sargent and Ponicsan had brought to the material, but his financial demands, which included equal profit-sharing with Streisand, were rejected by the studio. When Ritt and Streisand agreed to delay filming until October, Dreyfus agreed to co-star.

For the part of Claudia's stepfather, Arthur Kirk, offers were made to George C. Scott, Burt Lancaster, Robert Mitchum, Kirk Douglas, Richard Widmark, and

Gregory Peck, with whom Streisand had also long wanted to work. The part eventually went to Ritt's friend Karl Malden from the Group Theatre, but only after Streisand insisted, to Ritt's embarrassment, that Malden audition for it. The cast was rounded out with other impressive actors: Maureen Stapleton (Mrs. Kirk), Eli Wallach (Dr. Morrison), James Whitmore (the judge), Robert Webber, and Leslie Nielsen.

Streisand prepared for her role as an incarcerated mental patient by visiting the neuropsychiatric wings of various hospitals, sometimes in company with Ritt. *Nuts* finally commenced principal photography on October 20, 1986, with a direct cost budget of $21.5 which eventually escalated to well over $27 million.

The set was rife with tension, which made the film the most unpleasant of Ritt's career. Streisand, who was used to giving orders, especially after *Yentl,* constantly interfered with Ritt during production. Unused to such treatment, Ritt became increasingly annoyed at Streisand's constant suggestions for retakes or changes in the set and lights. She also wanted final cut. The problems escalated when Ritt became convinced that Streisand, who was committed to preparing her *One Voice* concert for HBO, was giving less than her full attention to the film.

Nuts does not look like any other Ritt film. Rather than the small, intimate atmosphere that characterizes much of his work, it has a big and expensive feel despite the confinement of most of its action. Even more unusual is that the film's narrative is repeatedly interrupted by flashbacks to the events leading up to the manslaughter charge against Claudia Draper, a dramatic device Ritt had never used before.

The story concerns the plight of Claudia, a high-priced prostitute, who has killed one of her clients, she contends, in self-defense. The film, however, focuses not on her potential guilt, which the flashbacks disprove, but on her ability to stand trial. Her stepfather, Arthur Kirk, wants to have her institutionalized rather than subjecting her to the ordeal of a trial. Claudia, however, claims that she is sane enough to stand trial and insists on a hearing to determine her mental capacity. Her stepfather, it is revealed, has his own motivations for wanting her discredited, for he molested her as a child and into her adolescence. Ritt's film, like the play, centers on the sanity hearing.

Taking place entirely in the courtroom, the play is divided into three acts. The first act deals primarily with the testimony of Dr. Herbert Rosenthal (renamed Morrison in the film), a psychiatrist who declares that Claudia is unfit to stand trial. The second act focuses on the testimony of Mr. and Mrs. Kirk, and the third on Claudia's own testimony.

The film opens up the action with scenes in the hospital ward where Claudia is incarcerated, in her apartment, and in the hallway of the courthouse. There is also that series of flashbacks, detailing the killing of Allan Green (Leslie Nielsen), a client she meets at the bar and then invites to her apartment. The film also adds sequences introducing Aaron Levinsky and showing how he became Claudia's lawyer. In an early scene, Clarence Middleton (William Prince), a high-priced lawyer hired by the Kirks, tries to persuade the judge that Claudia is unfit to stand trial. When the judge insists that he consult with his client, an argument ensues and Claudia punches Middleton in the nose. Needing another lawyer immediately, the judge turns to Levinsky, a legal-aid attorney in the room on another matter, and prevails upon him to take over the case.

Claudia, like other Ritt protagonists, is an outsider, here challenging the court's definition of "normal." The hearing she demands succeeds in exposing the Kirks' family secrets, including Claudia's repressed hatred of her father and resentment of her mother. Her affluent upper-middle-class upbringing has only disguised the reality of her sexual abuse by her stepfather, which contributed to the destruction of her marriage and her descent into prostitution.

Unlike other Ritt protagonists, who are confined by social and/or political systems, however, Claudia is primarily a prisoner of the psychological traumas inflicted by her family. And while the film touches very lightly on abuses in mental hospitals, manipulation of the legal system, and the feminist issues raised by the aggressive Claudia's success in a man's world, the film is essentially a psycho-drama that builds to the not very surprising revelation of child molestation.

Streisand's performance, although powerful at times, is too calculated and too strident to command sympathy. Although supposedly dosed with Thorazine and dressed in a hospital gown and thongs, her character retains the aura of a movie star, and she never manages to look anything more than slightly de-glamorized. Streisand's Claudia is so clearly stronger than the sleazy prosecuting attorney and the less than brilliant psychiatrist that there is never any doubt that she will win her case. The flashbacks to the killing are presented early on in the film to assure the audience that Claudia was acting in self-defense and that there are no grounds for the manslaughter charge. Her certain innocence and her obvious strength of character undercut any potential tension or suspense.

The film's pleasures are instead mostly to be found in the work of a first-rate supporting cast, particularly Eli Wallach, Maureen Stapleton, Karl Malden, and James Whitmore. Richard Dreyfuss delivers a very engaging performance, managing to hold his own with Streisand.

The film is interesting technically in that it offers more close-ups than any number of Ritt films combined. Elsewhere, Ritt utilized the device sparingly in order to make thematic points, reserving the close-ups, for example, of Russell in *Hombre*, Leamas in *Spy*, or Vince in *The Brotherhood*, for the purpose of emphasizing the characters' alienation or illuminating their sense of despair or isolation. He used the technique to great effect in *Pete 'n' Tillie* when Pete hears about his son's terminal illness, confirming the searing sense of loss in an unexpected, and therefore especially chilling, close-up shot of the sufferer's face at the moment of recognition.

In *Nuts*, however, the constant use of the close-up makes a somewhat claustrophobic film seem even more restricted. Though Ritt attempts to open up the film by moving among various locales, the primary setting is still the courtroom, where, because the proceeding is not a trial, there are no spectators other than the participants themselves. Ritt therefore zeroes in on each character with his camera as if to dissect him or her. Like *Pete 'n' Tillie*, this is an urban film featuring upper-middle-class characters, and one can only speculate whether Ritt's liberal use of the isolating close-up is a further indication of his disdain for the members of that social milieu, or whether he simply chose to counter Streisand's demand for close-ups by seeking to balance hers with numerous shots of the other players.

The final shots after the ruling, showing Claudia almost waltzing out of court, lifting a scarf from a clothing rack and embracing her freedom, oddly resemble a scene from a Streisand musical. Rather than relieving the feeling of confinement, they seem merely ludicrous. Whereas Topor's play closes with Claudia being remanded to the commissioner of corrections to await trial, the film's exploration of social hypocrisy and psychological alienation is cheerily resolved in a vision of Streisand in a hospital gown on a crowded New York street, still managing to be the center of attention.

Summing Up: *The Black Orchid* and *Stanley and Iris*

After the emotionally debilitating experience of *Nuts*, Ritt decided to take some time off from directing. Nothing piqued his interest until 1989 when he became involved with a project called "Union Street," which was eventually released as *Stanley and Iris* in 1990. It was to be his last film.

Unfortunately, *Stanley and Iris* was released with little fanfare, received lukewarm reviews, and disappeared from theaters shortly after it opened. Not even the box office appeal of Jane Fonda and Robert DeNiro managed to draw any audience to the film. Many critics claimed that Jane Fonda's glamour worked against her in the role of a struggling blue-collar worker in a cake factory, and they attacked her performance much as they had her portrayal of a down-and-out victim in *They Shoot Horses, Don't They?*

The main reason for the critical and public misperception of the film—and this was the fault of the filmmakers—was that it was marketed as a film about illiteracy. For although this theme was shoehorned into the story—it remains poorly integrated and unbalances the plot—the film's real strength lies in its remarkably detailed depiction of working-class life. Ritt had explored a similar East Coast milieu in *The Black Orchid* (1959), which also suffered from his indecision about the kind of film he wanted to make, and thus *The Black Orchid* serves as a useful point of comparison to Ritt's work in *Stanley and Iris*.

The Black Orchid—its working title was "The Flower Maker"—was Ritt's fourth film, released a year after *The Long Hot Summer*. It marked a return to the New York City locale of his film debut, *Edge of the City*. Produced by Carlo

Ponti and Marcello Girosi for Paramount, *The Black Orchid* had an engaging script by Joseph Stefano, and it starred Sophia Loren and Anthony Quinn.

Ostensibly, this piece was influenced by the realistic, working-class television dramas perfected by Paddy Chayefsky during the early 1950s. Ritt was, of course, familiar with such work, and he knew Chayefsky quite well; Ritt even starred as a union leader assassinated in a phone booth in one of his early teleplays, "Hello Mr. Lutz," an episode of the drama series *Danger*. He was also originally chosen to star in Chayefsky's *Marty*, perhaps the most famous television play of the fifties; and this play, too, would leave its mark on *The Black Orchid*.

Commenting on the suitability of such works for television, Chayefsky defined their naturalistic appeal: "They . . . deal with the world of the mundane, the ordinary, and the untheatrical. The main characters are typical, rather than exceptional; the situations are easily identifiable by the audience; and the relationships are as common as people. The essence of these . . . shows lies in their literal reality" (183).

Joseph Stefano was a lyricist-composer who had never watched a television program before tuning in to *Playhouse 90* one evening and deciding that he could work in television. He wrote a one-hour teleplay and, within two weeks, made a deal with Carlo Ponti. *The Black Orchid* was Stefano's first effort: "I'd never even read a screenplay. Somebody had to tell me about 'Long shots,' 'exterior,' and 'interior'" (Rebello 37). Stefano would also soon write an award-winning teleplay, "Made in Japan," for *Playhouse 90*.

The Black Orchid deals with Rose Bianco (Loren), the reclusive widow of a gangster, who is courted by a funny, outgoing widower, Frank Valenti (Quinn). Frank's humor and charm eventually break down Rose's reserve, and they fall in love. Their plans to marry are complicated by Frank's possessive daughter Mary (Ina Balin, in her film debut), who is engaged to marry Noble (Mark Richman). Mary's refusal to accept either Rose or the idea of her father marrying nearly destroys both her own engagement and her father's. Meanwhile, Rose is having problems with her young son, Ralphie (Jamie Baird), who regularly tries to run away from the work farm for delinquent youngsters in which he has been placed. Eventually, all these problems are resolved and everyone comes together.

What the film shares with Chayefsky's work is its close attention to physical detail, especially to the look and feel of New York City neighborhoods. The communal attachments shared by the immigrant group—like *Marty*, this film focuses on Italians—are developed alongside small, mundane family moments such as dinners, trips, engagement parties, wedding preparations, and house hunting. As in *Marty*, all the characters are preoccupied with getting married, settling down to the life rhythm of the community. Nothing momentous happens, yet the film has an edge, appearing at times ready to veer off in a direction more suited to Alfred Hitchcock or Fritz Lang than the early Paddy Chayefsky or Martin Ritt.

Stefano, who would adapt Hitchcock's *Psycho* for the screen a year later, here foreshadows some of the psychological phenomena explored on the surface in *Psycho*, among them the dangerous obsessive potential in the love of a child for a parent. Ina Balin may have been cast because of her resemblance to Loren, which Ritt emphasizes by positioning and filming them in similar ways. (Hitchcock made a practice of casting actors who looked alike to suggest pathological relationships, as in *Vertigo*, *Psycho*, and *The Birds*.) In *The Black Orchid* there is a strong suggestion that Frank's wife became insane and locked herself in her room, and when Mary, distraught over her father's engagement, runs up the stairs to her room, Ritt gives the staircase an eerie, ominous look that invests the scene with the potential for horror.

Stefano's subsequent involvement with *Psycho* perhaps explains why it is difficult at times to recognize the earlier work as a romantic comedy, for its oddly foreboding tone raises some doubt about the world these Italian immigrants have to contend with. The opening scenes certainly seem to promise a darker story line: eerie and haunting music, which begins behind the Paramount logo, continues into the opening shot, a medium close-up of the widow, Rose Bianco, who is dressed in black; she stares into the camera as, to her left, her son, Ralphie, is crying. As Rose turns to face her son, there is a cut to a coffin being loaded onto a hearse, followed by a long shot of mother and son walking behind the hearse through the city streets.

A car pulls up behind Rose and Ralphie, and then Ritt cuts to Rose in her black veil looking at the car. She does so a second time, appearing almost otherworldly as she whispers, "Murderers," at the figures in the car. Ritt then dissolves to the inside of the church, where a priest speaks about the dead man, a murder victim. As the priest recalls officiating at the couples wedding, Ritt cuts to a close-up of the veiled Rose and then dissolves to the scene of the marriage, the reception, and a brief moment outside the newlyweds' home. There Rose, still in her white wedding dress, tells her husband that he can make her dream come true by giving her a new house with many rooms and new furniture; he replies that this will take time.

Ritt then cuts back to the funeral and the priest, who declares that no one knows why Tony was murdered; but the cut suggests that Tony got in trouble with the mob, probably by embezzling money to satisfy his new wife. Rose, who came from Italy to become an American bride, wanted too much too fast, and her dream has been violently destroyed. The opening scenes thus imply, obliquely, the destructive potential of the American dream of wealth. Later, when it is revealed that Frank's wife became "ill" shortly after their child was born, the romantic image of marriage as a prelude to happiness—the dual goal of all the film's characters—is brought into question. Ritt's quick dissolve from Rose as exuberant, smiling bride to Rose as brooding, black-veiled widow suggests that the subsequent scenes will present a tale of loss and disillusionment.

The next sequence opens with the vibrant sounds of a player piano—winter has changed to spring, a street vendor is seen on the street, and the lighting is bright, signaling that the tone has shifted suddenly to a comic spirit of renewal. Rose, returning home in black, seems out of place in this cheerful setting, but her neighbor prevails upon her to come over for dinner to meet Frank Valente. Introduced while laughing with his neighbors over a card game, the personable Frank seems an unlikely match for the stone-faced and angry Rose. But he manages to soften her mood a bit and even invites himself on a Sunday bus trip to visit her son at the work farm.

The next scene, in Frank's brightly lit house, offers a strong contrast to Rose's home. Mary is making him breakfast, and as Frank tells her about his date with Rose, she becomes serious and upset. When Noble, her fiancé, arrives, she starts talking about staying with her father instead of moving to Atlantic City. Noble tries to break the mood, talking about his love, but Mary remains subdued. Again the music becomes ominous, replacing the light, playful tune that introduced the post-funeral scenes.

The scenes with Mary are contrasted with those introducing Ralphie. As Frank and Rose travel to the work farm by bus, Rose seems to be warming to Frank— she smiles and relaxes her manner. At the farm, she learns that Ralphie has tried to run away again and is now confined to his room, although she is allowed to visit him. Ralphie is first shown looking out a window at the countryside, as if dreaming of life in a rural environment, which will assume added importance as the film progresses. Rose tells him that she is beginning to trust men again and that she wants to introduce him to Frank to see if he meets with Ralphie's approval. Touched, he hugs his mother.

The remainder of the film follows this basic pattern of scenes alternating between Rose and Frank, Mary and Noble, Mary and Frank, and Rose and Ralphie. The complications become more dangerous as Mary's obsession with her father's marriage grows and Ralphie once more runs away from the farm. Mary locks herself in her room, duplicating her own mother's withdrawal, and this leads to a temporary rift in Frank and Rose's relationship. Rather too quickly, however, all the problems are resolved. Rose confronts Mary and manages to smooth things out. Frank comes across Ralphie as he is praying in church and takes him back to the farm. While Rose and Mary cook breakfast together, Frank takes care of Ralphie's problems at the farm. In the last two scenes, Frank, Rose, Mary, and Noble are reunited at the breakfast table, and then Frank, Rose, and Ralphie are seen leaving the farm together on their way to the new house Frank has bought in Somerville.

A number of scenes in this film are worthy of comment. After a surprise party, Mary, who is depressed over her father's new relationship, describes her reservations about marriage, and during this speech the haunting music associated with Mary earlier is heard again. Ritt then cuts to a shot of Mary walking home, picturing Mary in the same medium close-up composition that was used for Rose in the funeral scene. Later, when Mary visits Noble in Atlantic City to see their new home, she is dressed in black. In this scene she insists that they live with her father, which precipitates a quarrel.

The next scene opens in an ice cream parlor, where the white background and bright lighting contrast strongly with the previous scene. As Rose and Frank talk and laugh, their manner is reminiscent of the first scene between Frank and Mary. Frank tells Rose of his first wife's sickness and his dream of buying the house in Somerville for a second chance at life. He mentions that setting up a home there would enable Ralphie to leave the farm and live with them. Rose is moved, and she accepts his proposal. Ritt films much of this scene in shot–reverse shot, in medium close-ups of their faces. Rose is framed by trellises laced with flowers, which make her look like a bride, while behind Frank is a bowl of fruit. The mis-en-scène thus effectively suggests the couple's happiness and hopes for the future.

Another significant scene is that in which Frank talks with Ralphie and asks for his mother's hand, telling him about his plans for buying the house. They walk past a gate in the background, a reminder of the prison-like atmosphere of the work farm, but as Frank warms to his subject, they are beneath a large tree. The bucolic setting provides an evocative visual backdrop for Frank's dream of renewal in a country home. (*Stanley and Iris* features a similar scene, in which Stanley talks with the son of Iris, a widow whom he is courting.)

The recurrence of such rural scenes reflects Ritt's continuing fascination with the pastoral dream, which is always associated with emotional renewal, an important theme in much of his later work, especially *Norma Rae, Cross Creek, Murphy's Romance,* and *Stanley and Iris. The Black Orchid,* which finally allows its characters a second chance at happiness, thus offers an early instance of what would become a lasting preoccupation in Ritt's work. Many of these films also feature working-class characters whose earthy, elemental feelings permit them to forge close communal ties to their neighbors, unlike the jaded and alienated characters in a film such as *Pete 'n' Tillie.*

Ritt never had very much to say about *The Black Orchid*, commenting obscurely, "I didn't have any illusions about the film" (SMU 35). He enjoyed working with Sophia Loren, whom he called a "terrific lady," and with Anthony Quinn, although he had constantly to remind the actor that in film less is more. Quinn always appreciated Ritt's tutelage, and eight years later, when Ritt wanted to cast him in *The Brotherhood*, both regretted that it did not work out. *The Black Orchid* was an enormous success at the Venice Film Festival in 1958. In a telegram to Ritt, J. E. Perkins wrote that it received "the greatest public reception of any picture presented to date." Sophia Loren won the festival's Best Actress Award, and when the film opened in America, *Redbook* cited it as its best picture of the month in March of 1959.

Stanley and Iris, like *The Black Orchid*, is primarily a love story centered on family life and the concept of renewal through commitment. The differences between the two works obviously reflect changes in Ritt's style and temperament as well as the differing sensibilities of their screenwriters. Joseph Stefano's work has been marked by an interest in the irrational and the Gothic in juxtaposition with the mundane and the everyday. Ravetch and Frank, on the other hand, have, especially since the seventies, focused their attention on average working-class people involved in stories that have a liberal, progressive bent. This is the kind of story that Ritt was most comfortable with as well, whereas he had difficulty accommodating Stefano's Manichean vision to his own natural sympathy for his protagonists and their growing love. In *Stanley and Iris* Ritt was dealing with a story that reflected his own naturalistic bent, and he was also firmly in command of his style, as he had not been in 1959.

Like most of Ravetch and Frank's "adaptations," *Stanley and Iris* bears only a marginal relationship to its source novel, Pat Barker's *Union Street* (published in England in 1982 and in America a year later). The novel is set in the early 1970s in a grimy and impoverished unnamed town in England's industrial Northeast. Its two industries are a steelworks, which employs the men, and a cake factory, which employs or has employed most of the women. The novel is divided into seven sections, each named for a particular woman. The stories deal with rape, pregnancy, abortion, death, aging, making a living, and raising children. Social concerns such as the threat of automation, racial prejudice, and feeble-mindedness are touched on, but Barker's main focus is on the difficulty of existence in an industrialized slum and the heroic struggle for survival waged by some of these women.

Ravetch and Frank chose to scrap almost all of the characters except Iris King, who is portrayed in the novel as a kind of Earth mother and comforter to all the other women. Her section deals primarily with her anger over her youngest daughter's determination to have an abortion. The film's Iris is also kind-hearted, opening her home to her sister and her unemployed husband; but, although she does have to deal with her teenage daughter's pregnancy, there is no abortion. The cake factory setting is retained, though moved to a New England town, where the extreme poverty of Barker's locale is softened a bit; the film's characters are blue-collar workers who struggle but who live in nice neighborhoods and comfortable homes. The character of Stanley Cox is wholly Ravetch and Frank's invention. Although the husband of Muriel, one of the women in the novel, is unable to read, Barker makes little of this fact, devoting much of that episode instead to Muriel's efforts to cope with her husband's dying. This episode may have sparked Ravetch and Frank's interest, but the film's illiteracy story is essentially their original contribution.

Finding a location for filming presented some difficulty because there was considerable objections by veterans' organizations to the presence of Jane Fonda in their towns. Some veterans gave Fonda their support, but advance word of her coming, published in the local press of Waterbury, Connecticut, stirred much antagonism. After two weeks of shooting there, the remainder of the filming was done in Toronto.

The shoot was a pleasant one despite Ritt's need to watch his diet carefully because of his diabetes. He thoroughly enjoyed working with Jane Fonda, whom he considered a consummate professional, and after adjusting to Robert De-Niro's work habits, he cherished that association as well. DeNiro did not like to rehearse, feeling that repetition took the edge off his performance; he preferred the adrenaline rush of shooting from the hip. Ritt would let him take his time during a scene but then had to rein him in for being too leisurely. He explained, "I never like any of them [actors] to get comfortable. I like to keep them a little off center" (Cameron 46). Praising DeNiro as "an actor to the core," Ritt felt he gave an outstanding performance.

The opening of the film recalls Ritt's earlier work—a slow pan along a factory town reveals rows of identical houses jammed close together and a modern highway busy with traffic. The camera finally settles on a bakery just as the workers are leaving, and then it picks out Iris King. Ritt's strategy here differs from his insistent focus on the process of labor within the mill in *Norma Rae*. Here, although Ritt's camera occasionally moves into the factory, its primary concern is not the labor process itself but the woman it picks out from the crowd of workers. Her story of triumph over her mundane circumstances is the subject of this film.

Iris King is related to all of the heroines of Ritt's later work: she is a woman alone—her husband died some months earlier—who must persevere in the face of hardship. Like Emma Moriarty and Norma Rae, she has children to take care of and, in addition, she is supporting her unemployed sister and brother-in-law. She also eventually finds fulfillment in her growing love for Stanley Cox, and this relationship, like that of Frank and Emma and Murphy, is really the heart of the film.

Ritt introduces these various relationships and evokes the blue-collar atmosphere with the economy and precision that distinguish his best work. After Iris leaves the factory, Ritt shows her on a bus, ripping coupons out of a paper. When the bus stops, a passenger grabs her purse and runs off the bus; Iris, in pursuit, is followed by a good samaritan who turns out to be Stanley Cox. She chases the thief to a back alley, where barrels of industrial waste and a chain-link fence evoke the urban wasteland. Iris struggles with the thief, who throws her into the fence and then climbs over some barrels and other debris and escapes. When Stanley arrives, Iris is upset at the loss of her purse, which contained her paycheck, her driver's license, pictures of her children, and her rosary. Stanley helps calm her down and takes her home.

A series of quick scenes follow. First is a domestic scene in Iris's kitchen, in which the camera moves from dirty dishes piled up in the sink to Iris's extended family crowded around the kitchen table for dessert. Iris's sister Sharon (Swoozie Kurtz) is defensive about not having found a job. Her husband, Joe (Jamie Sheriden), talks about the unemployment line and then gets up to get a beer, which Sharon suspects that he has bought with money she was saving to get her teeth fixed. A fight ensues and he hits her; Iris sends the children out and tries to diffuse the tension. Iris's daughter then mentions that she needs to go to the hospital for a "scrape."

Ritt then cuts to a scene in the factory where the woman are talking about dating. One mentions that she wants to get pregnant so that she can get out of the factory. Iris responds that it won't work: "It takes two incomes." Another worker remarks that her husband is "Doin' time just like me." The suggestive sexual banter, with its cynical edge, is quite different from the romantic, wholehearted dream of marriage in *The Black Orchid*. The economic necessities of *Stanley and Iris* are harsher—these women realize that marriage does not bring with it security or even happiness, as Ritt's mis-en-scène seemed to promise in the earlier film. As the previous scene in Iris's house has vividly demonstrated, domestic life here is a struggle.

Ritt next interrupts his scenes of urban struggle to offer his final testament to the pastoral. Iris and some other workers are waiting for the bus when it passes them by with an "out of service" sign in the window. As the women vent their frustration, Stanley comes riding by on his bicycle and offers Iris a ride, which she happily accepts. Riding past a river, Stanley talks of leaving the city and buying a farm where he can grow his own food—his dream is reminiscent of Frank's desire to move to Somerville. Ritt's customary water backdrop sets up the film's most idyllic scene, as the optimistic talk, the river, the bicycle, and the emphasis on space and movement in long and medium-long shots create a refreshing sense of freedom and possibility.

Later in the film Stanley tells Iris of a vacation he once took to the Grand Canyon, dwelling on the splendor of being by himself as he walked the canyon and slept outside for six days and nights. Iris retorts that such isolation would drive her crazy and instead describes her ideal vacation as a night in a fancy Boston hotel room, ordering expensive room-service meals and having her bed turned down.

Stanley's connection with Frank Valente becomes even more explicit when Stanley takes a walk in a park with Iris's son. As they go, Stanley identifies the various trees, giving their Latin names and talking about them. The scene not only evidences Stanley's intelligence and learning despite his illiteracy but also further connects him with nature. The scene and its setting clearly recall Frank's talk to Ralphie under a tree, when he tells the boy of his love for Rose and his dream of moving to Somerville with his new family. In both films, Ritt interweaves the more poignant moments of his story with bucolic images.

Like *The Black Orchid*, this late film offers a number of subplots. The most affecting is Stanley's relationship with his father, movingly played by Feodor Chaliapin. Stanley lives with his father, but after losing his job as a cook in the cake factory, he must put the old man in a home. A montage of scenes shows Stanley giving his father a haircut, playing chess with him, sharing fruit—his devotion to his father is palpable, as is his shame at not being able to provide for him. The father's room at the retirement home is slightly reminiscent of Ralphie's room at the work farm, and both institutions are presided over by kindly, understanding individuals.

Although Ralphie runs away from the farm several times, he is finally rescued by his mother's marriage and restored to family life. Mr. Cox, however, dies at the home where, deprived of his only family, his health has deteriorated. Stanley learns of his father's death when he comes to visit bearing a plant, a symbol of life that comes too late. Humiliated that he can't even spell his father's name for the death certificate, alone and discouraged, he decides to ask Iris to teach him how to read and write.

The subplot of Stanley's relationship with his father is balanced by Iris's relationship with her daughter, Kelly (Martha Plimpton), as Ritt juxtaposes Stanley's scenes in the home with others showing Kelly in the hospital, finding out she is pregnant. Outraged, Iris slaps Kelly when she refuses to reveal the father. But Ravetch and Frank have modified this story from the novel, so that the film's mother and daughter are quickly reconciled and Kelly has the baby, which she names after her mother.

In an earlier version of the script, this story takes a harsher turn when it is revealed that Kelly has been having an affair with her uncle Joe and that he is the father of the baby. While this revelation would have been consistent with the tone of Barker's novel and would have provided the edge Stefano gave to *The Black Orchid*, it would be too jarring a note for the love story that Ritt wanted to emphasize in this film, and he wisely eliminated it here. In the final version, Iris's sister and brother-in-law simply disappear from the film, leaving this plot strand unresolved. The film's one sour note is that shortly after giving birth, Kelly drops out of school and joins her mother on the bakery assembly line, which, as Iris reminds her, "leads nowhere." There is some suggestion, however, that Kelly, like Ralphie, may be rescued by Iris's marriage to Stanley.

The film's main burden is the literacy theme. The scenes of Iris teaching Stanley how to read remain as stubbornly undramatic as those in which Ritt tried to highlight Marjorie Rawlings's writing. Here he struggles mightily to link Stanley's progress as a reader with the evolution of his love for Iris, but the character's illiteracy never really takes on any urgency. Stanley's achievement in finally learning how to read and write is gratifying, but that happiness is wholly eclipsed by the consummation of the love affair that is the emotional center of the film.

The plot resolves with the revelation that Stanley is in fact a brilliant and creative man, an inventor in his spare time. In one scene Iris visits him in his garage home and sees there an elaborate machine that he has invented to cool cakes quickly. Soon, Stanley's machine has attracted some notice, and he is eventually offered a job with an office of his own in Detroit. Again, in Ritt's world, Stanley's mastery of machines and his talent for invention represent a healthy balance to his pastoral dream. Demonstrating that the worlds of the pastoral and the modern must feed off one another if a successful synthesis is to occur, Stanley's invention indicates that despite his distaste for the modern world, he can accommodate aspects of it in order to survive.

The film concludes with Stanley flying off to Detroit and then surprising Iris by driving back one evening. His success is evident: he has a car, credit cards, and a health plan. He tells Iris that he has his eyes on a house with six bedrooms and one bathroom and that he wants her family to move into the house. Iris jokes that one bathroom won't be enough for such a large family and they will have to knock down a wall to add another one. Stanley remarks, "Anything is possible," as the film ends.

This emotionally satisfying ending replicates that of *The Black Orchid*, bringing Ritt's career full circle. Stanley and Iris, like Rose and Frank, Marjorie, Norma Rae, and Emma and Murphy, are offered a second chance for renewal and fulfillment. With hard work, love, and commitment, Ritt assures his audience, the American dream remains a possibility.

Stanley and Iris was heralded by Barbara Bush, who worked hard for the cause of illiteracy as First Lady, and was given a special screening at the White House. It was also chosen to open the U.S. Film Festival at Sundance, Utah, in 1990.

Despite this advance publicity, the film did not do well at the box office. It opened to mostly indifferent reviews and disappeared from local theaters soon afterward. It seems likely that the publicists' decision to market it primarily as a social problem film about illiteracy rather than a love story lessened its audience potential.

While filming *Stanley and Iris*, Ritt became interested in Joseph Stefano's *Two Bits*, an autobiographical story about a boy's relationship with his dying grandfather in Philadelphia. But after finishing *Stanley and Iris*, Ritt returned home sick with diabetes and a weak heart. He did little for months after the filming and then died of heart disease on December 8, 1990. *Two Bits* would be filmed some years later by James Foley, with Al Pacino in the starring role. Like *Stanley and Iris*, it opened to indifferent reviews and quickly disappeared.

CHAPTER 19

Conclusion

Martin Ritt had a remarkable Hollywood career. He was able to make small, character-driven, social films on a regular basis, turning out twenty-six movies from 1957 through 1990. Such success in the film business can be explained, in part, by Ritt's ability to play the game. Despite his reputation as a gruff individualist with outspoken leftist political opinions, he knew how to pitch his projects to the studios and how to present himself as a careful manager of money who brought his films in on time and occasionally even under budget. As his personal records indicate, Ritt planned his projects carefully, invariably having several future projects researched and in various stages of preparation, and he was never idle until overcome by the health problems that plagued him over the last decade of his life.

Ritt always knew what he wanted to do and whom he wanted to work with, which is not to say that he always got to make the films he wanted. When his personally favored projects fell through, Ritt often took on films that he liked but that lacked thematic depth, keeping busy with minor projects such as *Casey's Shadow* and *Pete 'n' Tillie*, whose modest virtues lacked the dramatic weight of his best work. He could also be surprisingly wrong-headed in his choice of material. Although Ritt knew that he had no facility for adapting stage plays, he agreed to direct *The Great White Hope*, and he allowed himself to be lured by Barbra Streisand's celebrity to take on *Nuts*, a project he could not control, ending up with a product that does not even look like a Martin Ritt film.

These lesser efforts point to an aspect of Ritt's career that has never received much attention. Writers of magazine and newspaper profiles liked to exaggerate Ritt's independent streak, portraying him rather simplistically as the blacklisted political radical who didn't play the Hollywood game, dressed in jumpsuits, and went his own way. Ritt himself helped to cultivate this image, and this "legendary" Ritt persona certainly had some basis in fact. But Ritt was not the maverick he was often made out to be. The same Martin Ritt who could make films like *The Front* and *Sounder* and *Norma Rae* was also very much a creature of the Hollywood system. He enjoyed the security of working for the studios. Walter Bernstein would occasionally try to prod him to become more independent, to use his reputation to set up his own production company, but Ritt shied away from such ventures, obviously preferring the safety of mediocre projects to the real risks of financing more ambitious ones.

Recognition of his cautious careerism, however, should not diminish appreciation of what Ritt was able to accomplish by working within the system. Throughout most of his time in Hollywood, he stayed away from the strictly genre pieces and the big-budget spectacles that could have guaranteed easy success. The movies Ritt did make share a small, intimate feel but lack a distinctive visual signature. Even films that should look "bigger"—*The Great White Hope* or *The Molly Maguires*—seem somehow scaled down, and this is because Ritt preferred to concentrate on his characters. He made movies about people. Invariably, they were people caught up in social or political issues that interested him, but it was observing his characters, as they react to challenge and grow, that was Ritt's central focus.

Emphasizing his aura of radical mystique and labeling him a creator of "social films" misconstrues Ritt's strengths as a storyteller. Ritt's films are not didactic; they do not announce that they are about big themes. Instead, powerful ideas and resonances emerge in them gradually and incrementally, through character and story. Even the impassioned personal polemic that is *The Front* takes as its protagonist a selfish, rather unsympathetic figure who must witness firsthand the results of hypocrisy, mendacity, and betrayal. The film builds its eloquent indictment of the blacklist by concentrating on the human behavior that charged the political climate. In an interview given to promote *Conrack*, Ritt commented: "It is not a matter of being identified with social consciousness films. . . . now it's not always political at all because you're very seldom dealing with political subjects. In "Conrack" it's in totally human terms. It is love story between a teacher and 21 kids. You will take out of it socially whatever your frame of reference is when you go in" (Light 18).

Ritt's story values and attention to character were honed in the writing process. He worked hard on the screenplays with his writers, and he valued the written word. Ritt had learned the value of well-written scenes in his earliest days in the theater, when he performed in plays by Clifford Odets, Irwin Shaw, and Maxwell Anderson and directed others by Arthur Miller, Ben Hecht, and Sidney Kingsley. Writers enjoyed working with him because he respected their craft; Ritt's films were written by some of Hollywood's best: Irving Ravetch and Harriet Frank, Walter Bernstein, Lonne Elder III, Julius Epstein, Joseph Stefano, and Lewis John Carlino.

Ritt's acting and theater training turned him into one of the most respected actor's directors in Hollywood. Top film stars wanted to work with him. Because of his reputation, he could attract Robert DeNiro and Jane Fonda to a modest project like *Stanley and Iris*, and Barbra Streisand requested him for *Nuts*. His other films are a who's who of Hollywood superstars: Paul Newman, Joanne Woodward, Richard Burton, Orson Welles, Sidney Poitier, Walter Matthau, Sally Field, Yul Brynner, Frederic March, James Earl Jones, Melvyn Douglas, and Patricia Neal. Having learned the actor's craft from fellow Group Theatre members such as Elia Kazan, Robert Lewis, Lee J. Cobb, John Garfield, and Sanford Meisner, Ritt later taught at the Actor's Studio where, under the leadership of Lee Strasberg, "method acting" became a seminal theory for actors. There Ritt taught Paul Newman, Joanne Woodward, Anthony Franciosa, Lee Grant, and others.

Ritt's method as a director was to let his actors act, allowing them to develop complex and layered characterizations. Never one to use editing techniques to overwhelm an actor's performance, he preferred to let his camera follow the actor through the process of building a character. The result is acting that appears natural and real, achieved through an ideal fusion of the medium with the actor's craft. This naturalistic approach carried over to his lighting as well, for Ritt invariably preferred a subtle use of light that supported the mood of a scene to any effect of high-contrast lighting that might distract an audience from the movement of the story and the arc of the actor's performance.

Ritt's films are also memorable for their faithful portrayal of the look, feel, and sounds of working-class life. He preferred to film on location, never choosing a setting for its pictorial qualities alone; instead, he mined location for its authenticity. In conjunction with the naturalistic acting and lighting, Ritt's ability to exploit setting made the world of his films seem real. One need only look at the Bannon home in *Hud*, the Kings' kitchen in *Stanley and Iris*, the Morgans' farm in *Sounder*, or the Websters' home in *Norma Rae* to appreciate the authenticity of Ritt's rendering of place. The audience's sense of inhabiting a world rather than observing one is the hallmark of Ritt's style. His look is so unobtrusive that often the boundaries between fiction and documentary are obliterated, and this vernacular effect is heightened by the leisurely narrative rhythms of his editing. Ritt's best work offers the aesthetic pleasure of a well-told story enacted by believable characters in an authentic environment.

Ritt's films are a record of his dialogue with America, reflecting a lifelong struggle with the concepts of individualism and self-reliance and their relationship with community. Most of his protagonists are loners, outsiders at war with a system from which they feel isolated. From the very beginning his work focused on these outsiders: Axel Nordman in *Edge of the City*, Ben Quick in *The Long Hot Summer*, Rose Bianco in *The Black Orchid*, Ram Bowen in *Paris Blues*, Jovanka in *Five Branded Women*, and Nick Adams in *Hemingway's Adventures of a Young Man*—all are estranged from family and community. In the early films, Ritt invariably allows these characters a measure of reconciliation that knits them back into the social fabric. Rose Bianco and Ben Quick are granted marriages that will reverse the alienating patterns of the past. Like Quentin Compson in *The Sound and the Fury*, they find happiness and contentment as Ritt changes the mood at last and resolves their stories in the comic spirit of reconciliation and reclamation.

The early films reveal Ritt's interest in characters who bring their personal problems to bear on the social world they inhabit. Their emotional isolation is caused not only by removal from the community but also by some psychic wound inflicted by parents or family. This combination of external rebellion and spiritual pain makes Ritt's protagonists more difficult and complex than those caught up in most sociopolitical dramas. The early films fall short of Ritt's later achievement, however, because he did not ultimately control the projects and often had to subvert his themes to commercial necessity, contriving happy endings that undercut the integrity of the stories. And with the exception of *The Long Hot Summer*, Ritt was not able to express in these early works the deep sense of place and the feel of a social world that would mark his best work. The recurrent themes and character types are staked out, however, as are the political and social issues that would constitute his quarrel with America.

The Long Hot Summer is the most fully integrated of Ritt's early films and the one that forecasts most dramatically his later career. Ben Quick is an outsider, rejected by society because of his father's crimes. Ben, however, recognizes society's rules and knows how to manipulate them. It is by playing the game better than anyone else that he becomes successful. He is greedy and manipulative like Will Varner, and he is capable of cheating the townspeople; but he can also be charming and he has the insight to admit the error of his ways. Ben finally seems a better man than the society he is welcomed into at the film's end, and although the happy ending satisfies emotionally, a more objective view suggests that he might have done better to have remained on the outside.

Ritt's films of the 1960s are his most despairing—dark visions of violence and betrayal. Unable to resolve the rigidity of his society with the impulsive nature of the individual, or the humane and ethical impulse with the amoral profit motivation of a postindustrial, corporate system, Ritt lashed out at the loss of personal responsibility in the conformist ethic of the modern world. The despair that had been lurking below the surface of *Edge of the City, The Black Orchid,* and *No Down Payment* and that had erupted, albeit incoherently, in *Hemingway's Adventures of a Young Man* was unleashed amid the tumult of the sixties, and it produced Ritt's most powerful, most unsparing examination of the American experience.

Ben Quick was in some ways the model for Hud, protagonist of Ritt's first great film. Like Ben, Hud does not really oppose the society from which he stands apart, but while Ben manipulates this corrupt society, Hud represents it. He only seems to be an outsider because society does not want to acknowledge him, but every trait that Ritt despised in the American character is represented in Hud—greed, rapaciousness, and the unchecked individualism that leads to selfishness. He is contrasted to his father, Homer Bannon, a man of honor and integrity who believes that he is a representative American. But this blindness to the diseased reality of his society, symbolized in part by the plague that ravages his ranch, makes inevitable Homer's defeat by his son, who is the true exemplar of his modern race. Hud will turn his father's land to the oil wells that symbolize the triumph of unbridled capitalism. Hud's instincts are not to be softened, as Ben's are, by love and marriage. Hud remains isolated and alone; he is the fore-runner of the corporate man that Ritt abhorred.

Vince Ginneta of *The Brotherhood* is Hud's worthy successor. Whereas Hud's betrayal leads indirectly to his father's death, Vince's defection to the service of an anonymous conglomerate makes him the actual executioner of his brother, Frank, a small businessman who prefers the old Mafia ways. When Vince kills his brother for the corporation, the act not only resonates as fratricide but also carries overtones of patricide, both because Frank practically raised him after their father's death and because Vince is in effect putting an end to the Old World values that nurtured his growth.

Hombre, although it touches on racial themes, is at its core a work in the same vein of cultural narrative, reflecting the transition of America from an agrarian society to an industrial one. John Russell, a half-breed Indian who, although raised by a white father, is more at home on the frontier than in the town, embodies an America whose values are shifting with the coming of the railroad.

Like Homer Bannon and Frank Ginneta, Russell is eventually destroyed by a society that no longer prizes what he represents. Ritt characterizes the barren spirit of the emerging modern society in his depiction of the landscape traversed by Russell and his fellow stagecoach passengers. Unlike the majestic Monument Valley of John Ford's Westerns or the awesome vistas of Anthony Mann's, Ritt's American scene is a vast wasteland of emptiness and abandonment, a fit setting for the lost pilgrims Russell leads and eventually dies for.

In Ritt's historical chronology, *The Molly Maguires* follows up the transitional movement of *Hombre* and delves deeper into the abuses of industrialism. The coal mine bosses of nineteenth-century Pennsylvania are bleeding their workers dry; the Mollies are a renegade group dedicated to sabotaging the mines in the hope of improving the labor conditions and the lives of their working-class community. Ritt presents a confrontation between one Irish immigrant intent on rising in the world and another who fights for the dignity and the well-being of his fellow workers. McParlan, an ancestor of Hud who has mastered the selfish ethic of the American system, informs on his friend Kehoe to obtain a financial reward and a promotion to a managerial position with the agency that polices the activities of the community.

The Great White Hope, released in the same year as *The Molly Maguires,* also chronicles the destruction of an outsider by the modern hierarchy of power. Jack Jefferson, a black heavyweight champion, refuses to play by the rules of the white boxing establishment or to serve as a role model for blacks. His insistence on maintaining his sense of self seals his doom with a racist society bent on destroying him. Jefferson eventually loses everything: his money, his championship belt, his wife, and his rebellious spirit.

Pete 'n' Tillie (1972) serves as a transitional step from the violent mood of the sixties toward the comparative serenity of Ritt's later years. An unsuccessful mixture of pathos and humor, darkness and light, it centers on the comeuppance of a cynical, rather callous rogue with an aberrant sense of humor. Pete Seltzer, a motivational researcher, is, like Hud and Vince Ginetta, in step with the corporate world he serves, remaining emotionally detached from his job and cheating on his wife. After the death of their son, Pete and Tillie's marriage disintegrates, but Ritt brings them together at the end as they attempt to put their lives back together.

Sounder, released in the same year, provides a more successful breakthrough. Ritt's major exploration of the African American experience, it offers a powerful demonstration of his ability to meld a sense of place with beautifully drawn characters in a well-structured story. The equal of *Hud* as an expression of his fluent cinematic style, the story of the sharecropper's family and their struggles against racism and economic hardship delivers Ritt's most eloquent plea for creation of a diverse and democratic community. In the Morgans' commitment to the values of family, education, and hard work, he celebrates not only the strength of a unique culture, but also the endurance of the American dream. Ritt's vision here reflects the central tension, defined by Gunnar Myrdal in *An American Dilemma,* between the nation's lofty ideals and its history of wrongs perpetrated against minorities. Myrdal characterized this conflict between ideal and reality as a struggle for America's "soul," and he recognized the invigorating effect of incorporating outsider groups into the social fabric as a "spiritual convergence" (13). These concepts might serve as a gloss on Ritt's mature films of the seventies and eighties.

The energies of diversity and convergence are also evident in Ritt's portrayals of women; three of his best works feature strong heroines. *Norma Rae, Murphy's Romance,* and *Stanley and Iris* all share stylistic qualities with *Sounder;* all demonstrate an extraordinary feel for the texture of blue-collar lives. As he did in *Hud,* Ritt captures the look of the homes and the frustration inherent in striving but not quite succeeding. At the center of each of these dramas is a woman who struggles to find fulfillment in a world that has previously allowed her no room for personal growth.

Norma Rae Webster's battle to focus her aimless life involves both remarriage and a courageous plunge into union organizing; her coming of age represents a merging of the private with the social and public aspects of life. Norma Rae's growth into moral, social, and ethical responsibility marks her as a heroine, and it relates her experience to that of Emma Moriarty in *Murphy's Romance.* Another divorcée, Emma gradually learns to accept the iconoclastic Murphy as a worthier mate than her charming cad of an ex-husband, and her emotional growth coincides with her developing strength and resolve as an independent businesswoman. Like Norma Rae, Emma triumphs in undertaking a second marriage that reflects her maturity and reinforces her bond with the community. The "humanism" that Ritt strove to inject into his later work is the central element of *Stanley and Iris,* a love story about a strong woman whose determination to teach a reclusive man how to read and write is infused with the democratic values of the American dream.

Significant steps toward the affirmative spirit of these films were Ritt's two most personal works, *The Front* and *Cross Creek.* By making *The Front,* he was able to exorcise artistically the ordeal of the blacklist; the act of informing, an important motif in many of Ritt's earlier films, no longer figures in those made after 1976. In collaboration with Walter Bernstein, he chose a comic approach over any more "maudlin and sentimental" treatment, effectively structuring the story as a testing of the idea of community (McGilligan, "Ritt Large" 44). Mirroring the larger culture, Howard Prince is an underachiever whose selfishness and dreams of easy success prevent any acceptance of social responsibility. Like Norma Rae, Howard matures into political activism, having discovered, through his relationship with Florence Barret and Hecky Green, his own social and communal conscience.

Ritt articulated his artistic credo in *Cross Creek* (1983), chronicling the evolution of Marjorie Kinnan Rawlings as a writer and independent woman. Leaving her husband and her life in the East to find herself and her artistic vocation in the backwaters of Florida, Marjorie is reborn as an artist by learning the rhythms, the sounds, and the feel of the natural world. And she grows, as do all Ritt's later heroines, by developing a mature romantic relationship with a man who is rooted in the community.

Ritt's final films, especially *Cross Creek,* offer a significant thematic culmination to the evolution of his art. All of the films made after *The Front* are set in rural environments. (*Nuts* is the sole exception, but that project did not originate with him and was less his film than Barbra Streisand's.) In framing his portraits of individual struggles for survival and redemption, Ritt repeatedly rejects urban centers to present the prospects of personal and cultural rediscovery in a movement back toward an agrarian past. Ritt saw in the modern cityscape a failure to create an environment for individual fulfillment; in his films, the postwar industrial world is a place of isolation and personal displacement.

Even Ritt's darkest films usually allow a glimpse of serenity by placing the protagonist in a scene by the water, always a symbol of regeneration and harmony. In Ritt's very first film, Tyler speaks of "being ten feet tall" while enjoying lunch by the water. In such moments, suggestive of some former Edenic existence, man seems free to dream of a simpler life where the basic values and beliefs of the American idea might be realized in communion with nature.

Ritt's father settled in America after working as a second mate on the Hamburg Steamship Line. In the process he learned several languages and visited a number of American ports. In looking toward the water, Ritt may therefore have reimagined a journey of discovery, the unfolding of an earlier America whose values were rooted in the land and in individual communal responsibility. His retreat from the modern urban landscape suggests an attempt to reconstruct and reaffirm the American adventure by discovering it anew, as do many of his later protagonists. The construction in his films of a democratic aesthetic for the common man thus coincides with rediscovery of the awesome possibilities of the American experience.

Of the generation that came to maturity in the thirties, Ritt remarked, "My generation was totally committed to humanism" (McGilligan, "Ritt Large" 39). In his films, that commitment translates as an affirmation of individual and collective redemption, equality of opportunity, and the promise of America as a sanctuary for diverse and disadvantaged seekers of a new world. The journey from despair to hope that characterizes Martin Ritt's career as a filmmaker represents his refusal to let go of this "humanism" and his enduring belief in the democratic ideal.

Appendix 1:
Martin Ritt's Theater Work

Golden Boy by Clifford Odets, 1937 and 1938 (actor and later asst. stage manager)
Plant in the Sun by Ben Bengal, 1938 (actor)
The Gentle People by Irwin Shaw, 1938 (actor)
The Time of Your Life by William Saroyan, 1939 (actor)
Two on an Island by Elmer Rice, 1940 (actor)
No for an Answer by Marc Blitzstein, 1941 (actor)
The Criminals by Ferdinand Bruckner, 1941 (actor)
Eve of St. Mark by Maxwell Anderson, 1942 (actor)
Music at Work, a variety of music and dance scenes, supervised by Marc Blitzstein, 1942 (actor)
They Should Have Stood in Bed by Leo Rifkin, Frank Tarloff, and David Shaw, 1942 (actor)
Afton Water by William Saroyan, 1942 (actor)
Winged Victory by Moss Hart, 1943 (actor)
Yellow Jack by Sidney Howard, 1944 and 1947 (director)
Mr. Peebles and Mr. Hooker by Edward Paramore Jr., 1946 (director)
The Big People by Stanley Young and Nancy Wilson Ross, 1947 (director)
Eastward to Eden by Dorothy Gardner, 1947 (director)
Set My People Free by Dorothy Heyward, 1948 (director)
The Winslow Boy by Terence Rattigan, 1949 (director)
The Man by Mel Dinelli, 1950 (director)
Cry of the Peacock by Jean Anouilh, 1950 (director)
The Temptation of Maggy Haggerty by James McGee, 1952 (director)
Maya by Simon Gantillon, 1953 (actor)
Men of Distinction by Richard Condon, 1953 (actor)
Detective Story by Sidney Kingsley, 1953 (director)
Boy Meets Girl by Bella Spewack and Sam Spewack, 1954 (director)
The Front Page by Charles MacArthur and Ben Hecht, 1954 (director)
Golden Boy by Clifford Odets, 1954 (director)
The Flowering Peach by Clifford Odets, 1954 (actor; assisted Odets with direction)
Put Them All Together by Theodore Hirsch and Jeannette Patton, 1954 (director)
Born Yesterday by Garson Kanin, 1955 (actor)
The Two Mrs. Carrolls by Marguerite Veiller, undated (director)
A Memory of Two Mondays and A View from the Bridge by Arthur Miller, 1955 (director)
A Very Special Baby by Robert Alan Aurthur, 1956 (director)

Appendix 2
Martin Ritt's Filmography

Edge of the City, MGM, 1957 (released in England as *A Man Is Ten Feet Tall)*
No Down Payment, Twentieth Century Fox, 1957
The Long Hot Summer, Twentieth Century Fox, 1958
The Sound and the Fury, Twentieth Century Fox, 1959
The Black Orchid, Paramount, 1959
Jovanka E L'Altri (Five Branded Women), Paramount, 1960
Paris Blues, United Artists, 1961
Hemingway's Adventures of a Young Man (also known as *Adventures of a Young Man),*
     Twentieth Century Fox, 1962
Hud, Paramount, 1963
The Outrage, MGM, 1964
The Spy Who Came in from the Cold, Paramount, 1965
Hombre, Twentieth Century Fox, 1967
The Brotherhood, Paramount, 1968
The Great White Hope, Twentieth Century Fox, 1970
The Molly Maguires, Paramount, 1970
Pete 'n' Tillie, Universal, 1972
Sounder, Twentieth Century Fox, 1972
Conrack, Twentieth Century Fox, 1974
The Front, Columbia, 1976
Casey's Shadow, Columbia, 1978
Norma Rae, Twentieth Century Fox, 1979
Back Roads, Warner Brothers, 1981
Cross Creek, Universal, 1983
Murphy's Romance, Columbia, 1985
Nuts, Warner Brothers, 1987
Stanley and Iris, MGM, 1990

Martin Ritt appeared as an actor in the following:

Winged Victory, Twentieth Century Fox, 1944 (directed by George Cukor)
The End of the Game, Twentieth Century Fox, 1976 (directed by Maximilian Schell)
The Slugger's Wife, Columbia, 1985 (directed by Hal Ashby)

Martin Ritt made appearances in the following documentaries:

Hollywood on Trial, Lumiere, 1977
The Group Theatre, PBS, 1985
Fifty Years of Action, Directors Guild of America Golden Jubilee Committee, 1986

Notes

Chapter 1: Discovering a Vocation

1. The biographical information in this chapter comes mostly from interviews with Adele Ritt and from Jackson's *Picking Up the Tab*.

Chapter 5: Ernest Hemingway and Jerry Wald

1. The suggestions Wald made for a title prior to Hemingway's death have nothing to do with the author. In a memo to Ritt, dated July 24, 1961, Wald recommends "Illusion of Immortality, Reap the Whirlwind, Clouds of Glory and Light of Common Day." He even suggests re-using "The Breaking Point," his title for the remake of *To Have and Have Not*. The simple "A Story by Hemingway" is his only overt reference to the source material (RC 7-24-61).

2. Final page of A. E. Hotchner's script labeled "Revised Final" and dated "October 17, 1961, completed: October 23, 1961," 141. All page references refer to this script.

3. The source for this episode is "A Pursuit Race," by Hemingway, which is not one of the Nick Adams stories.

4. Hotchner's script, see note 2.

5. This account is quoted from a story created to publicize the Newman/Ritt partnership and announce that the first film would be *Horseman Pass By*, later changed to *Hud*. It is dated February 27, 1962, and is in the Ritt Collection.

Chapter 6: The Death of the Western Hero

1. I have consulted two versions of the screenplay for *Hud*. One is undated; the other is published—see Ravetch and Frank. Page numbers cited in the text refer to the published version.

2. For a more detailed analysis of the novel and film, see Simon 14–23.

Chapter 9: "I Believe in America"

1. "Montezuma" was a potentially interesting project that received some time and effort. Dalton Trumbo wrote a 205-page preliminary script, dated February 5, 1965 (part of the Ritt Collection). It was to be an epic film, like *Spartacus*, about Cortez, whom Trumbo describes as in "his late 30s, an intellectual who is also a man of action, fanatically religious who is no stranger to cynicism . . . an adventurer and statesman, brave but not ashamed to run for his life." The film deals with his attempts "to instruct the heathen in the true faith, to explore and map the western coastlands and cultivate trade and com-

merce." Ritt was undoubtedly excited by the prospect of working with Trumbo, but the project never got much beyond the stage of the initial script and an outline of the sets that would be needed.

2. Memo from Peter Bart, May 19, 1967. He asks if it wouldn't be more dramatic and realistic if the younger brother was an "urbane Mafia type" in contrast to the older brother's more predictable personality. The article referred to is by Fred P. Graham, "U.S. Crime Study Sees Cosa Nostra as Growing Peril" (May 15, 1967). The article is included in the Ritt Collection (RC).

3. Lewis John Carlino, "In Search of Origins: The Brotherhood." This is included in the files for the film in the Ritt Collection (RC). There is no date or source.

4. One of Douglas's early suggestions for the role, made in a letter to Ritt (June 24, 1967), was Robert Redford. In the Ritt Collection (RC).

5. According to Douglas, he and Papas staged and improvised this scene. He writes about this in his autobiography: "When Marty came to shoot it, he didn't change a thing, just shot it exactly as we rehearsed it" (Douglas 371–72). Douglas repeated this story to me during our interview.

6. These scenes are included in the final shooting script for *The Brotherhood* in the Herrick Library. The script is not dated though there are some revised pages dated October 10, 1967.

7. "New Movies: Black Handiwork," *Time*, January 24, 1969, 62.

8. "It is really the juxtaposition of these two elements that concerns the theme of *The Brotherhood*." Letter from Kirk Douglas to Joseph Friedman, Vice President of Publicity and Advertising, Paramount, October 16, 1967, Herrick Library.

Chapter 10: The Valley of Death

1. Information on the production was obtained from the following sources: The "Press Kit" for the film; "Official Bulletin" of the International Alliance of Stage Employees, no. 466 (winter 1969–70): 4; and Lightman.

2. Walter Bernstein's "Treatment," which is not dated, is in folder #153, in the Ritt Collection (RC). All other references to Bernstein's "Treatment" are to this document.

3. From Bernstein's script for *The Molly Maguires* dated "revised 4/22/68" with other pages dated as "revised 5/1/68." This copy was sent to me by Adele Ritt. There is also a script in the Ritt Collection (RC).

4. "Stanley Kauffmann on Films," *New Republic*, February 21, 1970, 20.

Chapter 11: The African American Experience

1. Both quotes in this paragraph are from a publicity interview generated by Gordon Armstrong, National Publicity Director, Twentieth Century–Fox Film Corp. It was obviously intended for distribution to critics and other members of the media. It is not dated and was not published. Ritt made a similar comment to the *Philadelphia Inquirer* on August 6, 1973, 4-B.

2. It seems that Lawrence Turman wanted to begin with a prologue, stating that the

film was based on history while detailing some of the parallels with actual events. Sackler objected, "I think it creates a weakness where none exists, announcing we call on history for support" (RC, July 4, no year). Darryl F. Zanuck later vetoed the idea of a prologue. Turman wrote to Sackler on July 19, 1970, informing him of Zanuck's decision. The released film does state, "Much of what follows is true," before the credits begin.

3. Roscoe C. Brown Jr., "A Teacher's Guide for *Sounder.*" There is no publication information printed on this 7-page guide. It was presumably published by Twentieth Century Fox and Radnitz/Mattel Productions as promotional material for the film. The quote used here is on the first page under the heading "The Production."

4. This review was included in the files on *Sounder* in the Ritt Collection. The section is titled "*Ms.* on the Arts" and the title of the review is "Film Find: A Really Good Movie about Blacks." The entry is not dated and the page numbers are not reproduced.

5. Recounted in a telephone interview with author on February 8, 1996.

6. Pat Conroy, "Pat Conroy (and Hollywood) Presents Pat Conroy and His Kids." The essay is reprinted from *Learning, The Magazine for Creative Teaching.* There are no page numbers. This was included in the files on *Conrack* in the Ritt Collection (RC).

7. Conroy, "Pat Conroy (and Hollywood)."

Chapter 15: A Portrait of the Artist

1. The quotes from Robert Radnitz come from the press information packet provided by Universal. The packet contains eight stapled releases on the film, the director, the producer, and various stars. It is dated August 9, 1983. Much of the material was repeated by Radnitz to me during an interview on February 3, 1996. All quotes by Radnitz are from the press material or the interview.

2. Dalene Young wrote *Marilyn*, an examination of the Monroe legend, and *Will There Really Be Morning?* about Frances Farmer. What really caught Radnitz's attention, however, was a television drama called *Christmas: Coal Mine Miracle.*

3. Radnitz, press information packet (see note 1).

4. Radnitz told me that the script I read was not the "final shooting script." He said that there were other versions that came after the one I read (Interview).

5. Perkins's advice to Marjorie is based on an incident in Radnitz's own life. His first wife, Joanna Crawford, was a writer and Radnitz was struck by letters she sent him about her childhood and experiences growing up in the Amish country in Pennsylvania. Like Perkins, he recommended that she write of these experiences. The result was the novel *Birch Interval,* which Radnitz later turned into a film in 1977 which also featured Rip Torn.

Works Cited

Action. "Martin Ritt: Conversation." (March/April 1971): 27–29.

Adams, Michael. "How Come Everybody down Here Has Three Names? Martin Ritt's Southern Films." In *The South and Film*, ed. Warren French. Jackson: University Press of Mississippi, 1981.

American Film Institute (AFI). "Seminar with Martin Ritt." TS of seminar Ritt gave at the American Film Institute, Beverly Hills, Calif., February 22, 1974.

Armstrong, William H. *Sounder*. 1969. Reprint, New York: Harper & Row, 1972.

Barker, Pat. *Union Street*. 1982. Reprint, New York: Ballantine, 1990.

Barson, Michael. "Martin Ritt." In *The Illustrated Who's Who of Hollywood Directors*. Vol. 1, *The Sound Era*. New York: Farrar, Straus & Giroux, 1995.

Bart, Peter. "There Are Spies and Spies." *New York Times*, January 2, 1966.

Bentley, Eric. *Thirty Years of Treason: Excerpts from the Hearings before the House Committee on Un-American Activities, 1938–1968*. New York: Viking, 1971.

Berkowitz, Stan. "Martin Ritt: A Shaper of the Medium Is Now Its Critic." *Emmy Magazine* (July/August 1985): 40–48.

Bernstein, Walter. "Treatment for the Molly Maguires." Folder #153, Martin Ritt Collection. Margaret Herrick Library of the Motion Picture Academy of Arts and Sciences, Beverly Hills, Calif.

———. Interview with author. March 18, 1992.

———. *Inside Out: A Memoir of the Blacklist*. New York: Alfred A. Knopf, 1996.

Brady, Frank. *Citizen Welles: A Biography of Orson Welles*. New York: Charles Scribners' Sons, 1989.

Bragg, Melvyn. *Richard Burton: A Life*. Boston: Little, Brown & Co., 1988.

Broehl, Wayne, Jr. *The Molly Maguires*. Cambridge: Harvard University Press, 1965.

Cameron, Julia. "True Ritt." *American Film* 15, no. 2 (November 1989): 43–48.

Cawelti, John. *The Six-Gun Mystique*. Bowling Green, Ohio: Bowling Green University Popular Press, 1970.

Ceplair, Larry, and Steven Englund. *The Inquisition in Hollywood: Politics in the Film Community, 1930–1960*. Garden City, N.Y.: Anchor Press/Doubleday, 1980.

Chase, Donald. "Martin Ritt and the Making of *Norma Rae*." *Millimeter*, June 7, 1979, 45.

Chayefsky, Paddy. *The Collected Works of Paddy Chayefsky: The Television Plays*. New York: Applause Books, 1995.

Ciment, Michel. *Kazan on Kazan*. New York: Viking Press, 1974.

Clurman, Harold. *The Fervent Years: The Story of the Group Theatre and the Thirties*. New York: Hill and Wang, 1957.

Conroy, Pat. *The Water Is Wide.* 1972. Reprint, New York: Bantam, 1987.

Considine, Shaun. *Mad as Hell: The Life and Work of Paddy Chayefsky.* New York: Random House, 1994.

Cook, Bruce. "Norma Rae's Big Daddy." *American Film* 5, no. 6 (April 1980): 52–58.

Denby, David. "Gentility—This Time American Style." *New York* 16 (October 3, 1983): 88.

Denison, D. C. "The Interview: Martin Ritt." *Boston Globe Magazine,* June 15, 1988, 7–8.

DeVries, Peter. *The Cat's Pajamas and Witch's Milk.* Boston: Little, Brown & Co., 1968.

Douglas, Kirk. *The Ragman's Son.* 1988. Reprint, New York: Pocket Books, 1989.

Farber, Stephen. ' "Cross Creek: The Story of a Writer's Love of the Land." *San Francisco Sunday Examiner and Chronicle,* October 2, 1983, 22–23. Reprinted from the *New York Times,* September 18, 1983.

Faulkner, William. *The Sound and the Fury.* 1929. Reprint, New York: Vintage, 1956.

———. *The Hamlet.* 1931. Reprint, New York: Vintage, 1959.

Field, Sidney. "*Outrage:* A Print 'Documentary' on Hollywood Filmmaking." *Film Quarterly* 18, no. 3 (spring 1965): 13–39.

Flender, Harold. *Paris Blues.* New York: Ballantine Books, 1957.

Goldfarb, Lyn, and Anatoli Ilyashov. "Working Class Hero: An Interview with Martin Ritt." *Cineaste* 18, no. 4 (January 1992): 20–23.

Gow, Gordon. *Hollywood in the Fifties.* New York: A. S. Barnes & Co., 1971.

Harnisch, Larry. "Murphy's Romance on Location in Arizona." *American Cinematographer* (November 1985): 28–32.

Higham, Charles. *Hollywood Cameramen: Sources of Light.* Bloomington: Indiana University Press, 1970.

Jackson, Carlton. *Picking Up the Tab: The Life and Movies of Martin Ritt.* Bowling Green, Ohio: Bowling Green State University Popular Press, 1994.

Kael, Pauline. "Hud, Deep in the Divided Heart of Hollywood." In *I Lost It at the Movies.* New York: Little, Brown & Co., 1965.

Kanin, Fay, and Michael Kanin. *Rashomon.* New York: Random House, 1959 (also published by Samuel French, 1987).

Kawin, Bruce F. *Faulkner and Film.* New York: Frederick Ungar Publishing Co., 1977.

Kazan, Elia. *A Life.* New York: Alfred A. Knopf, 1988.

Kinney, Nancy S. "Cross Creek." In *Magill's Cinema Annual 1984,* 116–20. Englewood Cliffs, N.J.: Salem, 1985.

Kramer, Hilton. "The Blacklist and the Cold War." *New York Times,* October 3, 1976, sect. 2, 1, 16–18.

Laurence, Frank M. *Hemingway and the Movies.* Jackson: University Press of Mississippi, 1981.

Leiferman, Henry P. *Crystal Lee: A Woman of Inheritance.* New York: MacMillan, 1975.

le Carré, John. *The Spy Who Came in from the Cold.* 1964. Reprint, New York: Bantam, 1989.

———. " 'The Spy'—From the Cold to the Screen." *This Week Magazine* April 4, 1965, 12–13.

————. "To Russia, with Greetings." *Encounter* 26, no.5 (May 1966): 6.

Leonard, Elmore. *Hombre.* 1961. Reprint, New York: Ballantine, 1991.

Light, Russell J. "Ritt Discusses *Hud, Sounder,* and *Conrack.*" Iconoclast, April 5–12, 1974, 18, 22.

Lightman, Herb A. "Photographing 'The Molly Maguires' without Arc Lighting." *American Cinematographer* (April 1970): 306–10, 344–46.

Marx, Leo. *The Machine in the Garden.* New York: Oxford University Press, 1964.

McGilligan, Pat. "Ritt Large." *Film Comment,* February 22, 1986, 38–46. Reprinted in *Tender Comrades: A Backstory of the Hollywood Blacklist,* by Patrick McGilligan and Paul Buhle. New York: St. Martins Press, 1997.

————, ed. *Backstory 2: Interviews with Screenwriters of the 1940s and 1950s.* Berkeley: University of California Press, 1991.

McMurtry, Larry. *Horseman, Pass By.* 1961. Reprint, New York: Penguin, 1979.

Miller, Arthur. *Timebends: A Life.* New York: Grove, 1986.

Myrdal, Gunnar. *An American Dilemma: The Negro Problem and American Democracy.* 2 vols. 1942. Reprint, New York: Harper Colophon, 1962.

Navasky, Victor S. *Naming Names.* New York: Viking, 1980.

Peper, William. "Man Who Made the Spy Come In." *New York World-Telegram and Sun,* December 17, 1965.

Phillips, Gene D. *Hemingway and Film.* New York: Frederick Ungar Publishing Co., 1980.

————. *Fiction, Film, and Faulkner.* Knoxville: University of Tennessee Press, 1988.

Pollock, Dale. "23 Films, 23 Struggles for Cross Creek Director." *Los Angeles Times,* October 6, 1983, sect. 6, 1, 9.

Radnitz, Robert. Interview with author. February 3, 1996.

Ravetch, Irving, and Harriet Frank Jr. "Hombre," June 29, 1965.

————. Hud, Norma Rae, *and* The Long Hot Summer: *Three Screenplays by Irving Ravetch and Harriet Frank Jr.* New York: New American Library, 1988.

Rawlings, Marjorie Kinnan. *The Yearling.* New York: Scribners, 1938.

————. *Cross Creek.* New York: Scribners, 1942.

Rebello, Stephen. *Alfred Hitchcock and the Making of Psycho.* 1990. Reprint, New York: Harper Perennial, 1991.

Red Channels: The Report of Communist Influence in Radio and Television. New York: Counterattack, 1950.

Rickey, Carrie. "The Long Hot Career." *Fame* (Winter 1990): 34–40.

Riese, Randall. *Her Name Is Barbra.* 1993. Reprint, New York: St. Martin's Paperbacks, 1994.

Ritchie, Donald, ed. *Rashomon.* New Brunswick, N.J.: Rutgers University Press, 1987.

Ritt, Martin, Collection (RC). Margaret Herrick Library of the Motion Picture Academy of Arts and Sciences, Beverly Hills, Calif.

Sackler, Howard. *The Great White Hope.* New York: Dial Press, 1968.

Sarris, Andrew. "Woody Allen Excorcises the Not-so-Grand Inquisitors." *Village Voice,* October 4, 1976, 121.

Schott, Max. *Murphy's Romance.* New York: Harper & Row, 1980.

Simon, Roger. "Intertexuality and the Western: The Case of *Hombre* as Novel and Film." In *Varieties of Filmic Expression,* ed. Douglas Radcliff-Umstead, 14–23. Kent, Ohio: Romance Languages Dept., Kent State University, 1989.

Smith, Henry Nash. *Virgin Land: The American West as Symbol and Myth.* Cambridge, Mass: Harvard University Press, 1950.

Smith, Wendy. *Real Life Drama: The Group Theatre and America, 1931–1940.* New York: Alfred A. Knopf, 1990.

Southern Methodist University (SMU). "Martin Ritt Interview," conducted by Ronald L. Davis, July 13–14, 1987. Oral History Collection, A80.154. Degolyer Library, Dallas, Tex.

Spada, James. *Streisand: Her Life.* New York: Ivy Books, 1996.

Stone, Judy. "There's Them People in the Mine, and Them People on the Hill . . ." *San Francisco Sunday Examiner and Chronicle,* July 28, 1968.

Tomkins, Jane. *West of Everything: The Inner Life of Westerns.* New York: Oxford University Press, 1992.

Topor, Tom. *Nuts.* New York: New American Library, 1986.

Wald, Jerry. "Faulkner in Hollywood." *Films in Review* 10, no. 3 (March 1959): 129–33.

———. "From Faulkner to Film." *Saturday Review,* March 7, 1959, 16, 42.

———. "Screen Adaptation." *Films in Review* 5 (1954): 62–67.

Watts, Stephen. "Shooting a 'Spy' in the Cold." Undated, in clipping file. Martin Ritt Collection. Margaret Herrick Library of the Motion Picture Academy of Arts and Sciences, Beverly Hills, Calif.

Weinstein, Wendy. "Martin Ritt Journeys Down 'Cross Creek.' " *Film Journal* 86 (October 28, 1983): 12, 119.

Whitaker, Sheila. *The Films of Martin Ritt.* London: British Film Institute, 1972.

Yakir, Dan. "A Special Way of Life." *Horizon* 26 (October 1983): 45–47.

Zolotow, Maurice. "A Day at the Races with Marty Ritt (and a Cameo by Walter Matthau)." *Los Angeles Magazine* (October 1978): 164–66, 293–300.

Index